Accountability for Human Rights Violations

This book analyses how open source evidence can be harnessed to enhance accountability for human rights violations in Kenya. Building upon existing literature that has demonstrated its potential to radically transform the way investigations are conducted and how information is collected and analysed, it argues for the development of a legal framework to facilitate the use of open source evidence in court. This framework is developed by incorporating best practices gleaned from a comparative analysis of the national jurisprudence from leading common law jurisdictions and an assessment of prevailing international standards. The research supporting it further incorporates primary data from a systematic case study, a survey and key informant interviews targeting legal practitioners, criminal investigators and members of the judiciary in Kenya. In examining and proposing a standardised and reproducible framework for the determination of the admissibility of open source evidence in domestic legal proceedings within a common law legal system, the work will be a valuable resource for academics, researchers and policy-makers working in the areas of International Human Rights Law, International Criminal Law, Evidence Law, Law and Technology, Comparative Law and Accountability Studies.

Claire Adionyi is an Advocate of the High Court of Kenya. She holds an L.L.M. in International Human Rights Law from the University of Groningen, the Netherlands, and a PhD in Law from the University of Pretoria, South Africa. She is currently a Lecturer at Strathmore Law School in Nairobi, Kenya.

Accountability for Human Rights Violations

Harnessing Open Source Evidence in Kenya

Claire Adionyi

Routledge
Taylor & Francis Group
LONDON AND NEW YORK

First published 2027
by Routledge
4 Park Square, Milton Park, Abingdon, Oxon OX14 4RN

and by Routledge
605 Third Avenue, New York, NY 10158

Routledge is an imprint of the Taylor & Francis Group, an informa business

British Library Cataloguing-in-Publication Data
A catalogue record for this book is available from the British Library

ISBN: 978-1-041-29603-4 (hbk)
ISBN: 978-1-041-29605-8 (pbk)
ISBN: 978-1-003-77034-3 (ebk)

DOI: 10.4324/9781003770343

Typeset in Galliard
by Deanta Global Publishing Services, Chennai, India

To my parents Dr Peter Itapara Ochieng and Mrs Rosemary Imatata Omuse Ochieng.
You are my reason.

Contents

Figures

Table

Boxes

Acknowledgements

My first and most sincere gratitude is to my Heavenly Father, God Almighty – "Promises" by Maverick City Music *et al.*

To my mom and dad, God has been so kind and merciful to grant me the privilege of having you as my parents. Thank you.

Felix, Metrine, Collins, Eve, Haggai – you are my whole world.

Nakita, Pharrell, Liam, Enzi, Oz – little lights of mine, I hope this inspires you to shine ever so brightly.

To my friends and colleagues who assisted me on this journey, Dr Joe Kilonzo, Fiona Njeri Mwaura and Caroline Wanjugu Gichuki, thank you.

To the Routledge (Taylor & Francis) and Deanta Global Publishing Services team, thank you sincerely.

Abbreviations

CCTV	Closed Circuit TV
CD	Compact Disc
CEA	Canadian Evidence Act
CPIA	Criminal Procedure and Investigations Act
CPS	Crown Prosecution Services
DCI	Department of Criminal Investigations
DRC	Democratic Republic of Congo
FDLR	Democratic Forces for the Liberation of Rwanda
GA	General Assembly
HTML	Hypertext Markup Language
ICC	International Criminal Court
ICJ	International Court of Justice
IPOA	Independent Policing Oversight Authority
IDF	Israeli Defense Forces
KICA	Kenya Information and Communications Act
NGO	Non-Governmental Organisation
ODPP	Office of the Director of Public Prosecutions
OHCHR	Office of the High Commissioner for Human Rights
OPT	Occupied Palestinian Territory
OTP	Office of The Prosecutor
PW	Plaintiff Witness
TWAIL	Third World Approach to International Law
UN	United Nations

Foreword

Since the establishment of the current world order, the protection of human rights is appreciated as a legal obligation. Under international law, states have the primary responsibility to protect and fulfil the fundamental rights of all persons within their jurisdiction. This duty is not rhetorical. It is grounded in both treaty and customary international law, and it demands the adoption of appropriate legislative, procedural and institutional measures that guarantee fair, effective and prompt access to justice.

In Kenya, this responsibility is granted constitutional force under Article 21 of the 2010 Constitution, which requires the state to observe, respect, protect, promote and fulfil the rights and fundamental freedoms in the Bill of Rights. The promise of the 2010 Constitution is therefore inseparable from the demand for accountability. Human rights and fundamental freedoms only become meaningful when violations are investigated, adjudicated and remedied through credible and principled legal processes.

It is within this context that the contribution of *Accountability for Human Rights Violations: Harnessing Open Source Evidence in Kenya* becomes timely, important and welcome. The author speaks to an area of growing significance in contemporary adjudication: the use of open source evidence in the pursuit of justice. Today, due to increased digital communication, citizen documentation and the rapid circulation of information, the evidence of human rights violations has largely become publicly accessible. Photographs, videos, satellite imagery, social media posts and other forms of open source material are reshaping how facts are both documented and contested.

To rely on open source evidence in court processes requires rigour, integrity and adherence to evidentiary standards. This is because the integrity of the judicial process is anchored on clear evidentiary standards, procedural fairness and fidelity to dictates of the Constitution and the rule of law. This book carefully situates the discussion within Kenya's evidentiary framework while conscious of the fact that the Evidence Act applies to all branches of law. By focusing on the evidentiary process instead of a single substantive field, the author underscores a critical truth; that accountability is not just about moral clarity but also about proof.

This book's approach to the question of accountability is both doctrinal and comparative. It examines how other domestic jurisdictions have approached the admissibility and assessment of open source evidence, and it draws instructive lessons from the practice of international courts and tribunals. In doing so, this work invites a critical reflection on how the Kenyan Judiciary can responsibly adapt to the evolving forms of evidence without compromising established safeguards.

As courts face the increasingly sophisticated forms of documentation, questions of authenticity, reliability, chain of custody, and digital integrity will become even more important. This book does not however provide simplistic answers. Instead, it offers a careful, principled approach to engaging these challenges within the bounds of existing legal standards, while remaining open to thoughtful development.

In bridging constitutional and international obligations, evidentiary doctrine and technological change, this book speaks to judges, practitioners, scholars, investigators and policy makers. It is both a welcome and necessary contribution to the ongoing effort to ensure that the promise of human rights protection is matched by effective mechanisms of accountability based on open source evidence.

I therefore commend this book to all who are committed to strengthening the rule of law and to ensuring that justice in Kenya remains both principled and responsive in a rapidly evolving world.

Justice Isaac Lenaola,
Judge of the Supreme Court of Kenya and President,
Residual Special Court for Sierra Leone (RSCL)

1 Introduction

Introduction

As a matter of international law, states have the primary responsibility to protect their populations from human rights violations and also have the obligation under international conventional and customary law to see that those responsible for these violations are held accountable.[1] The international legal obligation of states to respect, protect and fulfil enjoins state parties to ensure access to justice and proper investigations and effective remedies. States therefore remain ultimately accountable in guaranteeing this protection to citizens, whether in times of peace or conflict. This responsibility has a pedigree traceable to international human rights principles.

An aspect of ensuring that affirmative measures are adopted to protect human rights is the requirement for states to enact and enforce legislation or to adopt other appropriate measures to secure the respect of human rights by individuals and other entities.[2] Specifically, this obligation requires states to adopt "appropriate and effective legislative … procedures and other appropriate measures that provide fair, effective and prompt access to justice."[3] It is based on this responsibility that this book proffers the hypothesis that open source evidence, which has been demonstrated – as will be seen in subsequent discussions – as having the potential of radically transforming the way investigations are conducted and how information is collected and analysed, can enhance accountability for human rights violations in Kenya.

It is important to emphasise the fact that human rights can be violated and/or perpetrated by both individuals, whose conduct criminal law seeks to

1 Overall International Humanitarian Law, International Human Rights Law, International Criminal Law, the Geneva Conventions and the Convention on the Prevention and Punishment of the Crime of Genocide oblige member states to prevent those crimes or violations and ensure that the attendant norms are respected.

2 United Nations General Assembly, Basic Principles and Guidelines on the Right to a Remedy and Reparation for Victims of Gross Violations of International Human Rights Law and Serious Violations of International Humanitarian Law (Basic Principles and Guidelines), A/RES/60/147, 21 March 2006.

3 Basic Principles and Guidelines (n 2 above).

DOI: 10.4324/9781003770343-1

regulate, and by other entities such as government bodies, whose conduct is regulated under the framework of the Bill of Rights as contained in Chapter Four of the Constitution of Kenya, 2010. For this reason, this book will primarily focus on an analysis of how open source evidence can be harnessed to enhance accountability for human rights violations through this lens, that is, holding both individuals and other entities, such as the state, accountable.

Definition of Terms

Before delving further into these discussions, it is prudent to situate this book. Accordingly, it is imperative to clarify some terminology and to provide a definition of how these terms have been conceptualised for the purposes of this book. In particular, it is of the essence to define the meaning of the term "open source evidence" and to clarify the breadth of its usage herein, given the many definitions that this term possesses.[4] Similarly, the terms "authentication;" "verification" and "reliability" are defined. It would be very remiss not to acknowledge that these definitions are not perfect as they cannot cover absolutely everything. However, these definitions are tailor-made to suit this book's objective.

Open Source Evidence

Open source information has been defined as encompassing publicly available information that any member of the public can observe, purchase or request without requiring special legal status or unauthorised access.[5] In this book, the focus is on user-generated information – a variety of media content uploaded by end users – that has been derived from online platforms such as YouTube, Facebook and Twitter.[6] Additionally, the definition of open source information as employed in this book distinguishes itself from data that has been made

4 See for instance, OHCHR & Human Rights Center, University of California, Berkeley, Berkeley Protocol on Digital Open Source Investigations: A Practical Guide on the Effective Use of Digital Open Source Information in Investigating Violations of International Criminal, Human Rights and Humanitarian Law (Berkeley Protocol), para.6.; K Stavrou, "Open-Source Digital Evidence in International Criminal Cases: A Way Forward in Ensuring Accountability for Core Crimes?," Opinio Juris. Available: http://opiniojuris.org/2021/01/26/open-source-digital-evidence-in-international-criminal-cases-a-way-forward-in-ensuring-accountability-for-core-crimes/, accessed 11 November 2023; E De Busser, "Open Source Data and Criminal Investigations: Anything You Publish Can and Will Be Used Against You" (2014). Available: http://rjh.ub.rug.nl/ GROJIL/article/download/31124/28431, accessed 11 November 2023.

5 Berkeley Protocol (n 4 above) para. 6. Open source information is to be distinguished from closed source information, which has been defined as information with restricted access or access that is protected.

6 P Jordi & K Pawel, "User-Generated Information System" (2017). Available: https://www.researchgate.net/publication/316996069_User-Generated_Information_System, accessed 11 November 2023.

public without the consent of the owners, such as information that has been hacked, leaked, exposed by security vulnerabilities or posted by a third party without proper permissions.

Open source information is to be distinguished from open source intelligence, which has been defined by the Berkeley Protocol as being a subcategory of open source information that is "collected and used for the specific purpose of aiding policymaking and decision-making, most often in a military or political context" as opposed to being used in investigations for purposes of a judicial process.[7] Open source information then becomes open source evidence once the former has been used for information and evidence gathering functions in an open source investigation.[8]

The Berkeley Protocol defines open source evidence as open source information that contains evidentiary value and may be admitted in order to establish facts in legal proceedings.[9] It has also been defined as information that is publicly available and generally acquired through the internet that may include, but is not limited to, social media content, images, videos and audio recordings on websites.[10]

This book emphasises the use of the term open source evidence as relating to that which is digital and/or available online only.[11] Furthermore, the book only focuses on instances where open source information is imputed with evidentiary value in the absence of a witness. For this reason, and given the fact that within the Kenyan context – as demonstrated by the findings from the data collection – the predominant iteration of open source evidence in legal proceedings is evidence from social media platforms, the term social media evidence is used synonymously with open source evidence in this book. This is especially in Chapter 4, which chapter draws directly from primary data from the survey and the systematic case study.

This book recognises that there are other types of open source evidence, such as satellite imagery, NGO reports, media reports, *inter alia*, but these are not categorically present within the Kenyan context, as shown by the findings from the data collection.[12] This context-specific focus is important as it

7 Berkeley Protocol (n 4 above) para.8.

8 Berkeley Protocol (n 4 above) para.8. Where open source investigation is simply defined as the use of open source information for information and evidence gathering functions.

9 Berkeley Protocol (n 4 above) para.8.

10 Stavrou (n 4 above).

11 De Busser (n 4 above).

12 See for example, these writings/court decisions for further elaboration on the various iterations of open source evidence: L Freeman, "Prosecuting Atrocity Crimes with Open Source Evidence: Lessons from the International Criminal Court," in S Dubberley, A Koenig and D Murray (eds) *Digital Witness: Using Open Source Information for Human Rights Investigation, Documentation, and Accountability,* Oxford University Press (2019) p 52; Transcript, Al Hassan (ICC-01/12-01/18-T-027-Red-ENG), Trial Chamber X, 21 September 2020; Judgment and Sentence, Al Mahdi (ICC-01/12-01/15-171), Trial Chamber VIII, 27 September 2016; Decision on "Prosecution's Fifth Request for the Admission of Evidence from the Bar

aligns this book with the theoretical framework that underpins it, that is, the Third World Approaches to International Law (TWAIL) framework.[13] The TWAIL framework's clarion call is that whenever international standards are being used to influence municipal practice, these standards must take into consideration the prevailing circumstances of the specific municipal jurisdiction under consideration, as opposed to transplanting legislations as was the case in post-colonial times. The TWAIL framework is discussed extensively later in this chapter under the theoretical framework section.

Authentication

The Evidence Act of Kenya has not defined the term "authentication" and neither has the term been explicitly defined in case law by Kenyan courts. However, the closest definition that can be inferred within the Kenyan context is found in the case of *Republic v Mark Lloyd Steveson*, where the court equated authentication to " the proponent must prove that the evidence is what the proponent claims it to be."[14] On the other hand, innumerable definitions of the term have been provided within the milieu of the law of evidence. For instance, *Black's Law Dictionary* has defined the term as " the provision of evidence sufficient to support a finding that the matter in question is what its proponent claims it to be."[15] This definition is very similar to the Kenyan court's definition, above, as the focal point appears to be the issue of "is what the proponent claims it to be." Conversely, from an author's perspective, Pattenden provides a legal definition of the term as referring to "the process of convincing a court that a 'thing' (tangible evidence) matches the claims made about it."[16]

However, due to this multiplicity in definitions, this book favours the definition that has been provided by the Berkeley Protocol as it is one that is closely aligned to the open source evidence discourse. Accordingly, "authentication" is herein defined as "the ability to demonstrate that a digital item

Table", Bemba *et al.* (ICC-01/05-01/13-1524), Trial Chamber VII, 14 December 2015. See further, "Prosecution's Fifth Request for the Admission of Evidence from the Bar Table," Bemba *et al.* (ICC-01/05-01/13-1498), 30 November 2015, paras. 17–18.

13 It has been defined as a broad dialect of opposition to the traditional configuration of international law, its Eurocentric origins, colonial and imperial legacies and argues for a more inclusive international law. See, JT Gathii, "The Agenda of Third World Approaches to International Law (TWAIL)" in J Dunoff and M Pollack (eds) *International Legal Theory: Foundations and Frontiers*, Cambridge University Press (2019), p 31.

14 [2016] eKLR. This case has been discussed in detail in Chapter 4.

15 Black's Law Dictionary, Minnesota: West Publishing, 5th ed.

16 R Pattenden, "Authenticating 'things' in English Law: Principles for Adducing Tangible Evidence in Common Law Jury Trials," International Journal of Evidence & Proof (2009) Vol. 12.

remains unchanged from when it was collected. It requires that a digital item remains unchanged from when it was collected."[17]

Verification

Similarly, this book favours the definition that has been provided by the Berkeley Protocol. Accordingly, verification is defined as referring to the "process of establishing the accuracy or validity of information that has been collected online."[18]

Reliability

For the purposes of this book, reliability is defined, based on the definition in the Berkeley Protocol, as referring to the "ability to perform consistently, dependably or as expected."[19] Therefore, the reliability of open source evidence would be demonstrated.

> through information concerning the nature and characteristics of the evidence, the purpose of creation, contemporaneousness, and whether there is sufficient information to allow for a proper evaluation of sources, including whether the source was in a position to accurately and objectively record or recollect information concerning the facts and circumstances of the case, and the means used to compile the data or information in question.[20]

Situating the Scope of the Book

This book focuses on open source evidence within Kenya's judicial process and does not exclusively focus on a specific branch of law; that is, neither civil nor criminal law, but rather targets the overall evidentiary process in light of the fact that the Evidence Act – the principal law that governs the process of adducing evidence in court – is not specific to any branch but has an overarching mandate covering all branches of law. However, in light of the fact that this research's overarching objective is to enhance accountability for human rights violations in Kenya, as highlighted in the introduction, there will be, inevitably, a significant focus on cases from the Constitutional and Human

17 Berkeley Protocol (n 4 above) para. 160.
18 Berkeley Protocol (n 4 above) para. 176.
19 Berkeley Protocol (n 4 above) para. 23.
20 *The Prosecutor v Al Hassan Ag Abdoul Aziz Ag Mohamed Ag Mahmoud*, Defence Response to Prosecution's Second Request for the Admission of Documentary Evidence from the Bar Table, No. ICC-01/12-01/18, 26 April 2021, para. 5. See also, *Katanga and Ngudjolo*, ICC-01/04-01/07-2635, para. 27.

Rights Division and the Criminal Division in the subsequent systematic case study under Chapter 2.

Similarly, in as much as the book will engage in a comparative analysis with other domestic jurisdictions and also look to the practice of international courts and tribunals for best practice on the use of open source evidence, the Kenyan judicial evidentiary process is the focal point. The challenges of translating such standards to the Kenyan context are acknowledged and will be addressed accordingly in forthcoming discussions.

Another important point of note on the breadth of this book is that its primary focus is on the evidence itself and not the investigation. That is, the investigatory process will only be discussed to the extent to which it has a bearing on the verification and the consequent authenticity of the said evidence – in line with the need to ensure fair trial guarantees.

Additionally, as stated above, the book only focuses on instances where open source information is imputed with evidentiary value in the absence of a witness.[21]

A Brief Overview of the Emergence and Use Open Source Evidence in Practice

In light of the realisation that news often spreads faster on social media than through conventional media, and the unprecedented autonomy that comes with self-publishing, it has been observed that citizens are increasingly uploading vast amounts of digital imagery and videos to social media platforms to spread awareness of atrocities and human rights violations.[22] The Syrian conflict presents an apt example of this fact where it is reported that since protests erupted in 2011, millions of videos and images of violations have been captured and disseminated by actors such as Syrian victims, eyewitnesses and in some instances the perpetrators themselves, using mobile phones and social media.[23] So big is this information that Beth Van Schaack noted that more hours of video footage now exist of the Syrian conflict than the actual length in hours of the conflict itself.[24]

This phenomenon led to the establishment of organisations whose aim is to support actors in their efforts to document human rights violations through

21 This means that the user-generator will not be identified, nor will they be available to the inquiry.

22 N Mehandru & A Koenig, "Open Source Evidence and the International Criminal Court," *Harvard Human Rights Journal* (2019). Available: https://journals.law.harvard.edu/hrj/2019/04/open-source-evidence-and-the-international-criminal-court/, accessed 11 November 2023.

23 Syria Justice & Accountability Centre, "Violations Database." Available: https://syriaaccountability.org/database/, accessed 11 November 2023.

24 A Koenig & L Freeman, "Strengthening Atrocity Cases with Digital Open Source Investigations," Lieber Institute West Point (2021) Available: https://lieber.westpoint.edu/strengthening-atrocity-cases-digital-open-source-investigations/, accessed 11 November 2023.

open source intelligence such as Bellingcat.[25] Bellingcat is emblematic of the other side of this coin, that is, the presence of "independent international collective of researchers, investigators and citizen journalists using open source and social media investigations to probe a variety of subjects."[26] The presence of these actors and organisations has led to justice and accountability in various instances such as the bringing of historical crimes to a domestic court in the Democratic Republic of Congo by eyeWitness, TRIAL and WITNESS. In this case, two commanders of the Democratic Forces for the Liberation of Rwanda were found guilty of crimes against humanity and their victims were awarded reparation.[27] Part of the evidence that was admitted and consequently relied on was "digital photography that had been captured with the eyeWitness app, a ready-for-court technology developed to streamline the documentation of international crimes."[28] This material was therefore instrumental in proving legal points as it demonstrated the extent of the mass graves which the court could not visit due to security reasons.[29]

The presence of this type of evidence within a domestic jurisdiction within Africa has also recently been seen in South Africa where investigators and prosecutors used digital evidence, that is, voice notes that were being circulated on WhatsApp, to secure a conviction against a senior member from Operation Dudula.[30] This further points to the rise of user-generated digital evidence as an aid to accountability for human rights violations efforts.

So much has this rise been that the International Criminal Court (ICC) issued its first arrest warrant based entirely on evidence collected from social

25 See also, The Syrian Archive. Available: https://syrianarchive.org/en/about; Syria Justice and Accountability Centre's Database Software, "Bayanat." Available: https://syriaaccountability.org/database/; and eyewitness. Available: https://www.eyewitness.global/. All were accessed 11 November 2023.

26 Bellingcat. Available: https://www.bellingcat.com/, accessed 11 November 2023.

27 *Ndayambaje Gilbert and Nizehimana Evariste*, Tribunal Militaire de Garnison Bukavu (Bukavu Military Tribunal), RP No. 1215/2017, RMP No. 6043/YM/017, 2018; AS Macumu, "Bringing Historical Crimes to Domestic Court in the Democratic Republic of Congo," eyeWitness. Available: https://www.eyewitness.global/Bringing-historical-crimes-to-a-domestic-court-in-the-DRC, accessed 11 November 2023.

28 C Gabriele, K Matheson, RV Llorente, "The Role of Mobile Technology in Documenting International Crimes: The Affaire Castro et Kizito in the Democratic Republic of Congo," Journal of International Criminal Justice (2021) Vol. 19, 1, pp 107–130. It is important to reiterate here that even though the "eyeWitness" app is a closed source tool, this case is important as it highlights the importance of open-source intelligence and it also provides a good example of the use of mobile technology to document evidence that was accepted by a court of law in the Global South.

29 A Irwin, "Digital evidence opens doors to human rights probes," SciDev.Net, 20 March 2019.

30 K Allen, "Digital evidence – A step forward for South Africa: As police and prosecutors test new legislation, what are the challenges of using digital evidence?," Institute of Security Studies, 11 September 2023. Operation Dudula is a South African vigilante group that is against the presence of foreign nationals in South Africa.

media against Mahmoud Mustafa Busayf Al-Werfalli on 15 August 2017 and consequently heralded a new era in open source evidence in light of the fact that the ICC is often lauded as a standard setter.[31] The significance of this decision is that the collection and use of evidence in the ICC is regulated, *inter alia*, by Articles 54, 68 and 69 of the Rome Statute and Chapter Four of the Rules of Procedure and Evidence. However, none of these sources specifically address the use of open source evidence and, as such, the issuance of Al-Werfalli's arrest warrant signalled the willingness of this Court to align itself to the realities of today.[32] The willingness by the ICC to admit open source evidence, despite the lack of explicit reference to it in the operative laws, is one that should be borne in mind throughout this book as ultimately it is this book's contention that explicit inclusion of open source evidence within the Kenyan law of evidence is not necessary. But rather, in similar fashion with the ICC, the pre-existing laws can be interpreted to enable such admission.

It is worth noting, however, that the ICC had dealt with open source evidence prior to this in the *Al Mahdi* case, where the Prosecutor's evidence included:

> satellite images from before and after the destruction; archive photographs taken at different times; audio recordings found on the internet containing statements from members of armed groups; video recordings on the internet which show the destruction at the time of the attack; a geolocation report from an expert witness, which made it possible to "locate with certainty" each video with regard to a precise mausoleum; an expert report ascribing dates and a time frame to the videos; 360-degree panoramic photographs.[33]

Similarly, some national jurisdictions have contended with open source evidence in their legal processes. For example, research that reviewed 28 member states of the European Union and Norway showed that "the use of online open source information in trial proceedings has increased considerably over the past few years."[34] In Sweden, a Stockholm District Court convicted a

31 *The Prosecutor v Mahmoud Mustafa Busayf Al-Werfalli*, Warrant of Arrest, ICC-01/11-01/17, 15 August 2017. Available: https://www.icc-cpi.int/CourtRecords/CR2017_05031.PDF, accessed 11 November 2023.

32 The ICC similarly has a Technology Advisory Board to help it understand how open source investigations could be applied to the ICC.

33 *Prosecutor v Al Mahdi*, ICC-01/12-01/15-T-4-Red-ENG, Transcript, 28–29, 22 August 2016. Available: https://www.icc-cpi.int/CourtRecords/CR2016_07244.PDF, accessed 11 November 2023.

34 Y Liao, "Investigating the Use of Online Open Source Information as Evidence in European Courts," ARES 2018: International Conference on Availability, Reliability and Security (2018). Available: https://doi.org/10.1145/3230833.3232812, accessed 11 November 2023.

Syrian national in 2017 (with a Swedish residency permit) to life in prison based in part on video evidence posted on Facebook.[35] In this case, the court used Facebook posts to establish a timeline to prove that the accused person violated international law by executing soldiers who were loyal to President Bashar al-Assad in 2012.[36]

At the regional level, the European court systems have also contended with open source evidence. For instance, the European Court of Justice dealt with open source evidence in the case of *Sharif v Council*, whereby the Council relied on some evidence from open sources as part of its case.[37] Similarly, the European Court of Human Rights saw the use of open source evidence in *Sanchez v France*, which related to comments that had been posted on Facebook.[38]

Open Source Evidence as Part of the Solution?

Indeed, open source evidence presents a number of advantages that would have the effect of either supplementing traditional evidence or, in the alternative, curing some of its weaknesses. As noted by various scholars, some of these advantages include: secured and verified open source evidence has the potential to cure some of the challenges that encumber traditional witnesses – such as intimidation or manipulation – by recording testimony that cannot be changed or recanted.[39] McDermott *et al.* have acknowledged the potential of open source evidence to democratise the collection of evidence as it "allows access to a much broader range of sources and voices than would normally be consulted through traditional methods of information gathering."[40] It also has the ability to provide immediate access to evidence, thereby preserving

35 Stockholm District Court, Case No.: B 3787-16, Judgment of 2017-02-16; "Swedish Court Hands Life Sentence to Syrian for War Crimes" The Local 16 February 2017. Available: https://archive.is/ZSWKF, accessed 11 November 2023. This conviction was based on the principle of "universal jurisdiction" which allows national prosecutors to pursue individuals believed to be responsible for certain grave international crimes such as torture, war crimes and crimes against humanity, even though they were committed elsewhere and neither the accused nor the victims are nationals of the country.

36 Stockholm District Court, Case No.: B 3787-16, Judgment of 2017-02-16; E Irving, "And So It Begins ... Social Media Evidence in an ICC Arrest Warrant," Opinio Juris, August 2017. Available: http://archive.is/XXRZ0#selection-93.0-93.64, accessed 11 November 2023.

37 Common foreign and security policy – Restrictive measures against Syria – Judgment [2019] EUECJ T-5/17 (04 April 2019).

38 Application no. 45581/15, Grand Chamber.

39 RJ Hamilton, "User-Generated Evidence," Columbia Journal of Transnational Law (2018) Vol. 57, 1. Available: https://ssrn.com/abstract=3124409, accessed 11 November 2023.

40 Y McDermott, A Koenig, D Murray, "Open Source Information's Blind Spot: Human and Machine Bias" in *International Criminal Investigations, Journal of International Criminal Justice* (2021) Vol. 19, 1, pp 85–105. Available: https://academic.oup.com/jicj/article/19/1/85/6214619, accessed 11 November 2023.

evidence that might otherwise be lost or destroyed by the time investigators get involved.[41]

These transformative changes denote the fact that open source evidence could easily be harnessed to be the solution. However, this process is a bit more nuanced as it is admittedly a challenge to convert open source information to open source evidence due to several unprecedented obstacles. These challenges relate to the pre-trial, the trial and the aftermath of the trial stages. The first problem relates to evidentiary issues as there is a lack of common standards and practices regarding the collection and analysis of open source information resulting in challenges in the admissibility of open source information as evidence.[42] These admissibility issues relate to biases and reliability as the information is oft collected by untrained individuals.[43]

Secondly, technological advancements make it easier for digital information to be interfered with resulting in questions about its credibility and authenticity.[44] During the trial stage, the problems to be contended with relate to fair trial rights considerations, the main one being the issue of exacerbating already significant equality of arms issues between the parties.[45] Lastly, generators of open source information are new actors in the investigatory ecosystem and do not enjoy the protection that traditional investigators have.[46] Therefore, questions as to whether these users fully comprehend the risks involved in the evidence collection are pertinent. And even though there is a measure of anonymity that may be guaranteed on online platforms,[47] the question as to who will be accountable if or when a user's safety is in jeopardy remains to be answered.[48]

Therefore, and as aptly noted by Alexa Koenig, "everyone knows there is a wealth of information out there in digital form. But no one knows, comprehensively, how to access it, how to preserve it, who to give it to and what to do with it, and then how to present it in a court."[49] For these reasons, open source investigations (and subsequently open source information) should, at the first instance, comply with applicable laws necessitating the need to have a baseline understanding of the said laws. This thus segues to a discussion of the operative laws in Kenya that relate to open source evidence.

41 Hamilton (n 37 above).
42 Stavrou (n 4 above).
43 Stavrou (n 4 above).
44 Stavrou (n 4 above).
45 Hamilton (n 37 above).
46 Hamilton (n 37 above).
47 See for example, Mark Ellis' (Director of International Bar Association) statement on anonymity of user generated content *via* user generated evidence apps where he noted that these apps offer users some anonymity, in M S Ellis, "Shifting the Paradigm – Bringing to Justice Those Who Commit Human Rights Atrocities," *Case Western Reserve Journal of International Law* (2015) Vol. 47, 1, pp 269–270.
48 Hamilton (n 37 above).
49 Irwin (n 29 above).

The Challenge of Harnessing Open Source Evidence

Open source evidence is changing the landscape of investigations and human rights processes, but there are various questions that have implications for the admissibility of open source evidence that need to be addressed in order for judicial processes to keep abreast of these changes. These questions include: what policies and procedures should be put in place to mitigate against risks such as the interest in holding perpetrators to account rather than concerns with the fair trial rights of the defendants?; does open source evidence exacerbate already significant problems regarding equality of arms between the state and those seeking justice for human rights violations?; and how have national jurisdictions dealt with the new challenges of the mass volume of data and the evidentiary value of open source evidence?

The dilemma then is how to design a process that will allow for these transformative changes by open source evidence while at the same time answering the various technical questions that are attendant to such a process. These issues include but are not limited to: the lack of standards and practices as the information is oft collected by untrained individuals resulting in issues of bias and reliability; technological advancements make it easier for digital information to be interfered with resulting in questions about its credibility and authenticity; and there are challenges in the admissibility of open source information as evidence due to the lack of common standards regarding the collection and analysis of open source information. A further challenge is that current research on the use of open source evidence in national jurisdictions is limited as most of the available research focuses predominantly on international investigations and trials.

There is therefore a need for research that has a broader scope, which will provide a framework as to how Kenya can interact with open source evidence in its legal processes.

As it will be demonstrated by the systematic case study, the necessity of using open source evidence as evidence in legal proceedings in Kenya continues to grow. For instance, the infamous police shooting criminal case of *R v Edward Kirui* that arose from the post-election violence in 2007 where the accused person was charged with murder and one of the crucial pieces of evidence before the High Court was open source material, specifically a video that captured the shooting.[50] Furthermore, there has been significant use of open source evidence in election petition cases, starting with the formative *Ndwiga Steve Mbogo v I.E.B.C & 2 others* election petition, on which this book's hypothetical case is based.[51]

Both cases disclose various instances in which there is either a violation or potential violation of human rights in Kenya which enjoins the Criminal

50 [2010] eKLR.
51 Election Petition no. 7 of 2017.

and the Constitutional and Human Rights Divisions. In order to ensure that there is effective and prompt access to justice in such instances as mandated by international human rights law principles, and keeping in mind this book's hypothesis, there is therefore a pressing need to clarify whether the Evidence Act is still effective and capable of grappling with the challenges that arise as a result of using open source evidence within such legal proceedings in Kenya.

Theoretical Framework

Third World Approaches to International Law

Thus far, an overwhelming majority of discourse relating to open source evidence has been from one geopolitical location, the Global North, or as James Gathii calls it, the first world.[52] This points to the fact that discussions and standard setting on the use of open source evidence in legal processes are currently only happening in this geopolitical location. This is despite the fact that the Global South, Africa to be specific, has been the site on which open source investigations have been carried out and continue to be carried out, and to that extent this region is contributing to the development of and the refining of the open source evidence discourse.

The second and equally important point that this book is alive to is the impact of transplanting laws without taking into consideration the specific context of a particular domestic system.[53] As was the case in Kenya, where British colonialism saw the transplanting of the British legal system, which resulted in the relegation of the indigenous systems.[54] Even though a discussion of the impact of this transplantation in Kenya is beyond the scope of this book, it is critical that such an exercise, a non-context specific transplantation of laws, is avoided. The most effective way of guaranteeing this is by ensuring that the theoretical framework that underpins this book is alive to such legacies and that it provides a proposal as to how to avoid such an exercise. It is based on this premise that this book relies on the Third World Approaches to International Law as a theoretical framework.

TWAIL is defined as a broad dialectic of opposition to the traditional configuration of international law, its Eurocentric origins, colonial and imperial legacies and argues for a more inclusive international law.[55] Makau Mutua

52 JT Gathii, "TWAIL: A Brief History of Its Origins, Its Decentralized Network, and a Tentative Bibliography," *Trade Law & Development* (2011) Vol. 3, p 34.

53 JA Yakubu, "Colonialism, Customary Law and the Post-Colonial State in Africa: The Case of Nigeria," *Africa Development* (2005) Vol. XXX, 4, pp 201–220.

54 It is interesting to note here that prior to independence, the Indian Evidence Act applied in Kenya as a result of this colonial transplanting and the cessation of its application only happened in 1872 with the coming into force of the Evidence Act, Laws of Kenya under its section 185 (1).

55 Gathii (n 13 above) p 31.

notes that TWAIL is driven by three basic, interrelated and purposeful objectives which are:

i. To understand, deconstruct and unpack the uses of international law as a medium for the creation and perpetuation of a racialised hierarchy of international norms and institutions that subordinate non-Europeans to Europeans;
ii. To construct and present an alternative normative legal edifice for international governance; and,
iii. To, through scholarship, policy and politics, eradicate the conditions of underdevelopment in the Third World.[56]

It is therefore, among other things, a school of thought that seeks to reject the diminishing of voices from the Third World in discussions about international law.

One of the main proponents of TWAIL, James Gathii, views TWAIL as a historically aware methodology in that it challenges the simplistic visions of an innocent third world and a colonising and dominating first world.[57] He posits that this methodology is situated within the assumption that it is not possible to detach modern forms of domination such as the concept of governmentality from older forms of domination such as colonisation.[58] In explaining this position further, Anthony Anghie argues that persisting issues such as racial discrimination, economic exploitation and cultural subordination can best be understood by re-examining the relationship between international law and colonialism.[59] He notes that doctrinal and institutional developments in international law cannot be understood as "logical elaborations of a stable, philosophically conceived sovereignty doctrine ... [but rather] as being generated by problems relating to colonial order."[60]

The underlying idea in Makau's, Gathii's and Anghie's conceptualisation of TWAIL is therefore the need for a distinctive approach to thinking about international law. This is because the current conceptions of international law are ones that Walter Mignolo observes as being confined to thinking from a certain geopolitical location – Europe – and which excludes other sites of knowledge generation such as the Third World.[61] On human rights and its

56 MW Mutua, "What Is TWAIL?," 94 Proceedings of the ASIL Annual Meeting (2000) 31. Available: https://digitalcommons.law.buffalo.edu/articles/560, accessed 11 November 2023.
57 Gathii (n 55 above) p 34.
58 JT Gathii, "Imperialism, Colonialism, and International Law," *BuFF. L. Rev.* (2007) Vol. 54, p 1013.
59 A Anghie, "Imperialism, Sovereignty and the Making of International Law," (2005) p 6–7.
60 Anghie (n 62 above).
61 W Mignolo, "The Geopolitics of Knowledge and the Colonial Difference," *The South Atlantic Quarterly* (2002) Vol. 101, pp 59 & 63–74.

decolonisation, Mignolo asserts that: the future demands thinking beyond the Greeks and eurocentrism and requires a radical reconceptualisation of the human rights paradigm and only then can the project of decolonising human rights be achieved.[62]

Therefore, for TWAILers, even though international law guarantees sovereign equality and self-determination, it is still the vessel through which the legacy of imperialism and colonial conquest is carried forward.[63]

Antony Anghie and B S Chimni coined the terms "TWAIL I" and "TWAIL II," where TWAIL I refers to the scholarship produced by that first generation of post-colonial international legal actors while TWAIL II refers to scholarship that "has broadly followed the TWAIL I tradition and elaborated upon it, while, inevitably, departing from it in significant ways."[64] Eslava notes that whereas the assignment of TWAIL I was to wrestle with imperialism at home, the struggle of TWAIL II and beyond is to "deal with the vestiges of formal empire and expanding multi-dimensional forms of informal imperialism."[65] Even more specifically on the sub-schools, Gathii holds that there exist several TWAIL strands that explore the roles of international law in constituting order and disorder.[66]

This book adopts the TWAIL strand that international law should be understood as a field of practice that influences everyday life at very localised levels and that there is therefore a need to expand its scope of inquiry into places and locales within which international law operates beyond the typical sites such as within international institutions and treaty regimes.[67] As noted by Gathii, the methodological stance adopted in this strand of TWAIL focuses on how international law constitutes and reconstitutes routines, spaces and objects including municipal laws.[68] This strand is the most relevant to this book given the emphasis it places on extending TWAIL scholarship beyond the traditional historical confines as well as going beyond its modes of self-representation particularly those termed by Anne Orford as a "heroic agent of progress, security, order, human rights and democracy."[69]

Luis Eslava and Sundhya Pahuja posit that international law and institutions get their power and authority because they transcend the boundaries between

62 W Mignolo, "Philosophy and the Colonial Difference," in E Mendieta (ed.) *Latin American Philosophy*, Indiana University Press (2003) p 85; W Mignolo, "The Many Faces of Cosmopolis: Border Thinking and Critical Cosmopolitanism," *Public Culture* (2000) Vol. 12, p 739.

63 Anghie (n 62 above).

64 A Anghie & B Chimni, "Third World Approaches to International Law and Individual Responsibility in Internal Conflicts," *Chinese Journal of International Law* (2003) Vol. 2, p 77.

65 L Eslava, "TWAIL Coordinates," 2 April 2019.

66 Gathii (n 13 above) p 13. See pages 12–21 for an elaboration of these strands.

67 Gathii (n 13 above) p 18.

68 Gathii (n 13 above) p 19.

69 A Orford, "Muscular Humanitarianism: Reading the Narratives of the New Interventionism,'" *European Journal of International Law* (1999) Vol. 10, pp 679–711.

the national and international, and it is as a result of this transcending that it becomes a part of the "everyday reality of people."[70] Noting this type of impact and the aims and objectives of this study to ultimately influence municipal laws with respect to open source evidence, this strand of TWAIL is best suited as it lays a foundation that will support consequent analysis. This is in cognisance of the accepted TWAIL position that international law is not always an instrument of colonial or post-colonial opposition, but it can, under certain circumstances, be an instrument for or a site of liberation, such as enhancing accountability for human rights violations through setting standards for open source evidence. It is, however, imperative that such standard setting is devoid of traditional hegemonic tendencies that are characteristic of international law.

Despite the fact that the TWAIL framework is principally geared towards an analysis of international law, in the sense that it is defined as a broad dialect of opposition to the traditional configuration of international law, while this thesis' overall objective is to borrow from international standards and practices of national jurisdictions in the Global North to influence national practice in Kenya, TWAIL is still best suited to support the research questions posed herein. This is due to the historically acknowledged fact that municipal laws tend to follow international law.[71] And as noted above, due to the fact that discussions and standard setting on the use of open source evidence in legal processes are currently, predominantly, taking place at the international stage and/or in the Global North, it is imperative that this book remains alive to the fact that, while relying on these best practices to develop a framework that will ultimately influence practice at the municipal level, awareness has to be brought to the effects of transplanting these standards and/or practices without taking into consideration the history of Kenya.

Particularly, the fact that historically laws have been transplanted from other jurisdictions without considering the unique circumstances in Kenya that would warrant a different approach and/or require the filtering of some of the standards and/or practices that are being borrowed from elsewhere. Therefore, this book's perspective of the TWAIL framework is its clarion call that these standards should take into consideration the prevailing circumstances of the specific municipal jurisdiction, that is, Kenya, as opposed to transplanting legislations as was the case in post-colonial times.

It is therefore because of this need to ensure that any proposed framework is informed by the idiosyncrasies of Kenya as a legal system, that a data collection exercise was conducted to determine, in the first instance, the insights

70 L Eslava & S Pahuja, "Beyond the (Post)Colonial: TWAIL and the Everyday Life of International Law," *Journal of Law and Politics in Africa, Asia and Latin America* (2012) Vol. 45, 195.

71 See generally, I Seidl-Hohenveldern, "Transformation or Adoption of International Law into Municipal Law," *International and Comparative Law Quarterly* (1963) Vol. 12, 1, pp 88–124.

of legal practitioners and judicial actors who were hypothesised to be having knowledge that would provide a clear picture of the *status quo* in Kenya *vis-à-vis* open source evidence by providing an insight into their experiences. And secondly, a systematic case study was conducted to ascertain how Kenyan courts have addressed the issue of open source evidence. This was then followed by a proposal of a context-specific framework which marries the findings from the data collection and the best practices that were gleaned from international standards and practices. An approach that mirrors the TWAIL framework's clarion call.

Structure of the Book

Chapter 1 provides an overall introduction to the book. Chapter 2 expounds on the available guidance on the use of open source evidence from the jurisprudence of other countries. To this end, a comparative analysis of the national jurisprudence from leading common law jurisdictions, that is, England and Wales, Canada and the United States of America, is conducted. The analysis seeks to determine how questions of admissibility and authentication of open source evidence have been dealt with in these jurisdictions. The aim of Chapter 2 is to glean best practices that could potentially influence the legal framework eventually proposed in Chapter 5.

The comparative analysis finds that these jurisdictions have had extensive interaction with open source evidence in their judicial processes, as denoted by the presence of considerable judicial evaluation of questions relating to its admissibility. Similarly, the comparative analysis shows that open source evidence is generally admissible in courts and has been predominantly categorised as documentary evidence. As expected, there are marked differences in the approaches taken by each jurisdiction in assessing admissibility of open source evidence. This divergence is logical, as rightly observed by McDermott, who notes that "there are few areas of practice that diverge so dramatically between different legal systems as that of admissibility of evidence.""[72]

As part of the endeavour to look to international standards and approaches to glean best practices, Chapter 3 examines international case law and the practice of UN human rights investigations, to equally consider the use of open source evidence in legal processes from international practice. This is done by examining the legal framework and relevant decisions of international criminal courts and tribunals. Further, official guidance from the OHCHR is also analysed; that is, both the "Commissions of Inquiry and Fact-Finding Missions on International Human Rights and Humanitarian Law: Guidance and Practice" and the "Berkeley Protocol on Digital Open Source Investigations"(Berkeley Protocol) are examined. Reports of UN-mandated human rights investigations,

72 Y McDermott, *Proving International Crimes*, Oxford University Press (Forthcoming 2024), see Chapter 3 generally.

such as the Independent International Commission of Inquiry on the Syrian Arab Republic and the Independent International Fact-Finding Mission on Myanmar (FFM), *inter alia*, are also reviewed. The overall aim of Chapter 3 is therefore to draw parallels between the discussed examples and to distil lessons that can inform the proposed framework for the use of open source evidence in Kenya.

Chapter 3 establishes that there is a steady development of international practice across various legal, policy and investigative processes that can be studied comparatively. Beyond the best practice gleaned from these discussions, the chapter also lends support to one of this research's main contentions: that open source evidence is a type of evidence the Kenyan legal system will have to contend with imminently, necessitating a framework for its use in legal practice.

Chapter 4 assesses whether Kenya's legal framework is suitable in relation to open source evidence. To answer this question, it is postulated that the best way to understand the *status quo* of a legal system is, first, to engage with that legal system's stakeholders, and second, to examine how its courts have pronounced themselves on the said issues. This approach is in line with the TWAIL framework's clarion call to ensure that the idiosyncrasies of a particular domestic legal system are understood before relying on international standards and practices to inform legal practice within it.This way, any unique circumstances that would warrant a different approach and thus require the filtering of some of the said standards and practices are made possible. Accordingly, a survey based on a hypothetical case is conducted, targeting defence counsel, prosecutors, police investigators and judges. A systematic case study is also conducted to assess how open source evidence has been used, and/or interpreted by courts, in legal proceedings in Kenya.

The analysis of the data shows that litigants and judicial actors in Kenya possess a good grasp of the concept of open source evidence. The data also reveal that the same standards apply when adducing "normal" digital evidence and open source evidence in Kenya. It is, however, evident, as this chapter demonstrates, that reliance on this legal framework to assess the admissibility of open source evidence, especially anonymously posted open source evidence, is not sufficient. It is on this basis that Chapter 4 concludes that there is a need for a legal framework that provides guidance on the admissibility of open source evidence in Kenya.

Chapter 5 determines how open source evidence should be litigated and judicially evaluated in Kenyan courts. This assessment establishes that section 78A of the Evidence Act provides a legal foundation for the admissibility of open source evidence in Kenya, while section 106B provides for the assessment of the weight to be apportioned to it. However, this legal framework is wrought with challenges that largely relate to the fact that these sections were conceptualised to cater for traditional digital and electronic evidence. Reliance on the current legal framework, despite these challenges, would have a deleterious effect on the use of open source evidence in legal proceedings in Kenya. To address these challenges, Chapter 5 proposes a tripartite framework that addresses both procedural and technical considerations.

Lastly, Chapter 6 provides the book's overall conclusion, followed by recommendations on how the framework proposed in Chapter 5 can be operationalised in practice.

Bibliography

Books

Anghie, A *Imperialism, sovereignty and the making of international law* (Cambridge University Press 2007).

McDermott, Y *Proving international crimes* (Oxford University Press 2023).

Book Chapters

Freeman, L 'Prosecuting atrocity crimes with open source evidence: Lessons from the International Criminal Court' in Dubberley, S; Koeing, A & Murray, D (eds) *Digital witness: Using open source information for human rights investigation, documentation and accountability* (Oxford University Press, 2019).

Gathii, JT 'The agenda of Third World Approaches to International Law (TWAIL)' in Dunoff, J & Pollack, M (eds) *International Legal theory: Foundations and frontiers* (Cambridge University Press 2019).

Jordi, PJ & Pawel, K 'User-generated information system' in Carayannis, EG (ed) *Encyclopedia of creativity, intervention, innovation and entrepreneurship* (Springer Science & Business 2017).

Mignolo, W 'Philosophy and the colonial difference' in Mendieta, E (ed) *Latin American philosophy: Currents, issues, debates* (Indiana University Press 2003).

Journal Articles

Aksamitowska, K 'Digital evidence in domestic core international crimes prosecutions: Lessons learned from Germany, Sweden, Finland and the Netherlands' (2021) 19 *Journal of International Criminal Justice* 189.

Anghie, A & Chimni, B 'Third world approaches to international law and individual responsibility in internal conflicts' (2003) 2(1) *Chinese Journal of International Law* 77.

Busser, ED 'Open source data and criminal investigations: Anything you publish can and will be used against you' (2014) 2(2) *Groningen Journal of International Law*.

Ellis, MS 'Shifting the paradigm—Bringing to justice those who commit human rights atrocities' (2015) 47(1) *Journal of International Law* 265.

Eslava, L & Pahuja, S 'Beyond the (post) colonial: TWAIL and the everyday life of international law' (2012) 45(2) *Journal of Law and Politics in Africa, Asia and Latin America* 195.

Freeman, L 'Digital evidence and war crimes prosecutions: The impact of digital technologies on international criminal investigations and trials' (2018) 41(2) *Fordham International Law Journal* 283.

Gabriele, C, Matheson, K & Llorente, RV 'The role of mobile technology in documenting international crimes: The affaire castro et kizito in the Democratic Republic of Congo' (2021) 19(1) *Journal of International Criminal Justice* 107.

Gathii, JT 'Imperialism, colonialism, and international Law' (2007 54(4) *Buffalo Law Review* 1013.

Gathii, JT 'TWAIL: A brief history of its origins, Its decentralized network, and a tentative bibliography' (2011) 3(1) *Trade Law and Development* 26.

Hamilton, RJ 'User-generated evidence' (2018) 57(1) *Columbia Journal of Transnational Law*.

Hiatt, K 'Open source evidence on trial' (2016) 125 *The Yale Law Journal* 323.

McDermott, Y, Koenig, A & Murray, D 'Open source information's blind spot: Human and machine bias in international criminal investigations' (2021) 19(1) *Journal of International Criminal Justice* 85.

Mehandru, N & Koenig, A 'ICTS, social media, & the future of human rights' (2019) 17 *Duke Law & Technology Review* 129.

Mehandru, N & Koenig, A 'Open source evidence and the International Criminal Court' (2019) 4 *Harvard Human Rights Journal.*

Mignolo, W 'The geopolitics of knowledge and the colonial difference' (2002) 101(1) *The South Atlantic Quarterly* 57.

Mignolo, W 'The many faces of cosmo-polis: Border thinking and critical cosmopolitanism' (2000) 12(3) *Public Culture* 721.

Mutua, MW 'What is TWAIL?' (2000) 94 *Proceedings of the ASIL Annual Meeting* 31.

Orford, A 'Muscular humanitarianism: Reading the narratives of the new interventionism' (1999) 10(4) *European Journal of International Law* 679.

Pattenden, R 'Authenticating things in English law: Principles for adducing tangible evidence in common law jury trials' (2009) 12 *The International Journal of Evidence and Proof* 273.

Rutenberg, I; Kiptinness, S & Sugow, A 'Admission of electronic evidence: Contradictions in the Kenyan Evidence Act' (2021) 18 *Digital Evidence and Electronic Signature Law Review* 37.

Seidl-Hohenveldern, I 'Transformation or adoption of international law into municipal law' (1963) 12(1) *International and Comparative Law Quarterly* 88.

Yakubu JA, 'Colonialism, customary law and the post-colonial state in Africa: The case of Nigeria' (2005) 30 *Africa Development* (2005) 4.

United Nations Documents

OHCHR & Human Rights Center UC Berkeley School of Law, 'Berkeley Protocol on Digital Open Source Investigations: A practical guide on the effective use of digital open source information in investigating violations of international criminal, human rights and humanitarian law' 2022 UN Doc HR/PUB/20/2.

United Nations General Assembly, 'Basic Principles and Guidelines on the Right to a Remedy and Reparation for Victims of Gross Violations of International Human Rights Law and Serious Violations of International Humanitarian Law,' 21 March 2006 A/RES/60/147.

Internet Sources

Allen, K 'Digital evidence – A step forward for South Africa: As police and prosecutors test new legislation, what are the challenges of using digital evidence?,' Institute of Security Studies, 11 September 2023.

Bellingcat https://www.bellingcat.com/about/.

Eslava, L 'TWAIL coordinates' Critical Legal Thinking, 2 April 2019 https://criticallegalthinking.com/2019/04/02/twail-coordinates/.

Irving, E 'And so it begins… social media evidence in an icc arrest warrant' Opinio Juris, 17 August 2017 http://archive.is/XXRZ0#selection-93.0-93.64.

Irwin, A 'Digital evidence opens doors to human rights probes' SciDevNet, March 2019 https://www.scidev.net/global/supported-content/digital-evidence-opens-doors-to-human-rightsprobes/.

Koenig, A & Freeman, L 'Strengthening atrocity cases with digital open source investigations' Lieber Institute West Point, 1 April 2021 https://lieber.westpoint.edu/strengthening-atrocity-cases-digital-opensource-investigations/.

Liao, Y 'Investigating the use of online open source information as evidence in European courts' International Conference on Availability, Reliability and Security, 27 August 2018 https://dl.acm.org/doi/abs/10.1145/3230833.3232812.

Stavrou, K 'Open-source digital evidence in international criminal cases: A way forward in ensuring accountability for core crimes?' Opinio Juris http://opiniojuris.org/2021/01/26/open-source-digitalevidence-in-international-criminal-cases-a-way-forward-in-ensuring-accountability-for-core-crimes/.

'Swedish court hands life sentence to Syrian for war crimes' The Local, 16 February 2017 https://archive.is/ZSWKF.

Syria Justice & Accountability Centre, 'Violations Database' https://syriaaccountability.org/database/.

The Syrian Archive, https://syrianarchive.org/en/about.

TRIAL International, 'Universal Jurisdiction Annual Review (UJAR) 2020: Atrocities must be prosecuted soundly and rigorously' 30 March 2020 https://trialinternational.org/latest-post/universal-jurisdictionannual-review-2020-atrocities-must-be-prosecuted-soundly-and-rigorously/.

Table of cases

International Criminal Court

The Prosecutor v Ahmad Al Faqi Al Mahdi, Trial Chamber VIII, ICC-01/12-01/15-171 27 September 2016.

The Prosecutor v Ahmad Al Faqi Al Mahdi, Trial Chamber VIII, ICC-01/12-01/15-T-4-Red-ENG 22 August 2016.

The Prosecutor v Al Hassan Ag Abdoul Aziz Ag Mohamed Ag Mahmoud, Trial Chamber X, ICC-01/12- 01/18-T-027-Red-ENG 21 September 2020.

The Prosecutor v Al Hassan Ag Abdoul Aziz Ag Mohamed Ag Mahmoud, Defence Response to Prosecution's Second Request for the Admission of Documentary Evidence from the Bar Table, No. ICC-01/12-01/18, 26 April 2021.

The Prosecutor v Germain Katanga, Trial Chamber II, ICC-01/04-01/07-2635 19 December 2010.

The Prosecutor v Jean-Pierre Bemba Gombo, Aime Kilolo Musamba, Jean-Jacques Mangenda Kabongo, Fidele Babala Wandu & AridoNarcisse , Trial Chamber VII, ICC-01/05-01/13-1498-Conf, 30 November 2015.
The Prosecutor v Jean-Pierre Bemba Gombo, Aimé Kilolo Musamba, Jean-Jacques Mangenda Kabongo, Fidèle Babala Wandu and Narcisse Arido, Trial Chamber VII, ICC-01/05-01/13-1524, 14 December 2015.
The Prosecutor v Mahmoud Mustafa Busayf Al-Werfalli, Warrant of Arrest, ICC-01/11-01/17, 15 August 2017.

European Court of Justice

Sharif v Council, (Common foreign and security policy - Restrictive measures against Syria), Judgment [2019] EUECJ T-5/17 04 April 2019.

International Tribunals

Ndayambaje & Evariste, RP No. 1215/2017, RMP No. 6043/YM/017, Military Tribunal Bukavu 21 September 2018.

National case law

Kenya

Ndwiga Steve Mbogo v I.E.B.C & 2 others, Election Petition no. 7 of 2017.
R v Edward Kirui [2010] eKLR.
Republic v Mark Lloyd Steveson [2016] eKLR.
Republic v Naomi Muthoni Mwaura [2018] eKLR.
Shekue Kahale Kombo v Governor Lamu County & 2 others [2022] eKLR.

Sweden

Stockholm District Court, Case No.: B 3787-16, Judgment of 2017-02-16.

2 Comparative National Jurisprudence on the Use of Open Source Evidence

Introduction

As open source evidence continues to take root, there is proof of its development as a practice within various legal and policy processes. As recognised by the theoretical framework underpinning this research, international practice influences national processes in multifaceted ways. Bearing this in mind, this chapter seeks to answer the research question, "what is the available guidance on the use of open source evidence from comparative national jurisprudence?" The first objective of the chapter is to draw guidance from these jurisdictions on how questions relating to the admissibility and authentication of open source evidence have been handled. The second objective of this chapter is to determine best practices within the context of open source investigations and how these can consequently influence the Kenyan practice.

These objectives will be met by assessing specific evidentiary themes and how they relate to open source evidence. These themes include authentication,[1] categorisation of open source evidence – specifically determining whether the form of open source evidence will impact its admissibility, and a consideration of exclusionary rules under the law of evidence that may impact the admissibility of open source evidence such as the rule against hearsay. This research proceeds on the premise that these are the most crucial themes in terms of assessing the admissibility of open source evidence.

It is important to highlight that whereas a discussion of how courts have discussed the theme of verification would be desirable, the case analysis in this chapter and as shall be seen in Chapter 4, discloses that the cases do not generally relate to verification. And in the instances that the cases do make reference to verification, it appears courts are using the term authentication to refer to both processes.

However, such an assessment is not a straightforward endeavour due to the special nature of open source evidence. That is, it is evidence that "bounces

1 As the majority of the cases discussed in this research bear upon the challenges of authentication vis-à-vis open source evidence.

DOI: 10.4324/9781003770343-2

around categories and is difficult to compartmentalise," necessitating a deeper understanding as to how best to approach questions regarding the rules of process, rules of admissibility and rules of reasoning.[2] As it is aptly noted that "social media evidence is legitimately many different kinds of evidence – from real to testimonial, from documentary to pictorial," because it blurs the categories of evidence to the extent that it defies any attempts at applying traditional rules of evidence, as they are.[3]

Based on the foregoing, the question whether the rules of evidence regarding the admissibility of open source evidence should be identical to traditional rules of evidence is important. In order to answer this question, it is prudent to first assess how other jurisdictions have handled these evidential considerations. Therefore, the cases that are analysed in the ensuing discussions are not necessarily identical to this research's main question, but they are enlightening as to how comparative national jurisdictions have grappled with these questions.

How Are Other National Jurisdictions Litigating and Judicially Evaluating Open Source Evidence?

There has been a considerable increase in the use of open source information in trial proceedings over the past years. For example, some European domestic courts in Sweden, Germany, Finland and Netherlands have used open source evidence to prosecute war crimes stemming from the conflicts in Syria and Iraq under the doctrine of universal jurisdiction. It is reported that these countries have used evidence from Twitter, Facebook posts, YouTube videos, among others, to triangulate and corroborate other evidence.[4] Digitally derived open source evidence has therefore proven to be instrumental in these prosecutions and, as a result, these countries have devised ways to effectively collect open source evidence, process it, analyse it, and share it.

At a regional level, the Democratic Republic of Congo's prosecution of two leaders of the Democratic Forces for the Liberation of Rwanda (FDLR) who had been accused of crimes against humanity also provides an example of the usage of open source evidence at a domestic level closer to Kenya. In this case, two commanders of the FDLR were found guilty of murder and torture as constituting crimes against humanity based on mobile device footage that contained photo and video evidence that was captured using the "eyeWitness to Atrocities" camera application.[5] The "eyeWitness to Atrocities" mobile

2 LA Silver, "The Unclear Picture of Social Media Evidence," *Manitoba Law Journal* (2020) Vol. 43, 3, p 121.
3 Silver (n 94 above).
4 Aksamitowska (n 89 above) p 192.
5 eyeWitness to Atrocities, "Bringing Historical Crimes to Justice in the Democratic Republic of the Congo" (2018). Available: https://www.eyewitness.global/Bringing-historical-crimes-to-a-domestic-court-in-the-DRC, accessed 11 November 2023.

camera app allows a user to record photos and videos that are embedded with the metadata needed to demonstrate their authenticity to a court.[6] It also provides for the transmission and storage of footage while creating a chain of custody to allow the photos to be used as evidence in court.[7] These images were taken to help prove contextual and material elements of the underlying offences of murder and torture and they contained embedded metadata that confirmed the locations of the graves and villages where these violations occurred, providing corroboration to other evidence.[8]

It should be noted that the above examples have only been included in this research insofar as these countries provide evidence of a growing state practice in the collection, processing and analysis of open source evidence in legal processes at the domestic level. This is because their use as a comparative study from whence to distil best practices is limited due to various factors. These factors range from the fact that the European countries are civil law systems, meaning there is already a fundamental departure in the existing evidentiary processes and an attempt to borrow from it to influence the use of open source evidence in a common law country can only lead to further confusion and legal challenges. Additionally, and as already noted, these countries have used open source evidence to prosecute international crimes at the domestic level under the principle of universal jurisdiction – in the case of the European countries, this does not therefore provide a good basis to distil best practice to influence domestic level adjudication of municipal laws.

For these reasons, the next sections will focus solely on the usage of open source evidence in common law jurisdictions. Due to its relationship with Kenya, a systematic case study of England & Wales will be conducted based on the search terms that have been set out under the research methodology section.[9] These are: Facebook, Twitter, YouTube, "open source evidence," and "social media evidence." This systematic study will then be augmented by an analysis of secondary material that will include a discussion of key cases from leading common law jurisdictions, specifically Canada and the USA.[10]

6 Welcome to eyewitness, https://www.eyewitness.global, accessed 11 November 2023.

7 Welcome to eyeWitness, https://www.eyewitness.global, accessed 11 November 2023.

8 eyeWitness to Atrocities (n 97 above).

9 The Evidence Act that was enacted at independence on 10 December, 1963 only underwent comprehensive amendments in 2010 (and enacted in 2012). Also, Kenya still maintains close relations with England and Wales in terms of borrowing of precedents and influence in legal practice.

10 While the inclusion of some examples from the Global South in the case study would have been desirable, regrettably, as at the time of writing, there was not sufficient information to support this inclusion beyond the current brief references.

Admissibility of Open Source Evidence in England and Wales

Introduction

Evidence from social media has been used in courts in England and Wales for various reasons. It has been used to prove the guilt of accused persons by prosecutors; for instance, in *Khan v R*, content from Blackberry messages, Facebook and Instagram was part of the evidence under consideration.[11] In *Burns v R*, material found on electronic media that was discovered on an account that "was not locked and so could be readily accessed by any user of the internet" was used to assess the appellant's state of mind and intention, resulting in his conviction.[12] This evidence has also been used to determine whether social media identification constitutes lawful identification,[13] and to determine questions relating to violations of international humanitarian law, among other usages.[14]

It is worth noting, however, that in some cases, lower courts have been very dismissive of open source evidence. For instance, in the *Campaign Against Arms Trade, R (On the Application Of) v The Secretary of State for International Trade* case referenced above, an English Divisional Court dismissed the challenge brought by the applicant on the grounds that, "open source material [that is, NGO reporting] is only part of the picture."[15] The Court of Appeal, however, set aside the lower court's decision and, by extension, gave credence to open source evidence whereby the court noted, *inter alia*, that in instances where OSINT material can prove the missing aspect of a case's hypothesis or can corroborate a witness's testimony, it helps to build a stronger case and there is therefore every reason to strive to put it before the Court.[16]

Even more importantly, the question of admissibility of open source material that had been posted anonymously was considered in England and Wales in the case of *Amjad v R*. The facts of the case, as noted by the Court of Appeal, were that a search of the appellant's home revealed a large quantity of anti-western publications and a notebook containing his handwritten list of fitness requirements for a Mujahideen fighter. The Crown argued, *inter alia*,

11 [2015] EWCA Crim 1816.

12 [2017] EWCA Crim 1466.

13 See for instance the case of *R v Crampton* [2020] EWCA CRIM 1334 and *R v Phillips* [2020] EWCA CRIM 126. In acknowledging that indeed a social media identification is not a formal procedure, the same can still be admitted as evidence as long as the weaknesses of such an identification process are pointed out to the jury; *T v R* [2012] EWCA Crim 2358, where content from Facebook was being used to support the defence's case, *inter alia*.

14 *Campaign Against Arms Trade, R (On the Application Of) v The Secretary of State for International Trade* [2017] EWHC 1754 (Admin).

15 [2017] EWHC 1754 (Admin), para.86. See also, D Minogue, "Digital Accountability Symposium: Harnessing User-generated Content in Accountability Efforts for International Law Violations in Yemen," *Opinio Juris*, 18 December 2019.

16 [2017] EWHC 1754 (Admin), para. 134. See also, Minogue (n 106 above). It should be reiterated here that the open source material that was being referenced is NGO evidence.

that in the context of other anti-western documents in the appellant's home, his handwritten list of fitness exercises was intended to be of assistance to someone planning to commit an act of terrorism. This was on the basis of an internet search by the police that revealed a similar list of fitness requirements in a document "Crusaders War on Iraq" and in a Wikipedia reference to its author Yusef Al Aliyi as a terrorist. The issue was therefore whether the page had been written as part of a fitness regime – the appellant's case – or whether, by showing how to get fit for war, they could further acts of terrorism by the appellant or someone else – the Crown's case.[17]

Arguing successfully for the reliance on open source material, the Crown contended that:

> to establish the intention behind the document it should be permitted to rely on open source material. Even though it did not have an expert witness to describe that material, it argued that it was significant that the document found in open source research, and which it argued was strikingly similar to the appellant's list, featured in two places online and both sources ascribed it to Yusuf, a terrorist.[18]

The defence argued that it was wrong to admit the material because its source was unsafe as the Wikipedia author was unknown. Specifically, the appellant's ground of appeal before the Court of Appeal Criminal Division was:

> The judge was wrong to admit the open source material relating to the source and to the author of the original list. There was no power at common law or in reliance on the Criminal Justice Act 2003 or on the Coroners and Justice Act 2009 to admit anonymous hearsay.[19]

In dismissing the Appeal, the Court of Appeal noted that the trial judge was right in ruling that there did not exist hearsay because "the jury was not invited to conclude that the internet-derived material amounted to the truth."[20]

The relevant laws in England and Wales include the Criminal Justice Act 2003,[21] the Police and Criminal Evidence Act 1984, which is the law that gives the police power to secure evidence as part of a criminal investigation,[22] and

17 [2016] EWCA Crim 1618.
18 [2016] EWCA Crim 1618.
19 [2016] EWCA Crim 1618, para. 14. See also, D Minogue, S Allen, C Andrews-Briscoe & Y McDermott, "Putting Principles into Practice: Reflections on a Mock Admissibility Hearing on Open Source Evidence," Global Legal Action Network & Bellingcat (2020). Available: https://cronfa.swan.ac.uk/Record/cronfa63763, accessed 11 November 2023.
20 [2016] EWCA Crim 1618, para. 36.
21 The Civil Evidence Act of 1995, for civil matters.
22 Since this research focuses predominantly on the criminal aspect of conduct, the Civil Evidence Act will not be discussed as it goes beyond the scope of the research.

the Police, Crime, Sentencing and Courts Act, which received Royal Assent in April 2022, and its sections 37 to 44 deal with the extraction of information from electronic devices.[23]

Section 134 (1) of the Criminal Justice Act 2003 addresses the issue of proving a statement in a document whereby a document has been defined as anything in which information of any description is recorded. This brings evidence from social media platforms within the definition of documents.[24] Furthermore, in *Marlton v Tektronix UK Holdings Ltd*, databases, backup tapes and servers were held as being documents clearly bringing open source output within the purview of documents.[25]

Authentication of Open Source Evidence in England and Wales

In order to provide proof of the said documents, section 133 of the Criminal Justice Act prescribes that:

> Where a statement in a document is admissible as evidence in criminal proceedings, the statement may be proved by producing either –
>
> (a) the document, or
> (b) (whether or not the document exists) a copy of the document or of the material part of it, ***authenticated in whatever way the court may approve***.[26]

Authentication in England and Wales is therefore determined "in whatever way the court may approve." However, this does not provide much guidance as to what an applicable standard can be. This has led to the conclusion, by some authors, that authentication in England and Wales lacks a common standard resulting in ambiguity.[27] This lack of a common standard and/or clear guidance on the authentication of electronic evidence has been ascribed to various reasons. O'Floinn and Ormerod connect it to the lack of a clear standard under section 133 as above,[28] while Gauthier ascribes it to the complexity of the pieces of legislation that deal with the admissibility of computer-generated

23 J Goldstraw-White, "Legal and Policy Framework for Digital Forensics: A Resource for Practitioners," A Policy and Practice Briefing from the Digital Forensics and Social Media project funded by the Dawes Trust (2022).
24 M O'Floinn & D Ormerod, "Social Networking Material as Criminal Evidence," *Criminal Law Review* (2012) Vol. 7, p 3. See also for example, *R v Thames Magistrates Court, ex parte Da Costa & Co* [2002] EWHC 40 (Admin), where a hard disk was defined as being a document.
25 [2003] EWHC 383 (Ch).
26 The Explanatory Notes to the Act state that section 133 "corresponds to the position under section 27 of the Criminal Justice Act 1988, whereby a statement in a document can be proved by producing either the original document or an authenticated copy."
27 See for instance, O'Floinn & Ormerod (n 114 above) p 7.
28 O'Floinn & Ormerod (n 114 above) p 7.

evidence.[29] On the other hand, Mason and Stanfield attribute it to the fact that "traditional rules look at individual documents rather than the digital system in which digital data are created."[30] The resultant situation is therefore that authenticity is determined on a case-by-case basis in England and Wales.[31]

However, there is an overarching requirement that for evidence to be admitted it must be authentic, where authentic has been defined as being, "what it purports to be."[32] The *Kay v R* case, for example, was an appeal against a conviction for the offence of rape on the ground, *inter alia*, that "fresh evidence in the form of Facebook messages is now available that go directly to A's credibility. And that edited and misleading copies of the Facebook messages were adduced at trial." The appeal was upheld due largely to the fact that the lower court relied on evidence from Facebook that had not been adequately authenticated.[33] This is because the Facebook messages were not what they purported to be as they had been edited to favour the complainant's version of the story. The *Kay* decision also highlights the importance of ensuring there is continuity in evidence, that is, chain of custody, for data that has been derived from devices as this would have been the only way for the first instance court to ensure that the said Facebook messages had not been manipulated.

To demonstrate the place of technical evidence to authenticate electronic evidence, the court in *Nobel Resources SA v Gross* noted that:

> Prior to the start of the trial Mr. Gross attempted to cast doubt on the reliability or authenticity of the SMS evidence. However the technical evidence subsequently served by Noble explaining: (a) how the SMS messages were identified and recovered; (b) that it was not possible to alter an SMS message on a BlackBerry once it has been received or sent; and (c) that it would be very difficult to alter data on a server back-up, meant that when it came to trial there was no realistic attack by Mr. Gross on the reliability or authenticity of the SMS messages or any suggestion to the effect that they had been doctored or deleted.[34]

29 J Gauthier, "The Admissibility of Computer-Generated Evidence: An Overview," (2015). Available: https://www.yumpu.com/en/document/view/51956479/the-admissibility-of-computer-generated-evidence-an-overview, accessed 11 November 2023.

30 S Mason & A Stanfield, "Authenticating Electronic Evidence," in S Mason and Seng (eds), *Electronic Evidence*, University of London (2017) 4th edn, pp 193–260.

31 S Mason (ed), Electronic Evidence, LexisNexis Butterworths (2012) 3rd ed, p5.01 – 5.37; O'Floinn & Ormerod (n 114 above) p 7; Pattenden (n 16 above) pp 273–302.

32 Mason & Stanfield (n 120 above) p 193.

33 [2017] EWCA Crim 2214, para. 20.

34 2009] EWHC 1435 (Comm) para 60. It should be noted that this is a civil case; however, it provides a good clarification of the English & Wales courts' position on authentication. In *Bussey Law Firm PC v Page*, [2015] EWHC 563 (QB), the court established the standard of balance of probabilities and noted that: The likelihood is, in the absence of any convincing explanation to the contrary, that the posting from Mr Page's account was authored or authorised by him. It is extremely improbable that anyone successfully hacked into that account on

The import of this decision is that proper authentication can result in the admissibility of open source evidence and that the testimony of an expert can authenticate electronic evidence. It further shows the type of information that an expert witness would, for instance, have to show the court in order to prove this authenticity.

In *Amjad v R*, the court upbraided the Crown for its failure to call expert evidence to authenticate the open source evidence, and it noted:

> We were surprised the Crown made no effort to canvass expert evidence at least capable of establishing the provenance of some if not all open source material and perhaps of establishing authenticity and accuracy. Had it been able to lead any such evidence the court might have been better served. For all we know the Recorder might not have added, or might have tempered, his final caution to the jury.[35]

This case also highlights the risk of the lack of proper authentication – " the Crown did not have an expert witness to describe that material" – and for this reason, the court directed the jury that "it could not convict solely on the basis of the open source evidence." The direction given to the jury warned against the possible dangers arising from such evidence and the limited use to which it could be put. The Recorder emphasised that there was no evidence of who created the articles or when."[36]

It is, however, essential to emphasise at this point that the nature of the particular electronic evidence will ultimately determine the authentication requirements. This was noted by Mason and Stanfield, who quoted Lord Griffith, where he observed that:

---

27 January 2012 with a view to posting the words complained of. There is no evidence that anyone did so on that date and, moreover, no reason why anyone with a grudge against the Claimants should attempt to go down that route in any event. Why Mr Page should himself choose to attack the Claimants is also unclear, but the most likely explanation would appear to be a purely financial one. I do not need, however, to come to a conclusion on motive since it is not essential to the Claimants' cause of action. All I need say is that the overwhelming probability is that he is responsible for the posting from his account on the date in question and for its remaining accessible thereafter. There is simply no other reasonable explanation.

35 [2016] EWCA Crim 1618, para. 37. The jury had been warned about the dangers of the research, but were entitled to use the material to assist if struck by the similarity between the document on Wikipedia and another separate article. The Recorder would also admit the material with heavy caveats. The jury was further directed that it could not convict solely on the basis that the open source evidence showed that the Appellant's list of training requirements was identical to that attributed to a terrorist. The direction warned against the possible dangers arising from such evidence and the limited use to which it could be put. The Recorder emphasised that there was no evidence of who created the articles or when. (see para. 12–13).

36 [2016] EWCA Crim 1618, para. 13.

> Computers vary immensely in their complexity and in the operations they perform. The nature of the evidence to discharge the burden of showing that there has been no improper use of the computer and that it was operating properly will inevitably vary from case to case. I suspect that it will very rarely be necessary to call an expert and that in the vast majority of cases it will be possible to discharge the burden by calling a witness who is familiar with the operation of the computer in the sense of knowing what the computer is required to do and who can say that it is doing it properly.[37]

This is an important qualification given the diverse nature of open source evidence. In consonance with this position, Mason and Stanfield further note that "the tests of authenticity for digital data ... will vary, depending on the source and type of the data."[38]

This also appears to be the position taken by the court in *R v Mawji (Rizwan)* where the court refused the appellant's contention that "the provenance of the email could not be certain as it was relatively easy to produce a document that had nothing to do with the email address," and that for this reason, there should have been evidence that proved the audit trail.[39] The court noted instead that the way through which this evidence was presented in court, through the oral testimony of the victim, was sufficient to allow for its admission. In agreeing with this court's position, Mason and Stanfield observed that, "the email did not have to be authenticated in the way suggested by the appellant because of the circumstances surrounding the events and the other evidence in the case."[40] As the authenticity of a document in electronic format can be tested in other ways, for instance, by analysing the metadata.[41]

However, the court in *R v Skinner* noted the difficulty of authenticating "pages from the internet" due to the frequency at which they can be altered, in which case the court was discussing the admissibility of a website screenshot.[42] Therefore, in order to assess the relevance of any factual representation contained therein that may result in its inadmissibility, evidence of the provenance of the printout's content must be adduced.[43]

The court in *Khan* further revealed authentication markers in discussing the authentication of screenshots when it noted that:

37 Mason & Stanfield (n 120 above) p 203, discussing *R v Shephard* [1993] AC 380, 387.

38 Mason & Stanfield (n 120 above).

39 [2003] EWCA Crim 3067.

40 Mason & Stanfield (n 120 above) p 218.

41 A Stanfield, "The Authentication of Electronic Evidence," Queensland University of Technology (2016) p 204.

42 [2005] EWCA Crim 1439.

43 See, *Essen v DPP* [2005] EWHC 1077, para. 8. See also, Pattenden (n 16 above).

> no doubt the expectation of both this court and the parties was that the BlackBerry would be provided and subjected to proper analysis; and also that Jane would enable access to her Facebook account to provide some prospect of an investigation whether the images said to come from Choudhury's Facebook and Instagram postings in fact do so. PC Mark Evans, a specialist investigator of electronic evidence, was made available to examine whatever was produced by the appellant in compliance with this court's order.[44]

An apt summary of what is entailed in authenticating what has been termed as "complex systems" and can thus be applied to open source evidence as the authenticity threshold in England and Wales has been provided by Mason, and it includes:

1. The data (both the content and associated metadata) relied upon in any legal proceedings can be shown to be an accurate representation of the prevailing and existing state of those data at the time relevant to the legal proceedings.
2. If the data have changed, for whatever reason, there is an accurate and reliable method of documenting the changes, including the reasons for any such changes from the moment they were identified (and possibly seized) as potential evidence in legal proceedings.
3. The continuity of the data can be demonstrated between the moment the data were obtained for legal purposes and their submission as an exhibit in legal proceedings.
4. Any techniques that were used to obtain, secure and process the data can be shown to have been appropriate for the purpose for which they were applied.
5. The technical and organisational evidence demonstrates that the integrity of the data is trustworthy, and can therefore be considered to be reliable and complete (insofar as the data can be complete), which in turn will depend on the circumstances surrounding the data at the time they were identified as being potentially relevant in legal proceedings.[45]

44 [2015] EWCA Crim 1816, para. 9.

45 Mason & Stanfield (n 120 above) p 247. This is the standard that has been included in a "Draft Convention on Electronic Evidence" as proposed by Mason – which has been said to be the first treaty dealing with the status of electronic evidence, covering civil and criminal proceedings; the investigation and examination of electronic evidence, and general provisions regarding the recognition and admissibility of electronic evidence from foreign jurisdictions and was published in 2016. An important clarification to make here is that even though this proposed Draft Convention focuses on electronic evidence, the same standards can be transposed herein given that open source evidence falls under the electronic and digital evidence framework in Kenya. The second, yet very critical clarification is the fact that this proposed Draft Convention has been drafted by Stephen Mason in consultation with various stake-

As far as the best evidence rule is concerned, it has been noted that it is no longer applicable in the electronic environment due to the fact that originals do not exist *per se*.[46] This position has received judicial assent in *R v Governor Ex p Osman (No 1)* where the court noted:

> this court would be more than happy to say goodbye to the best evidence rule. We accept that it served an important purpose in the days of parchment and quill pens. But since the invention of carbon paper and, still more, the photocopier and the telefacsimile machine, that purpose has largely gone. Where there is an allegation of forgery the court will obviously attach little, if any, weight to anything other than the original; so also if the copy produced in court is illegible. But to maintain a general exclusionary rule for these limited purposes is, in our view, hardly justifiable.[47]

And this is even more true for open source evidence where the original only exists in "nanoseconds" and beyond the metadata the copies remain the same.[48] To support the position, the Court of Appeal observed that the relevance of the best evidence rule has long since expired, noting that in instances where a party seeks to rely on secondary evidence of the contents of a document, it was up to the court to decide, based on the circumstances of the particular case, the weight to be attached to that evidence, if any.[49] The Court of Appeal further noted:

> Where the party seeking to adduce the secondary evidence could readily produce the document, it may be expected that (absent some special circumstances) the court will decline to admit the secondary evidence on the ground that it is worthless. At the other extreme, where the party seeking to adduce the secondary evidence genuinely cannot produce the document, it may be expected that (absent some special circumstances) the court will admit the secondary evidence and attach such weight to it as it considers appropriate in all the circumstances. In cases falling

holders such as the Institute of Advanced Legal Studies. It is therefore more of a proposal as opposed to an instrument that has been drafted under the aegis of a responsible international law-making organ.

46 See, L Duranti and A Stanfield, "Authenticating Electronic Evidence," in S Mason and D Seng (eds) *Electronic Evidence,* University of London (2017) 4th edn, p 247; O'Floinn & Ormerod (n 92 above) p 3.

47 [1990] 1 WLR 277 (DC) at 308B-C.

48 See, Duranti & Stanfield (n 136 above).

49 *Masquerade Music Ltd v Springsteen* [2001] EWCA Civ 563, para. 64–85. Even though this is a civil case, the principle applies to criminal matters too. Mason and Seng note that this change has also affected the Criminal Justice Act 2003 in S Mason and D Seng, "The Foundations of Evidence in Electronic Form," in S Mason and D Seng (eds), *Electronic Evidence,* University of London (2017) 4th edn, pp 64–67.

> between those two extremes, it is for the court to make a judgment as to whether in all the circumstances any weight should be attached to the secondary evidence.[50]

For these reasons, the court adjudged the "admissibility" of secondary evidence of the contents of documents as being entirely dependent upon whether or not any weight is to be attached to that evidence, in the first instance.[51] And secondly, whether or not any weight is to be attached to such secondary evidence is a matter for the court to decide, taking into account all the circumstances of a particular case.[52]

Does the Form of Open Source Evidence Impact Its Admissibility?

Another equally important issue for consideration under authenticity is the form of the open source evidence and whether this impacts its categorisation. The question here being whether screenshots of social media postings can be admissible. As demonstrated by the systematic case study, screenshots are admissible as real evidence. This was the holding in the *Skinner* case, for instance, where the court in discussing the admissibility of screenshots of a website and recognising them as real evidence noted that, in instances where screen images have been produced in evidence by the original author and adduced as such, they would be admissible as real evidence.[53] The court further observed that electronically copying such content would not render them hearsay based on the fact that such a process is entirely supported by an electronic process.[54]

Nevertheless, the admissibility of screenshots is subject to the presence of a demonstrable link between the material contained in the screenshot and the subject matter and secondly, the screenshot must be authenticated. This was the position in *Khan v R* where the issue of authentication of screenshots was raised where the appellants sought to rely on material in the screenshots as evidence in support of the appeal.[55] The screenshots were held as being unreliable as there had been no demonstrable link between them and the accused.[56] The court noted that there was no date on the said messages and further "there appears to have been no attempt to secure any device which might provide proper evidence in the sense of being able to demonstrate that the messages and images of which Jane had provided screenshots came from Choudhury."[57]

50 *Masquerade Music Ltd v Springsteen* [2001] EWCA Civ 563, para. 64–85.
51 *Masquerade Music Ltd v Springsteen* [2001] EWCA Civ 563, para. 64–85.
52 *Masquerade Music Ltd v Springsteen* [2001] EWCA Civ 563, para. 64–85.
53 *Skinner* [2005] EWCA Crim 1439; [2006] Crim. L.R. 56 at [21].
54 *Skinner* [2005] EWCA Crim 1439; [2006] Crim. L.R. 56 at [21].
55 [2015] EWCA Crim 1816.
56 [2015] EWCA Crim 1816.
57 [2015] EWCA Crim 1816.

In discussing the challenges associated with presenting evidence in the form of screenshots as done in this case, the court made the following observations:

> Photographs of the kind shown in the screenshots can be copied in from various sources, which include Facebook and other social media sites or uploaded from the internet. The screenshots appear to be from a mobile phone, but carry no date or time, and no confirmation of who the message is from … Without access to the telephone or to the BlackBerry Messenger account, it is not possible to check which BlackBerry Messenger PIN number was used to send any message, or when it was sent, or to whom that PIN belonged. A person can set up many accounts and "talk" to him or herself.[58]

Ultimately, the court rejected this evidence, noting that the lack of supporting information that would enable any meaningful investigation to identify the relevant accounts was an effective block to their usage.[59]

The court also rejected an application for Jane to "attend to give evidence orally *de bene esse* to help inform the question whether her evidence is credible, albeit that she would be unlikely to shed any light on the authenticity of the communications she says she received." The rejection was based on the fact that the court thought it would be a pointless exercise as "Jane cannot deal with the important question of authenticity, even if her evidence is otherwise capable of belief."[60]

Categorisation of Open Source Evidence in England and Wales

Videos, films, photographs and sound recordings are mostly admitted as evidence that speaks for itself, that is, as real evidence.[61] The accuracy of this audio-visual material will therefore affect the weight apportioned to it as evidence.[62] It has been noted that the weight and admissibility of such material may overlap, thereby making it relevant to discuss the categorisation of open source evidence as it goes to the root of open source evidence's admissibility.[63] Open source evidence is categorised as a document under section 134 (1) of the Criminal Justice Act as discussed above, and although electronic evidence has very different characteristics to paper, "the rules of evidence that have developed with respect to the authentication of evidence, particularly documentary evidence, are still highly pertinent to electronic evidence."[64]

58 [2015] EWCA Crim 1816, para.10.
59 2015] EWCA Crim 1816.
60 [2015] EWCA Crim 1816, para.16.
61 Pattenden (n 16 above). See also Minogue *et al.* (n 109 above).
62 *R v Williams* [2006] EWCA Crim 2148, para. 55.
63 Pattenden (n 16 above).
64 Mason & Stanfield (n 120 above) p 193.

This categorisation as real evidence, that is, evidence that "could be directly analysed as a primary source or 'thing'" after verification, instead of being treated as "any kind of statement made by a person" is important especially for anonymously posted content.[65] This is because, without such categorisation, it would be difficult to justify the admission of open source evidence, especially video evidence, if the "creator is not available to testify, because it would be hearsay if introduced as evidence of the truth of its contents."[66]

This allows for a segue into the discussion of the categorisation of open source evidence as hearsay evidence and the potential impact of such a categorisation on its admissibility.

Open Source Evidence as Hearsay?

Due to its potential impact on admissibility and reliability of open source evidence, especially in common law countries, the rule on hearsay is one that also requires due consideration in that hearsay evidence is inadmissible unless it falls within the accepted exceptions.[67] The basis for these exceptions is that it is presumably admissible since it incorporates sufficient findings of necessity and reliability.[68]

Section 114 (1) of the Criminal Justice Act 2003 defines hearsay as a statement not made in oral evidence that is, evidence of any matter stated. Section 115(2) of the same Act goes ahead to define a statement as any representation of fact or opinion made by a person by whatever means including a representation made in a sketch, photo fit or other pictorial form.[69] As noted by Minogue *et al.*, there are two questions to ask in as far as hearsay and open source evidence is concerned, that is, is there a hearsay issue? If so, do any of the exceptions apply?[70]

Audio-visual open source evidence is not hearsay if it is not being relied upon for the truth of their content, and this was the position of the court in *Amjad v R*, where the ground of appeal was:

> the judge was wrong to admit the open source material relating to the source and to the author of the original list. There was no power at common law or in reliance on the Criminal Justice Act 2003 or on the

65 Minogue *et al.* (n 109 above).
66 Minogue *et al.* (n 109 above).
67 These exceptions include: admissions by opposing party litigants, the business records exceptions to the hearsay rule, and the *res gestae* exception – most notably the "statement of present mental state exception" and the "excited utterance exception." See sections starting from 116 of the Criminal Justice Act 2003.
68 *R. v Starr* [2000] 2 S.C.R. 144, 2000 SCC 40.
69 Criminal Justice Act 2003.
70 Minogue *et al.* (n 109 above).

Coroners and Justice Act 2009 to admit anonymous hearsay. Despite warnings to the jury, the admission led to an unsafe conviction.[71]

Ruling that the probative value was significant and that it did not contain hearsay, the Court stated that the material on the internet had not been relied on for truth but rather to show the similarity to that which was possessed by the Appellant.[72] The Court further observed that if the said material had images of individuals demonstrating exercises rather than words, the Crown would have still advanced its case in the same way, that is, relying on the striking similarity of the fitness poses. In which instance, the Court noted that it would be odd to describe such images as hearsay and thus ruled that there was no hearsay and no anonymous hearsay issue in this case.[73] In holding that it was not essential to the Crown's case that the information online was true and accurate, the Court held that the evidence from the internet was adduced to "support the contention that the exercises and fitness regime were not innocent but derived from sources associated with the terrorist cause" rather than the fact that this information was true.[74] The Court further observed that it was enough that the information contained descriptions of training exercises in terms so similar to those in the Appellant's possession as to rebut coincidence.[75]

The converse is also true; open source evidence will be excluded as hearsay if there is no witness to testify as to its contents on the grounds that there would be no way to test its reliability.[76]

The same holds true for text-based open source evidence, that is, they will fall under the categorisation of "statements" as under section 115 of the Criminal Justice Act 2003 and will not constitute hearsay if they are not relied on for the truth of the matter stated.[77] The contrary is also true; if these statements are submitted for the truth of the matter stated without a witness to authenticate the said material, it will constitute hearsay.[78]

In noting that the complexity of the hearsay rule increases where digital evidence is concerned, Gallavin and Mason pointed, for instance, to the fact that a communication written by a person and stored in a digital form is capable of being a statement for the purpose of the hearsay rule whereas "statements" derived from software code are not, as they are derived from a digital process.[79]

71 [2016] EWCA Crim 1618.
72 [2016] EWCA Crim 1618, para. 32–33.
73 [2016] EWCA Crim 1618, para. 32–33.
74 2016] EWCA Crim 1618, para. 32–35.
75 [2016] EWCA Crim 1618, para. 32–35.
76 D Seng & S Mason, "Hearsay" in S Mason and D Seng (eds), *Electronic Evidence and Electronic Signatures*, University of London (2021) 5th edn, p 86.
77 O'Floinn & Ormerod (n 114 above) p 9.
78 O'Floinn & Ormerod (n 114 above) p 9.
79 C Gallavin & S Mason, "Hearsay" in S Mason and D Seng (eds), *Electronic Evidence and Electronic Signatures*, University of London (2021) 5th edn, p 71.

For this reason, they suggest that there should be a distinction between the content of text messages and emails; the presentation of raw data (for instance, the metadata in Gmail, Hotmail, graphs, charts, presentations); and the presentation of information derived as a consequence of action by software code (for instance, conclusions resulting from predictive logic and the presentation of computer-generated conclusions and advice drawn from data).[80]

Another important opinion on this issue is the one made by the UK Law Commission with respect to the admissibility of a computer print-out on whether it is hearsay and whether the print-out itself is relevant.[81] According to this Commission, the most important question to ask is, on what basis should such a type of evidence be excluded. In response, they proffered two views: the first view is that such evidence is hearsay in that it was made by the person who fed the data into the machine, and the second view is that, "the statement by the machine, properly understood, is conditional on the accuracy of the data on which it is based; and that, if those data are not proved to have been accurate, the statement therefore has no probative value at all" in which case the question of hearsay does not arise at all.[82] The UK Law Commission favours the latter view on the basis of the fact that it is important not to complicate the hearsay rule by extending it to statements that have been made by machines on the basis of human input.[83]

The courts appear to have held along similar lines. In *McDonald v R* the court found that a printout from a mobile phone service provider, Vodafone, was real evidence as opposed to documentary hearsay in an appeal case that was focusing on character evidence.[84]

Keeping in mind the foregoing discussion, this research contends that open source evidence is not hearsay if it is not being relied upon for the truth of their content and secondly, the hearsay rule should not be extended to information that has been produced by digital processes as this will inevitably result in further complicating the hearsay rule.

What follows is an examination of other leading common law jurisdictions with a specific focus on Canada and the USA. It should be noted that the ensuing discussions do not purport to be a comprehensive comparative study of the law of evidence in these jurisdictions. It is intended as a tool for pinpointing fitting approaches to admissibility of open source evidence from

80 Gallavin & Mason (n 163 above).
81 Law Commission, "Evidence in Criminal Proceedings: Hearsay and Related Topics," (1997) 245.
82 Law Commission (n 165 above) paras 7.48–7.49.
83 Law Commission (n 165 above) paras 7.48–7.49.
84 [2011] EWCA Crim 2933 para 42. See also, *R v Spiby*, [1990] 91 Cr App R 186, the court accepted an automated computer process that monitored telephone calls and a print-out of certain call details as real evidence because there was no human intervention in the production of the data and consequently held that it was not hearsay evidence.

whence best practices can be gleaned to consequently inform the proposed framework for Kenya.

Admissibility of Open Source Evidence in Canada

Introduction

The admissibility of open source evidence in Canada is governed by the Canada Evidence Act (CEA), whose provisions are more prescriptive compared to the England and Wales case.[85] In this context, this research will review the use of open source evidence at the discovery stage and admission at trial processes. The CEA contains various provisions on the admissibility of what it terms an electronic document under its section 31.8, and it has been defined as:

> means data that is recorded or stored on any medium in or by a computer system or other similar device and that can be read or perceived by a person or a computer system or other similar device. It includes a display, print out or other output of that data.

Section 31.8 of the CEA further defines data as: "representations of information or of concepts, in any form." When read together, these two definitions have been held as having a broad enough breadth to cover copies of all documents stored in a computer such as bulletin boards from Facebook and other social media such as tweets.[86] Another important definition is that of a computer system which has equally been defined under section 31.8 of the CEA as:

> Computer system means a device that, or a group of interconnected or related devices one or more of which,

(a) contains computer programmes or other data; and,
(b) pursuant to computer programmes, performs logic and control, and may perform any other function.

Canadian courts have interpreted these provisions as covering social media evidence. For instance, in the 2020 case of *R. v Richardson*, the Court held that:

> Facebook posts and messages, e-mails and other forms of electronic communication fall within the definition of an "electronic document." Home computers, smartphones and other computing devices fall within

85 Canada Evidence Act, R.S.C. 1985

86 DM Paciocco, "Proof and Progress: Coping with the Law of Evidence in a Technological Age," *Canadian Journal of Law and Technology* (2013) Vol. 11, 181, p 194.

> the definition of a "computer system." Likewise, MSN messages recorded or stored on a computer are "data" which falls within the definition of an "electronic document."[87]

Similarly, in *R v Ball*, a 2019 case, the question before the British Columbia Court of Appeal was whether the trial judge erred by admitting photographed Facebook messages without testing their admissibility.[88] On electronic evidence, this Court made a general observation that: "our general rules and principles of evidence law developed long before the advent of these technologies and, as a result, the law has had to adapt to facilitate the admission of electronic documents while screening for threshold authenticity and integrity. Building on established rules and principles, it has done so by imposing a complementary set of admissibility rules *via* statute and related jurisprudence."[89]

In answering the specific question, the Court held that the applicable statutory provisions for the above question are sections 31.1 to 31.8 of the Canada Evidence Act, noting that these provisions create a framework for the admission of all forms of "electronic document".[90] It was noted that "the admissibility of Facebook messages and other electronic communications recorded or stored in a computing device is governed by the statutory framework."[91] Therefore, and as pointed out by Wayne Gorman, a Court of Appeal Judge, the presence of these broad definitions guarantees that all forms of social media are subject to the admissibility criteria in the CEA, which in his opinion have been set at a minimal level.[92]

Authentication of Open Source Evidence in Canada

Admissibility under the CEA contains two related requirements, and the first requirement is that of authenticity under section 31.1. It provides that:

> Any person seeking to admit an electronic document as evidence has the burden of proving its authenticity by evidence capable of supporting a finding that the electronic document is that which it is purported to be.

This position was reiterated in the case of *R v Hirsch*, an appeal against a conviction and sentence and the charge followed from the posting, ostensibly

87 [2020] NBCA 35 at para. 22. This was before the New Brunswick Court of Appeal and does not necessarily speak on behalf of the entire country, but it discloses the presence of this practice within this legal system.
88 [2019] BCCA 32 at para. 65.
89 [2019] BCCA 32 at para. 65.
90 [2019] BCCA 32 at para. 66.
91 [2019] BCCA 32 at para. 67.
92 WK Gorman, "The Admissibility of Social Media Evidence in Canada, Part 2: The Canada Evidence Act," *A Court Review Column* (2021) Vol. 57, p 180.

on Mr Hirsch's Facebook account, of a message stating intentions to choke the complainant, Mr Hirsch's former girlfriend, and to shoot her.[93] The message was accompanied by a nude photograph of the complainant. The appeal alleged that the trial judge erred in law by relying on documentary evidence that had not been authenticated. The Court noted that:

> section 31.1 of the Canada Evidence Act merely requires the party seeking to adduce an electronic document into evidence to prove that the electronic document is what it purports to be. This may be done through direct or circumstantial evidence.[94]

An older case, *R v Cochrane*, that related to mainframe computers set out guidance that seems to have stood the test of time and holds true even for open source evidence today, as an aspect of electronic evidence, where the Lords held that:

> it was necessary that appropriate authoritative evidence should be called to describe the function and operation of the mainframe computer, including the extent to which it brought to bear information stored within it in order to validate a transaction and to enable an appropriate record to be made on the till roll. None of those matters were covered by any of the witnesses, and the judge had had to grapple with inadequate, and possibly, incorrect information. .... The Crown had failed to adduce adequate evidence to enable the court to properly rule that the till rolls were admissible evidence; and in the absence of the till rolls the Crown's case could not be proved.[95]

Therefore, the authenticity threshold for Canada is "evidence capable of supporting a finding that the electronic evidence sought to be admitted is what it purports to be."[96] This denotes the fact that the determination of the weight to be apportioned to an item is left to the judge at the end when balancing and weighing all the admitted evidence.[97] For that reason, the only consideration at the admission stage is some evidence that is logically probative of whether the electronic document is what it purports to be.[98] This test has been likened to the showing of a *prima facie* case for authenticity as opposed to full establishment of the same.[99]

93 Saskatchewan Court of Appeal, 2017 SKCA 14, para. 1.
94 Saskatchewan Court of Appeal, 2017 SKCA 14, para. 18.
95 [1993] Crim LR 48 Court of Appeal, Criminal Division.
96 *R. v Martin*, the Court of Appeal for Newfoundland and Labrador, [2021] NLCA 1 at para. 47
97 Gorman (n 175 above) p 181.
98 Gorman (n 175 above) p 181.
99 *R v JV*, 2015 ONCJ 837, para. 10.

This threshold has been noted as being low, in that it does not limit how or by what means it may be met and neither does it impose a particular standard for threshold admissibility.[100] In acknowledging the threshold test in section 31.1 of CEA, the Saskatchewan Court of Appeal in the case of *R. v Durocher* held that:

> The burden of proof to establish threshold authenticity for purposes of s. 31.1 is low and, once satisfied, the document is admissible and available for use by the trier of fact … To meet this threshold, the proponent need only provide sufficient evidence of authenticity from which the trial judge could reasonably find the document to be what it purports to be.[101]

The *Durocher* case concerned the procedure and standard of proof required for the admission of social media writings where the alleged author disputes having written them.[102] The relevant ground of appeal was that the trial judge admitted social media evidence as a full Crown exhibit without conducting a *voir dire* of his own motion to determine its admissibility.[103]

This low standard has invited both criticism and caution. In reiterating the risk that such a low threshold creates with regard to the special nature of social media evidence, Silver argues that open source evidence is not always textual "and is not, as argued, completely documentary. In fact, social media evidence, like photographs and digital recordings, is open to modification and fabrication."[104]

These sentiments have also been expressed by the Court of Appeal in the case of *R v Aslami* where the defence at trial had been that the accused had not sent the messages and that the same had been created to frame him.[105] In allowing the appeal, the Court noted that the trial judge erred by not recognising the inherent fallibility of the evidence of the electronic messages and by not rigorously evaluating its reliability and probative value. It held: "there was nothing in those messages that objectively established the appellant as the sender nor, as I have mentioned, was there any expert evidence offered regarding the functioning and reliability of the TextNow app."[106]

In relation to the Facebook messages, the Court held that these messages had no evidential value based on the fact that there was no evidence whatsoever that tied the appellant to these messages, other than the evidence of

100 Gorman (n 175 above) p 181. See also, LA Silver, "The Unclear Picture of Social Media Evidence," *Manitoba Law Journal* (2020) Vol. 43, 3, p 137.

101 [2019] SKCA 97, para. 82.

102 [2019] SKCA 97, para. 82.

103 [2019] SKCA 97, para.3.

104 Silver (n 183 above).

105 [2021] ONCA 249, para. 24.

106 [2021] ONCA 249, para. 24.

S.F.'s beliefs.[107] The Court highlighted the problem with relying solely on S.F.'s evidence given the animus that existed between the two of them which could result in false implication of the appellant.[108] Trial judges were therefore cautioned to be careful with electronic evidence of this type given the myriad of ways in which it could be manipulated.[109] The Court of Appeal emphasised the need for rigorous evaluation of such evidence both in terms of its reliability and its probative value.[110]

This caution was based on the fact that, in the Court's words, the *Aslami* case,

> demonstrates the risks associated with not paying adequate heed to the dangers that are associated with relying on text and other messages, absent expert evidence explaining how various pieces of software, or "apps", can be used to generate these messages, and how reliable the resulting messages are in different respects. Put simply, it is too easy to use various pieces of software to create, or manipulate, messages such that they can appear to be from someone when, in fact, they emanate from an entirely different person. Similarly, the timing of the messages can be altered to suit a particular purpose.

The second issue that CEA makes provision for and related to authentication is the best evidence rule and the presumption of integrity which are provided for under sections 32.1 and 31.3, respectively. Section 32.1 of the CEA states that the "best evidence rule in respect of an electronic document is satisfied by proof of the integrity of the electronic documents system by or in which the electronic document was recorded or stored."[111]

While section 31.3 in creating the presumption of integrity states that an electronic document will be deemed reliable and accurate if the person seeking to enter them establishes:

a) by evidence capable of supporting a finding that at all material times the computer system or other similar device used by the electronic documents system was operating properly or, if it was not, the fact of it not operating properly did not affect the integrity of the electronic document and there are no other reasonable grounds to doubt the integrity of the electronic documents system;
b) if it is established that the electronic document was recorded or stored by a party who is adverse in interest to the party seeking to introduce it; or

107 [2021] ONCA 249, para. 29.
108 [2021] ONCA 249, para. 29.
109 [2021] ONCA 249, para. 30.
110 [2021] ONCA 249, para. 30.
111 Gorman (n 175 above).

c) if it is established that the electronic document was recorded or stored in the usual and ordinary course of business by a person who is not a party and who did not record or store it under the control of the party seeking to introduce it.

It is critical to point out that this list is disjunctive, that is to say, that only the presence of one of the prerequisites is sufficient to trigger the presumption of integrity. This being a presumption, it follows therefore that evidence to the contrary can rebut it. It has been observed, however, that this presumption of integrity has the effect of reversing the traditional burden of proof from the prosecution to the accused person, which effectively raises fair trial questions and, more specifically, those that relate to equality of arms.

Authenticity and the best evidence rule standards will have been discharged in two ways. The first option is having a witness who is familiar with the original input of the information testify as to the accuracy of the said information, thereby fulfilling the requirement that the computer system in question correctly reproduced the information having functioned as it should. Secondly,

> if a document appears on its face to be what it is claimed, testimony that it is the document that was received or sent by email or text will be presumed to satisfy the authenticity and best evidence requirements, unless the opposing party raises a doubt about whether the computer system was operating properly.[112]

This was the holding in the Court of Appeal for Newfoundland and Labrador case of *Martin*, where the Court observed that section 31.3 (a): provides that integrity is presumed when, in the absence of evidence to the contrary, there is evidence capable of supporting a finding that the devices by or in which the electronic document was recorded or stored were operating properly.[113]

While elaborating on the best evidence rule, Paciocco notes that whereas at common law the best evidence rule focuses on promoting the use of original documents, its applicability to electronic documents from computer and similar devices is concerned with ensuring that an electronic document offered in court accurately reflects the original information that was input into a document as opposed to requiring original documents to be proved.[114] He further explains that, "to be clear, these best evidence rules are not concerned with whether the original information that was input was accurate information."[115] Here Paciocco gives an example of a document that contains inaccurate

112 Paciocco (n 169 above) p 193.
113 [2021] NLCA 1 at para. 60.
114 Paciocco (n 169 above) p 193.
115 Paciocco (n 169 above) p 193.

information, such as a forged document that has been adduced as a genuine document, which can still satisfy the best evidence rule.[116]

In consonance with this, Silver observes that the best evidence rule "seems out of place in the digital world."[117] She argues that:

> the best evidence rule in the digital world assures "the court that the document submitted is the same as the one that was input into the computer." But does it? There are no "originals" in the digital world; electronically stored information is just that, bits of data stored as a representation of a document. So too social media fits uncomfortably into the best evidence rule. By focusing on the end product as a document, the entire social media journey through the ethernet is ignored. Contextual nuances are removed in favour of the wrappings.

The consensus on the best evidence rule and the presumption of integrity in connection with open source evidence appears, therefore, to be that they give a "false sense" of integrity to a trial process that is nonexistent, and this is alluded to by the fact that they provide an evidentiary shortcut while failing to ensure substantive integrity of the adduced evidence.[118]

In conclusion therefore, in Canada, authentication is simply a matter of adducing some evidence that the item is what it purports to be. And this process does not require proof or accuracy of the item as that consideration is left within the domain of the determination of the weight of the item as opposed to its admissibility. Accordingly, open source evidence can be authenticated even if there is a dispute as to whether it is what it purports to be. And Paciocco so succinctly summarises the position as, "authentication for the purposes of admissibility is therefore nothing more than a threshold test requiring that there be some basis for leaving the evidence to the factfinder for ultimate evaluation."[119]

Does the Form of Open Source Evidence Impact Its Admissibility?

Another equally important issue for consideration under authenticity is the form of the open source evidence and whether this impacts its categorisation. Here too, the question is whether screenshots of social media postings can be admissible. The Court of Appeal for Newfoundland and Labrador in *R v Martin* considered the question of whether or not screenshots of a Facebook

116 Paciocco (n 169 above) p 193.
117 Silver (n 183 above) p 140.
118 Silver (n 183 above) p 140.
119 Paciocco (n 169 above) p199.

post by the accused person, provided to the police, can be admitted into evidence by the prosecution.[120] The relevant facts of the R v Martin case were:

> the Crown sought to introduce into evidence six screenshots depicting posts purportedly taken from the accused's Facebook page. The screenshots were provided to the police by an anonymous source. Some of the officers that testified were able to identify Mr. Martin and his apartment as being depicted in the screenshots from having had contact with him and from having been inside his apartment.

The trial judge concluded that the evidence was inadmissible and the accused was acquitted. The Crown appealed from acquittal. The Court of Appeal noted that the issues to be determined on appeal were whether the trial judge erred in excluding the screenshot evidence and therefore the Court's task was to determine whether the screenshot evidence was authenticated so as to meet the test for admissibility.[121] The Court of Appeal held:

> The fact that the purported Facebook posts were captured in screenshots and tendered as such, in the absence of credible evidence that screenshot technology could have or did alter the Facebook posts depicted in the screenshots, is immaterial. What requires authentication are the Facebook posts depicted in the screenshots, which appear to be posts from Mr. Martin's Facebook.[122]

The Court affirmed that the authenticity threshold requirement, as discussed in the foregoing, has been established and provided the following explanation for that holding:

> In this case there was no evidence to the contrary. Mr. Martin did not testify on the *voir dire*. Neither he nor anyone else said that any person had tampered with any system on which the Facebook posts were recorded or stored, or that the posts had been altered so as to interfere with the integrity of their contents. In other words, Mr. Martin did not advance any evidence to the contrary that would rebut the presumption of system integrity found in section 31.3(a) of the Act.[123]

In conclusion therefore, the Court of Appeal allowed the appeal, holding that Facebook posts fall within the definition of electronic documents in section 31.8 of the Canada Evidence Act and that the low threshold required

120 [2021] NLCA 1.
121 Gorman (n 175 above).
122 [2021] NLCA 1, para. 29.
123 [2021] NLCA 1, para. 70.

by the Act with respect to authentication and system integrity was met for the purposes of admissibility.[124]

Categorisation of Open Source Evidence in Canada

Another evidentiary issue that affects the admissibility of open source evidence in Canada is whether or not the categorisation of open source evidence is important, keeping in mind the import of section 31.7 of CEA. Section 31.7 provides that, "sections 31.1 to 31.4 do not affect any rule of law relating to the admissibility of evidence, except the rules relating to authentication and best evidence." The indication here is that for open source evidence to be admissible, it must first be admissible pursuant to other evidentiary considerations.[125]

Silver observes that categories abound in rules of evidence, noting that "connections between pieces of evidence often require connections between the rules of evidence" and that these connections have traditionally been viewed through categorisation.[126] Due to the fact that open source evidence can be many different kinds of evidence; that is, real, testimonial, documentary or pictorial, she argues that categorisation is important as it is the vehicle through which the law of evidence can give open source evidence "a familiar label, a category by which the lawyers and judges can comfortably apply the known rules of evidence for admissibility purposes."[127]

She provides four categorisations of open source evidence, that is, social media as real evidence, social media as image, social media as testimonial and social media evidence as documentary evidence.[128] Silver notes that social media started to be perceived as real evidence in 2014 with various decisions that proved this point emanating from courts. For instance, the *R v Bernard* decision before the Nova Scotia Supreme Court, where screenshots or photographs of Facebook Wall posts were admitted under the CEA, and the court noted that: "applying the regime to the screenshots is a matter of common sense as one should not be able to circumvent the admissibility rules for electronic information simply by taking a photograph of the information."[129] She notes that this explicitly categorised open source information as documentary electronic information.[130] It is important to note that the Kenyan court in

124 [2021] NLCA 1, para. 25 and para. 74.
125 Gorman (n 175 above).
126 Silver (n 183 above) p 120. An interesting finding here is that in Canada, academic writing, such as that of Lisa Silver, appears to have significantly influenced this process and her writing on categorisation has been referenced by some judges in their decisions, as seen in the above discussions.
127 Silver (n 183 above) p 122.
128 Silver (n 183 above) pp 122–133.
129 2016 NSSC 358.
130 Silver (n 183 above) p 124.

the *Steve Mbogo* case also contended with the use of screenshots as adduced evidence.

With respect to social media as image, Silver notes that this is when open source information is introduced into evidence as a photograph of the computer screen. This categorisation is important because photographic evidence is subject to different admissibility rules; that is, photographic evidence was considered more scientific, hence more objective than an eyewitness account. She, however, notes that "that self-same science provides a perfect platform for manipulation and fabrication of the image," raising intrinsic admissibility concerns with respect to the requirements of both authenticity and integrity threshold.[131]

Silver also notes that social media can also be pure testimonial evidence as she argues that, "although distilled to an animate hard piece of evidence like a document or photograph, Facebook messaging and even Instagram imagery involve a narrative that is crystallised into a written or textual conversation, either with one's self or with others. This diary-like quality of social media evidence suggests documentary evidence with a healthy dose of testimonial features." This ability of open source evidence to be categorised as testimonial evidence, she notes, adds to the confusion as to how to handle open source evidence.

Lastly, the categorisation of open source evidence as documentary evidence is based on the statutory electronic document admissibility regime under the CEA, which is based on the integrity of the computer and its ability to provide a *prima facie* admissibility process.[132] Silver notes that open source evidence became a part of this regime due to its "final resting place," which is the computer, and because, as discussed in the foregoing, the definition of electronic document was broad enough to encompass social media in its computerised form, hence packing open source information into what she terms the documentary scheme.

Open Source Evidence as Hearsay?

Due to its potential impact on admissibility and reliability of open source evidence, especially in common law countries such as Kenya, the rule on hearsay is one that also requires due consideration in that hearsay evidence is inadmissible unless it falls within the accepted exceptions.[133] The basis for these exceptions is that it is presumably admissible since it incorporates sufficient findings of necessity and reliability.[134] The *R v Khelawon* before the Supreme Court

131 Silver (n 183 above) p 130.

132 Silver (n 183 above) p 130.

133 These exceptions include: admissions by opposing party litigants, the business records exceptions to the hearsay rule, and the *res gestae* exception - most notably the "statement of present mental state exception" and the "excited utterance exception."

134 *R. v Starr* [2000] 2 S.C.R. 144, 2000 SCC 40.

of Canada is an interesting holding and one which may become relevant in assessing the admission of open source evidence – given its dynamic nature.[135] This is in instances when questions asked in court engage hearsay concerns and/or cause decision-making challenges with respect to how to deal with hearsay. The Supreme Court of Canada thus held that, in cases where hearsay evidence does not fall under a traditional exception, it may still be admitted if *indicia* of necessity and reliability are established.[136] The converse was also held as being true, that is, "in rare cases, hearsay evidence which falls under a traditional exception may be excluded on the ground that it lacks necessity and reliability in the specific circumstances of the case."[137]

In noting the importance of the impact of hearsay on admissibility of open source evidence, the New Brunswick Court of Appeal in *Richardson* held that:

> In addition to the threshold statutory requirements, electronic documents – like any other form of document – must satisfy common law rules to support the admission of their contents, such as … complying with rules applicable to hearsay evidence when documents are adduced for the truth of their contents.[138]

On its operation in relation to open source evidence, Paciocco rightly observes that:

> Computer Generated Information consisting of data created by a computer system is not hearsay even when offered to prove the facts it asserts. Admissibility depends on its reliability which can be established by expert evidence, or in appropriate cases, by taking judicial notice.[139]

He further notes that electronic documents containing statements of fact may still be admitted without the need for the hearsay exception to be triggered if, by their nature, they lead to relevant circumstantial inferences.[140]

In *R v Nde Soh*, the New Brunswick Court of Queen's Bench was called to determine whether Facebook chat statements, which were adduced in court as screenshots, attributed to the accused were hearsay.[141] The court held that "they constitute hearsay evidence since they contain statements not made directly by a witness actually present in the witness box; the Crown intends to introduce them in evidence at the trial to establish the veracity of the assertions

135 2006 SCC 57, [2006] 2 S.C.R. 787.
136 2006 SCC 57, [2006] 2 S.C.R. 787.
137 *R. v Simpson* 2007 ONCA 793, [2007] O.J. No. 4510.
138 [2020] NBCA 35, para. 24.
139 Paciocco (n 169 above) p 227.
140 Paciocco (n 169 above) p 228.
141 2014 NBQB 20.

they contain."[142] However, the Court proceeded to hold that the said evidence is admissible as electronic documents and as an exception to the hearsay rule.[143]

Similarly in *Durocher*, Facebook messages sent by the accused were admitted, but the accused argued that "this social media evidence was inadmissible based upon the hearsay prohibition."[144] In disclosing a difference in the rationale for admission, the Saskatchewan Court of Appeal stated that:

> Although there is consensus amongst academics that an admission constitutes admissible evidence, they differ on its rationale for admission: some contend it is an exception to the hearsay rule, yet others view it as part and parcel of the adversary system because the declarant is able to testify.[145]

The Court concluded, however, that:

> Statements made by Mr. Durocher in the Facebook messages are either not hearsay (because they were not adduced for the truth of their contents) or, if they are, they fell under a recognised exception to the hearsay rule and were presumptively admissible for the truth of their contents.[146]

Based on this evaluation, it is this research's position that as a matter of general rule, open source evidence should not be held as hearsay or should be admissible under an exception to the hearsay rule. And this is in order to avoid the complications that would arise with the classification of such information as hearsay – as has been elaborated extensively in the foregoing discussions on hearsay.

Admissibility of Open Source Evidence in the United States of America

Introduction

The January 6 2021 attack on the US Capitol by rioters is an apt example of the impact of the use of social media evidence in prosecutions.[147] Federal prosecutors charged more than 725 individuals using messages, photos and videos

142 2014 NBQB 20, para. 41.
143 2014 NBQB 20, para. 54.
144 The Saskatchewan Court of Appeal, [2019] SKCA 97
145 [2019] SKCA 97, para. 63.
146 [2019] SKCA 97, para. 68.
147 C Carpenter, "Click, Click, BOOM: The Digital Evidence Surge Behind Prosecuting Jan. 6 Rioters," Criminal Justice & the Rule of Law Democracy & Elections," March 2022. Available: https://www.lawfaremedia.org/article/click-click-boom-digital-evidence-surge-behind-prosecuting-jan-6-rioters, accessed 11 November 2023.

that had been posted on social media, which resulted in various criminal sentences.[148] For example, in the case of *United States of America v Russell James Peterson*, the Criminal Complaint stated:

> During national news coverage of the aforementioned events, video footage which appeared to be captured on mobile devices of persons present on the scene depicted violations of … law. The Facebook search warrant return attributable to Peterson's account also included the live stream videos Peterson's account made from inside the U.S Capitol … Based on open source research, your Affiant identified the location of the live stream from video ID ending in 3018 as streaming from the Crypt of the area of the U.S. Capitol.[149]

In Federal courts in the USA, admissibility of open source evidence is governed by Federal Rules of Evidence under Rule 901, which establishes the requirement that authentication is a condition precedent to the admissibility of non-testimonial evidence, under which open source evidence falls. Rule 104 (a) establishes the responsibility of the trial judge to make preliminary determinations regarding the admissibility of evidence, which would entail a determination of authenticity. While Rule 104 (b), "often referred to as the "conditional relevance rule," applies during the authentication process when there is a dispute of fact regarding whether an exhibit is authentic. For example, when the proponent of the evidence offers facts to establish authenticity that would be sufficient to persuade a reasonable jury by a preponderance of the evidence that the exhibit is authentic. At the same time, the party seeking to exclude the evidence is required to offer other evidence that could persuade a reasonable jury that the exhibit is not authentic."[150] Therefore, Rule 104(b) allocates the ultimate fact-finder responsibility to resolve disputes of fact, including genuine factual disputes regarding the authenticity of open source evidence.[151]

Admissibility of open source evidence in the USA appears to be clustered into what has been termed the Maryland Approach and the Texas Approach, and has been described as being "murky at best" in light of this

148 M Kunzelman, "Capitol Rioters' Social Media Posts Influencing Sentencings," Associated Press, December 2021.

149 United States District Court for the District of Columbia, Case No. AO 91 (Rev. 11/11), p 2–4. Available: https://www.justice.gov/usao-dc/case-multi-defendant/file/1367016/download, accessed 11 November 2023. It is important to note here that beyond the application for a search warrant, CCTV footage was also used to corroborate these videos.

150 PW Grimm, LY Bergstrom & MM O'Toole-Loureiro, "Authentication of Social Media Evidence," *American Journal of Trial Advocacy* (2013) Vol. 36, 433, p 440.

151 Grimm *et al.* (n 231 above).

split approach.[152] The Maryland Approach refers to the decisions in which courts are distrustful of open source evidence, determining that the odds that someone other than the alleged author of the evidence was the actual creator were too great.[153] This Approach therefore requires that the person adducing the open source material must affirmatively disprove the existence of a different creator in order for the evidence to be admissible.[154] On the other hand, the Texas Approach is more moderate in the sense that the burden of proving that the open source evidence was created or manipulated by a third party is placed on the objecting party.[155]

It is crucial to underscore the fact that these approaches are generally indicative of the practice in the states that follow the common law legal system and accordingly the cases that are analysed come from various appellate courts such as the California Court of Appeal, the Connecticut Appellate Court, the Arizona Court of Appeal, the Michigan Court of Appeal and of course the Maryland and Texas Appellate Courts.

In setting out the issues that need to be determined in order for digital evidence (under which purview open source evidence falls) to be admissible, the court in *Lorraine v Markel American Insurance Co* noted that these include relevance, authenticity, hearsay, the original writing rule, and probative value as compared with possible unfair prejudice.[156] This section will therefore focus on two issues, that is, authentication and its connection to relevance and hearsay.

Authentication Open Source Evidence in the USA

Authentication under the Maryland Approach

The Maryland Approach, which is generally considered as requiring a higher standard for open source evidence authentication, was demonstrated in the case of *Griffin v State*, before the Maryland Court of Appeal. In this classic case, the State adduced a MySpace profile, in the form of a printout, belonging to the defendant's girlfriend, Barber, to demonstrate that the said defendant's girlfriend had allegedly threatened one of the State's witnesses.[157] The printout displayed the name of the profile as "Sistahsouljah," and described details of the profile owner's life such as a birthday of 10/02/1983 and location of Port Deposit, and had a photograph of Griffin and Barber embracing.[158]

152 W Angus-Anderson, "Authenticity and Admissibility of Social Media Website Printouts," *Duke Law & Technology Review* (2015) Vol. 14, 1. The terms "Maryland Approach" and "Texas Approach" were first used in *Parker v State*, 85 A.3d 682 (Del. 2014) case.

153 Angus-Anderson (n 233 above).

154 Angus-Anderson (n 233 above).

155 Grimm *et al.* (n 231 above) p 455.

156 241 F.R.D. 534 (D. Md. 2007).

157 *Griffin v State*, 19 A.3d 415 (Md. App. 2011).

158 *Griffin v State*, 19 A.3d 415 (Md. App. 2011), para. 418.

The state used the lead investigator for the case, a Sergeant, to authenticate the pages instead of using Barber.[159] The investigator testified that he knew it was the girlfriend's page "through the photograph of her and Boozy on the front, through the reference to Boozy, the reference to the children, and her birth date indicated on the printout."[160] The defence counsel objected to the admission of the printouts "because the state could not sufficiently establish a 'connection' between the profile and posting and Ms. Barber."[161] The trial court admitted the printouts.

The defendant's ground of appeal was that the MySpace profile, in the form of printouts, was inadmissible because it was not properly authenticated.[162] The Maryland Court of Appeal noted:

> the picture of Ms. Barber, coupled with her birth date and location, were not sufficient "distinctive characteristics" on a MySpace profile to authenticate its printout [pursuant to Md. Rule 5-901, which is materially similar to Federal Rule of Evidence 901], given the prospect that someone other than Ms. Barber could have not only created the site, but also posted the "snitches get stitches" comment.[163]

The Court further observed that:

> "Authenticating electronically stored information presents a myriad of concerns because 'technology changes so rapidly, ... is 'often new to many judges,'" and "requires greater scrutiny of 'the foundational requirements' than letters or other paper records, to bolster reliability."[164]

It was further observed that:

> the identity of who generated the profile may be confounding, because 'a person observing the online profile of a user with whom the observer is unacquainted has no idea whether the profile is legitimate,'" and with "relative ease," a person "can create a fictitious account and masquerade under another person's name or can gain access to another's account by obtaining the user's username and password.[165]

Basing its holding on "the potential for abuse and manipulation of a social networking site by someone other than its purported creator and/or user,"

159 *Griffin v State*, 19 A.3d 415 (Md. App. 2011), para. 418.
160 *Griffin v State*, 19 A.3d 415 (Md. App. 2011), para. 418.
161 *Griffin v State*, 19 A.3d 415 (Md. App. 2011), para. 418.
162 *Griffin v State*, 19 A.3d 415 (Md. App. 2011), para. 417.
163 *Griffin v State*, 19 A.3d 415 (Md. App. 2011), para. 424.
164 *Griffin v State*, 19 A.3d 415 (Md. App. 2011), para. 423.
165 *Griffin v State*, 19 A.3d 415 (Md. App. 2011), para. 423.

the court concluded that a printout from a social media site "requires a greater degree of authentication than merely identifying the date of birth of the creator and her visage in a photograph on the site" to determine that the person whose birthday is listed and whose photograph appears on the site is both the creator of the site and the person who wrote the posting.[166]

Grimm *et al.* note that the Maryland Court of Appeals in *Griffin* set out a proper way to authenticate postings on social media sites and that it consisted of:[167]

i. Ask the purported creator if she indeed created the profile and also if she added the posting in question;
ii. search the computer of the person who allegedly created the profile and posting and examine the computer's internet history and hard drive to determine whether that computer was used to originate the social networking profile and posting in question; and
iii. obtain information directly from the social networking website that links the establishment of the profile to the person who allegedly created it and also links the posting sought to be introduced to the person who initiated.[168]

Another decision whose holding falls under the Maryland Approach is the *People v Beckley* before the California Court of Appeal where Beckley's girlfriend testified that she did not associate with gang members.[169] The prosecution rebutted this testimony by adducing the evidence of a photograph of the girlfriend displaying a gang hand signal; a detective "testified that he downloaded the photograph from Beckley's homepage on the internet website MySpace."[170] Beckley and his codefendants objected that the photograph "had not been authenticated but the evidence was admitted by the trial court.[171] The California Court of Appeal held that "the prosecution's failure to authenticate a photograph … downloaded from an internet website should have barred the photograph's admission."[172] Furthermore, the Court observed that, "no expert testified that the picture was not a 'composite' or 'faked' photograph," and "digital photographs can be changed to produce false images."[173]

In *State v Eleck* before the Connecticut Appellate Court, the defendant appealed his conviction on the ground that the trial court improperly excluded

166 *Griffin v State*, 19 A.3d 415 (Md. App. 2011), para. 423 - 424.
167 Grimm *et al.* (n 210 above) p 444.
168 *Griffin v State*, 19 A.3d 415 (Md. App. 2011), para. 427–428.
169 110 Cal. Rptr. 3d 362 (Ct. App. 2010), para. 365.
170 110 Cal. Rptr. 3d 362 (Ct. App. 2010), para. 365–366.
171 110 Cal. Rptr. 3d 362 (Ct. App. 2010), para. 366.
172 110 Cal. Rptr. 3d 362 (Ct. App. 2010), para. 364.
173 110 Cal. Rptr. 3d 362 (Ct. App. 2010), para. 366.

evidence that had been properly authenticated.[174] The said evidence was printouts of Facebook messages allegedly received from a State's witness, another attendant of the party adduced by the defendant.[175] The defendant personally testified as to the authenticity of the printouts, stating that the user name belonged to the witness, the profile contained photographs of the witness, and that he had downloaded and printed the messages himself.[176]

The State's witness admitted that the profile was hers, but claimed that her account had been hacked and she had not sent the messages in question.[177] The appellate court held that, "the Facebook printouts had not been properly authenticated because authenticating that a message came from a specific account is not sufficient evidence that it was authored by the account owner.[178] The messages themselves did not "reflect distinct information that only [the witness] would have possessed regarding the defendant or the character of their relationship."[179] The Court concluded that authorship had not been sufficiently authenticated.[180]

Another important point to note from the *Eleck* decision is the reasoning of the appellate court, thus: "an electronic document may continue to be authenticated by traditional means such as the direct testimony of the purported author or circumstantial evidence of 'distinctive characteristics' in the document that identify the author."[181]

Authentication under the Texas Approach

The Texas Approach is best demonstrated by the *Tienda v State* case which concerned an appeal of a murder conviction based on the ground that the trial court should not have admitted evidence from MySpace pages alleged to be managed by the defendant.[182] Each admitted MySpace page was linked to email addresses including Tienda's name or nickname, had a profile name matching either Tienda's name or nickname, listed Tienda's hometown as the location and contained photographs of a man who "resembled" Tienda.[183] The Court of Criminal Appeals compared *Tienda's* case to *Griffin's* case noting that in *Tienda*, "there were far more circumstantial indicia of authenticity

174 *State v Eleck*, 23 A.3d 818, 819 (Conn. App. Ct. 2011).
175 *State v Eleck*, 23 A.3d 818, 819 (Conn. App. Ct. 2011), para. 820.
176 *State v Eleck*, 23 A.3d 818, 819 (Conn. App. Ct. 2011), para. 820.
177 *State v Eleck*, 23 A.3d 818, 819 (Conn. App. Ct. 2011), para. 820.
178 *State v Eleck*, 23 A.3d 818, 819 (Conn. App. Ct. 2011), para. 822.
179 *State v Eleck*, 23 A.3d 818, 819 (Conn. App. Ct. 2011), para. 824.
180 Angus-Anderson (n 233 above) p 40.
181 *State v Eleck*, 23 A.3d 818, 819 (Conn. App. Ct. 2011), para. 823. It is important to highlight here that despite the difference between authentication and verification, the Court in Eleck has used the term "authentication" to describe both processes.
182 *Tienda v State*, 358 S.W.3d 633 (Tex. Crim. App. 2012), para. 634.
183 *Tienda v State*, 358 S.W.3d 633 (Tex. Crim. App. 2012), para. 634–636.

in this case than in Griffin."[184] The Court arrived at this conclusion based on the fact that:

> A combination of photographs, references to particular situations, and messages sent from accounts bearing the appellant's name – "taken as a whole with all of the individual particular details considered in combination" – was deemed sufficient for a reasonable jury to believe that Tienda created and maintained the profiles.[185]

While relying on the *Lorraine v Markel American Insurance Co* case,[186] the court stated that, "as with the authentication of any kind of proffered evidence, the best or most appropriate method for authenticating electronic evidence will often depend upon the nature of the evidence and the circumstances of the particular case."[187] It concluded by noting that whether Tienda's MySpace page had been fabricated was an "alternate scenario whose likelihood and weight the jury was entitled to assess."[188] A similar holding to this conclusion was in *the State v Assi* in which the Arizona Court of Appeal concurred that "the trial court need not determine whether the evidence is authentic, but only whether evidence exists from which the jury could reasonably conclude that the evidence is authentic."[189]

In a decision that seems to be intimating the threshold that is needed when assessing authenticity, it was noted in *People v Valdez* that there only has to be "a sufficient showing of authenticity of the writing to permit the trier of fact to find that it is authentic."[190] The Court in *Valdez* went ahead to distinguish the case from *Beckley* noting that

> unlike Beckley, there was evidence of the password requirement for posting and deleting content and pervasive consistency of the content of the page, filled with personal photographs, communications, and other details tending together to identify and show owner-management of a page devoted to gang-related interests.[191]

The Texas Approach can therefore be summarised as: "authentic evidence is admitted, clearly inauthentic evidence is excluded, and everything in between

184 *Tienda v State*, 358 S.W.3d 633 (Tex. Crim. App. 2012), para. 637.
185 *Tienda v State*, 358 S.W.3d 633 (Tex. Crim. App. 2012), para. 645.
186 241 F.R.D. 534 (D. Md. 2007).
187 *Tienda v State*, 358 S.W.3d 633 (Tex. Crim. App. 2012), para. 639.
188 *Tienda . State*, 358 S.W.3d 633 (Tex. Crim. App. 2012), para. 646.
189 No. 1 CA-CR 10-0900, 2012 WL 3580488 (Ariz. Ct. App. Aug. 21, 2012).
190 135 Cal. Rptr. 3d 628 (Ct. App. 2011).
191 135 Cal. Rptr. 3d 628 (Ct. App. 2011).

is conditionally relevant and admitted for the jury to make the final determination as to authenticity."[192]

It is important to highlight here that the cases discussed under the two approaches relied on "social media printouts" of profiles, which is only one form of open source evidence. However, as seen in the recent Peterson case that arose following the 6 January 2021 attack on the US Capitol, the same requirements would also apply to open source evidence that is in the form of video or images.

Categorisation of Open Source Evidence in the USA

Within the USA context, the literature only revealed a discussion of one aspect of the theme of categorisation, that is, the discussion of how the rule against hearsay relates to open source evidence. It is for this reason that this section does not contain similar discussions on the sub-themes of the form of open source evidence beyond the foregoing discussions that included a consideration of open source evidence that was adduced in the form of screenshots.

Open Source Evidence as Hearsay?

Gilliland observes that, in order to use hearsay rules to exclude or to use its exceptions to admit open source evidence, what is required is the application of the rules and exceptions in the same way they are applied to other evidence.[193] In *People v. Oyerinde*, the court held that the defendant's Facebook messages were not hearsay, but rather a party admission, because he sent them to another person.[194] From this decision, it can therefore be concluded that the availability of evidence on social media does not mean the test for a party admission has changed.[195] This conclusion is supported by the fact that the judge in *Oyerinde* applied the test as it would be applied to any other out-of-court statement and determined that such messages were not hearsay.[196] Another way in which this court also admitted Facebook messages sent to the defendant and another individual was under the "state of mind" exception to hearsay.[197] The court in *St. Clair v Johnny's Oyster & Shrimp, Inc* however noted that any evidence procured off the Internet is adequate for almost nothing, even under the most liberal interpretation of the hearsay exception rules found in Federal Rules of Evidence 807."[198]

192 Grimm *et al.* (n. 231 above) p 465.

193 J Gilliland, "The Admissibility of Social Media Evidence," Hein Online, Litigation (2013) 39, 20.

194 2011 Mich. App. Lexis 2104, (Mich. Ct. App. 29 November, 2011), para. 26–27.

195 Gilliland (n 274) p 21.

196 Gilliland (n 274) p 21.

197 Gilliland (n 274) p 21.

198 76 F. Supp. 2d 773 (S.D. Tex. 1999).

The main thrust of this section is that open source evidence is admissible as evidence in legal proceedings in all three jurisdictions; however, there is a difference in the approach taken to authenticate the said open source evidence. That is, in England and Wales, open source evidence is authenticated 'in whatever way the court may approve'; in Canada, the approach is that the adducer of the open source evidence is burdened to prove that the thing is authentic; whereas the USA has two approaches: the Maryland Approach, which sets out a higher standard of authentication, and the Texas Approach, which requires a lower standard, as enunciated above. This research favours the Canadian approach due to the fact that it aligns with traditional burden of proof standards, that is, the requirement that 'he who alleges must prove.' Thereby making it the approach that would make the integration of open source evidence within existing evidentiary standards and procedures facile.

Open Source Investigations in England and Wales

Introduction

As indicated in the introduction to this chapter and in order to reiterate the scope of this research, the main focus of this comparative analysis is England and Wales and this is due to the commonalities that exist between its legal system and that of Kenya.[199] Accordingly, this section analyses open source investigations within England and Wales to ascertain any replicable best practices. The issue of open source investigations in England and Wales predominantly focuses on questions relating to social media identification in the first instance, and the duty of disclosure in line with the reasonable lines of enquiry and the extent to which it relates to the respect for the right to privacy.

Social media communication is considered to fall under electronic communications in England and Wales and thereby covered by the legal framework that governs the latter.[200]

Legislative Framework for the Investigatory Process in England and Wales

In England and Wales, it is reported that there are currently at least 15 Acts of Parliament that need to be considered if social media data are used as evidence in court. These relate to two main themes: the first theme relates to the collection and review of potential evidence, and the second theme relates

199 Due to this scope and the fact that the primary focus of this research is not on open source investigations *per se* but rather what occurs in the courtroom, the investigatory procedures in Canada and the USA have not been included in this discussion.

200 Crown Prosecution Service, "Social Media and other Electronic Communications, Legal Guidance, Cyber /Online Crime," 19 December 2022. See also, Crown Prosecution Service, "Social Media: Reasonable Lines of Enquiry, Legal Guidance, Sexual offences," 23 November 2020, Updated: 3 August 2022.

to the subsequent disclosure and presentation of this evidence in court.[201] It was observed that the theme of privacy is one that runs throughout these two themes.[202]

The investigatory process in England and Wales is governed by an extensive legislative and regulative framework that applies from initially identifying, accessing, seizing, and extracting social media data, through to preserving, storing, transferring, examining, and analysing it, before its formal presentation as evidence in a court of law.[203] The legislative and regulative framework that governs this process of obtaining material from devices for the purposes of evidence and for disclosure in England and Wales includes:

- Sections 3(1)(a) and 23(1) of the Criminal Procedure and Investigations Act 1996 ("CPIA");
- The Code of Practice to the CPIA;
- The Attorney General's Guidance on Disclosure 2022;
- The Crown Prosecution Service's "Guidelines on Communication Evidence" and the "Guide to 'reasonable lines of the enquiry' and communications evidence"
- The Investigatory Powers Act 2016.

Furthermore, it is noted that investigators must also take into account other general laws that protect individuals, such as those relating to privacy and general human rights.[204] It is essential to note that, with the exception of the Police, Crime, Sentencing and Courts Act, which was given Royal Assent in April 2022 and whose sections 37 to 44 include details for the extraction of information from electronic devices,[205] no Acts of Parliament have been changed specifically to enable the inclusion of social media data. This is because, as aforementioned, data extracted from social media is considered to fall under electronic communications.[206]

In England and Wales, any material obtained by an open source investigator is capable of being used as evidence provided the following conditions are met: one, as long as the service provider can provide a statement or affidavit and two, there are no specific restrictions that have been placed on the material by the service provider.[207] Material obtained from a download of a device can

201 Goldstraw-White (n 113 above).
202 Goldstraw-White (n 113 above).
203 Goldstraw-White (n 113 above).
204 Goldstraw-White (n 113 above).
205 At the time of writing of this research, this part of the Act had not been brought into force.
206 Goldstraw-White (n 113 above).
207 Crown Prosecution Service (n 280 above). Where specific restrictions have been placed on the material's use in criminal proceedings and/or where a statement or affidavit is not provided by the provider, the material can be sought through MLA and therefore such material goes beyond the scope of this research.

be exhibited by the investigating officer and served as evidence and where a forensic examination of the device has been carried out there is a requirement that a statement is obtained from the technician as to how: the download has been conducted, that is, details of the software used, what has been searched for and any limitations on the results of the download such as whether or not it can be guaranteed that all deleted messages were retrieved.[208]

The justification of this requirement is that it will ensure that all parties understand the benefits and limitations of the open source material that has been provided, thereby upholding fair trial considerations. Additionally, if there was a manual download of open source material resulting from a manual examination of a device, the investigator must also provide a statement exhibiting any information found, including any screenshots taken during the examination.[209]

The Association of Chief Police Officers (ACPO) Good Practice Guide for Digital Evidence also lists four principles for digital evidence, which essentially apply to open source evidence, and these include:

> Principle 1: No action taken by law enforcement agencies, persons employed within those agencies or their agents should change data which may subsequently be relied upon in court.
>
> Principle 2: In circumstances where a person finds it necessary to access original data, that person must be competent to do so and be able to give evidence explaining the relevance and the implications of their actions.
>
> Principle 3: An audit trail or other record of all processes applied to digital evidence should be created and preserved. An independent third party should be able to examine those processes and achieve the same result.
>
> Principle 4: The person in charge of the investigation has overall responsibility for ensuring that the law and these principles are adhered to.[210]

These have been noted as being amongst the leading best practice advice.[211] However, it has been observed that they require an update given the passage of time and changes in technological advancements.[212] The need for an update is important because

208 Crown Prosecution Service (n 280 above).

209 Crown Prosecution Service (n 280 above).

210 The Association of Chief Police Officers (ACPO) Good Practice Guide for Digital Evidence, Version 5, October 2011, section 2.

211 G Horsman, "ACPO Principles for Digital Evidence: Time for an Update?," *Forensic Science International: Reports* (2020), Vol. 2, p 100076.

212 Horsman (n 291 above).

> there are now a wider range of more advanced investigative methods for data access and interpretation, coupled with a further understanding of the role which both traditional and novel forms of digital evidence can play in … investigation.[213]

Reasonable Lines of Enquiry

Considering the nature of open source evidence and more specifically that which relates to the vastness of open source material, questions relating to the concept of reasonable lines of enquiry are important. This is due to the fact that it provides an avenue through which to avoid overwhelming all the actors, that is, investigators, the prosecution, the defence and the court. Reasonable lines of enquiry are a duty under the CPIA Code of Practice that involves a consideration of: "what is expected to be found through the enquiry, to determine what is reasonable in the circumstances; how best to seek that information/material, taking a proportionate approach; and being able to explain why it is needed."

The overarching principle that guides the reasonable lines of enquiry *vis-à-vis* open source evidence is that for such an enquiry to be reasonable, "there must be something beyond a purely speculative search."[214] In the case of *R v CB and Mohammed*, which dealt directly with the issue of obtaining and reviewing material from digital devices, the court set out 'Issues of Principle' that investigators and prosecutors should consider when seeking to obtain material.[215] The most relevant principles to this research are the holding that: "digital material is no different from any other information or record and should be handled in accordance with established principles."

Similarly, it is required that the prosecutor has the following information from the investigator with respect to an open source investigation before presenting the same in court as evidence:

i. What method was used to interrogate the device, that is, a manual examination or a download, and an explanation as to why this method was used.
ii. Are there limitations of the method used? For instance, it does not contain deleted material, and it does not have access to the browser history.
iii. Were any date/time or other parameters used when interrogating the device, if yes, what were they?
iv. Were any search terms used when interrogating the device, if yes, what were they?[216]

213 Horsman (n 291 above). Horsman proposes eight new principles (see pages 3–4) but these will not be discussed *herein* as the ACPO remains the standing authoritative guide.
214 Crown Prosecution Service (n 280 above).
215 [2020] EWCA Crim 790.
216 Crown Prosecution Service (n 280 above).

In the *R-v-E* case, the court noted that,

> the Attorney General's Guidelines on Disclosure provide assistance on what amounts to a reasonable line of enquiry. The investigator must decide how best to pursue a reasonable line of enquiry in respect of such material, ensuring that the extent and manner of its examination are commensurate with the issues in the case.[217]

Further, in the Crown Prosecution Service's "Guidelines on Communication Evidence" and the "Guide to 'reasonable lines of the enquiry' and communications evidence", it was noted that:

> The examination of mobile devices belonging to the complainant is not a requirement as a matter of course in every case. There will be cases where there is no requirement for the police to take the media devices of a complainant or others at all, and thus no requirement for even a level 1 examination to be undertaken.[218]

The Guide further noted that:

> What represents a reasonable line of enquiry is an investigative matter for the police and whilst the prosecution will do what they can to assist in identifying potential further enquiries, that ought not to be taken by the police as definitive or exhaustive.[219]

In terms of securing the rights of an accused person, the CPS notes that, pursuant to the duty of the defence under rule 3.3 of the Criminal Procedure Rules to assist with case management, including identifying issues in the case and advising of any further information required, the defence should engage with the digital strategy being adopted and this includes suggesting reasonable lines of enquiry, search terms and date parameters, *inter alia*.

Conclusion

At the national level, there is evidence of the use of open source evidence in legal processes in some European countries such as Sweden, Germany, Finland and Netherlands. These countries have used evidence derived from digital open sources to prosecute domesticated international crimes under the concept of universal jurisdiction. The best practices that can be gleaned from these

217 [2018] EWCA 2426 (Crim), para. 21.

218 The Crown Prosecution Service's Guidelines on Communication Evidence" and the "Guide to 'reasonable lines of the enquiry' and communications evidence," para. 13.

219 The CPS (n 298 above) para. 19.

jurisdictions are therefore limited. This notwithstanding, their inclusion in this analysis is still relevant as they serve as an exemplification of the acceptance of this type of evidence in national judicial processes.

Conversely, a systematic case study of England & Wales was conducted. The choice of case study was influenced by the close relationship that exists between English and Kenyan laws by virtue of the colonial history. This study was supplemented by secondary data from other leading common law jurisdictions, specifically Canada and the USA. This analysis showed that the considered common law jurisdictions have had extensive interaction with open source evidence in their judicial processes. This is denoted by the presence of considerable judicial evaluation of questions of admissibility and reliability as pertaining to open source evidence. The analysis also showed that open source evidence is generally admissible as evidence in most courts which have predominantly categorised it as an electronic document.

On authentication, the analysis divulged that there appears to be two approaches. The first approach is simply a matter of adducing some evidence that the open source item is what it purports to be. Questions as to proof or accuracy of the open source item are left within the domain of the determination of the weight of the item. Therefore, open source evidence can be authenticated even if there is a dispute as to whether it is what it purports to be. The second approach is one which places a higher burden on the party that seeks to adduce the open source evidence item to prove, at the first instance, that the open source evidence has an *indicia* of authenticity in order for the evidence to be admissible.

Other themes were also found to be important considerations as they ultimately impact the admissibility of open source evidence by triggering the applicability of various evidentiary considerations as discussed. These include: the form of the open source evidence, as it was noted that the form of the open source material should not impact its admissibility as long as there is a presence of a demonstrable link between the material and the subject matter, and whether the screenshot was authenticated; the analysis established that open source evidence is predominantly categorised as a document, thus bringing it under the purview of the regime of documentary evidence, resulting in its being treated as real evidence; and lastly, the theme of hearsay was discussed whereby it was noted that open source evidence is not hearsay if it is not being relied upon for the truth of its content.

Open source investigations were also discussed in the context of England and Wales where it was seen that there exists an extensive legislative and regulative framework that governs these investigations. The concept of reasonable lines of enquiry was also discussed as being an important consideration that is essential to ensuring that actors involved in this process are not overwhelmed by increasingly large volumes of open source information.

Bibliography

Books

Mason, S (ed) *Electronic evidence* (LexisNexis Butterworths 2012).

Minogue, D, Siobhán, A, Andrews-Briscoe, C & McDermott, Y 'Putting principles into practice: Reflections on a mock admissibility hearing on open source evidence' in *International criminal law before domestic courts* (Vienna: MANZ Verlag 2023).

Book Chapters

Duranti, L & Stanfield, A 'Authenticating electronic evidence' in Mason, S & Seng, D (eds), *Electronic evidence* (Institute of Advanced Legal Studies 2017).

Gallavin, C & Mason, S 'Hearsay' in Mason, S & Seng, D (eds) *Electronic evidence* (Institute of Advanced Legal Studies 2017).

Mason, S & Seng, D 'The foundations of evidence in electronic form' in Mason, S & Seng, D (eds), *Electronic evidence* (Institute of Advanced Legal Studies 2017).

Mason, S & Stanfield, A 'Authenticating electronic evidence' in Mason, S & Seng, D (eds), *Electronic evidence* (Institute of Advanced Legal Studies 2017).

Minogue, D, Siobhán, A, Andrews-Briscoe, C & McDermott, Y 'Putting principles into practice: Reflections on a mock admissibility hearing on open source evidence' in *International criminal law before domestic courts* (Vienna: MANZ Verlag 2023).

Seng, D & Mason, S 'Hearsay' in Seng, D & Mason, S (eds) in *Electronic evidence and electronic signatures* (Institute of Advanced Legal Studies, University of London 2021).

Journal Articles

Aksamitowska, K 'Digital evidence in domestic core international crimes prosecutions: Lessons learned from Germany, Sweden, Finland and the Netherlands' (2021) 19 *Journal of International Criminal Justice* 189.

Angus-Anderson, W 'Authenticity and admissibility of social media website printouts' (2015) 14(1) *Duke Law & Technology Review* 33.

Gilliland, J 'The admissibility of social media evidence' (2013) 39 *Litigation* 20.

Gorman, WK 'The admissibility of social media evidence in Canada: Part 2: The Canada Evidence Act' (2021) 57 *Court Review: Journal of the American Judges Association* 180.

Grimm, PW, Bergstrom, YL & O'Toole-Loureiro, MM 'Authentication of social media evidence' (2013) 36 *American Journal of Trial Advocacy* 433.

Horsman, G 'ACPO principles for digital evidence: Time for an update?' (2020) 2 *Forensic Science International: Reports.*

Minogue, D, 'Digital accountability symposium: Harnessing user-generated content in accountability efforts for international law violations in Yemen' (2019) *Opinio Juris.*

O'Floinn, M & Ormerod, D 'Social networking material as criminal evidence' (2012) 7(7) *Criminal Law Review* 486

Paciocco, DM 'Proof and progress: Coping with the law of evidence in a technological age' (2013) 11(2) *Canadian Journal of Law and Technology* 181

Silver, LA 'The unclear picture of social media evidence' (2020) 43(3) *Manitoba Law Journal* 111.

Theses and Dissertations

Stanfield, AR 'The authentication of electronic evidence' unpublished PhD thesis, Queensland University of Technology, 2016.

National Legislation, Policies and Bills

Evidence Act, R.S.C. 1985, Canada.
Civil Evidence Act of 1995, United Kingdom.
Criminal Justice Act 2003, United Kingdom.

Internet Sources

Carpenter, C 'Click, click, boom: The digital evidence surge behind prosecuting jan. 6 rioters' *Lawfare*, 10 March 2022 https://www.lawfaremedia.org/article/click-click-boom-digital-evidence-surge-behindprosecuting-jan-6-rioters.

Crown Prosecution Service 'Social media and other electronic communications' 19 December 2022 https://www.cps.gov.uk/.

Crown Prosecution Service 'Social media: Reasonable lines of enquiry' 3 August 2022 https://www.cps.gov.uk/.

eyeWitness to Atrocities, 'Bringing historical crimes to justice in the Democratic Republic of the Congo,' 2018 https://www.eyewitness.global/Bringing-historical-crimes-to-a-domestic-court-in-the-DRC.

Gauthier, J 'The admissibility of computer-generated evidence: An overview' Ogilvy Renault S.E.N.C. https://docslib.org/doc/12991134/the-admissibility-of-computer-generated-evidence-an-overview.

Goldstraw-White, J 'Legal and policy framework for digital forensics: A resource for practitioners. A policy and practice briefing from the digital forensics and social media project funded by the Dawes Trust' September, 2022 https://perpetuityresearch.com/ wp-content/uploads/2022/09/Final-Legal-Procedural-and-Guidance.pdf.

Kunzelman, M 'Capitol rioters' social media posts influencing sentencings' *Associated Press*, 12 December 2021 https://apnews.com/article/media-prisons-social-media-capitol-siege-sentencing0a60a821ce19635b70681faf86e6526e.

Law Commission, 'Evidence in criminal proceedings: Hearsay and related topics' https://webarchive.nationalarchives.gov.uk/ukgwa/20241223105406/https:/lawcom.gov.uk/project/evidence-in-criminal-procedings-hearsay/.

The Crown Prosecution Service's 'Disclosure – Guidelines on communication evidence' 26 January 2018 https://www.cps.gov.uk/legal-guidance/disclosure-guidelines-communications-evidence.

Welcome to eyewitness https://www.eyewitness.global.

Table of Cases

National Case Law

United Kingdom

Amjad v Regina (2016) EWCA Crim 1618.
Campaign Against Arms Trade, R (On the Application Of) v The Secretary of State for International Trade (2017) EWHC 1754 (Admin).
Essen v DPP (2005) EWHC 1077.
Khan v R (2015) EWCA Crim 1816.
Marlton v Tektronix UK Holdings Plc (2003) EWHC 383 (Ch).
Masquerade Music Ltd v Springsteen (2001) EWCA Civ 563.
McDonald v R, (2011) EWCA Crim 2933.
R v Burns (2017) EWCA Crim 1466.
R v Carl Bater-James and Sultan Mohammed (2020) EWCA Crim 790.
R v Cochrane (1993) Crim LR 48, CA.
R v Crampton (2020) EWCA Crim 1334.
R v E (2018) EWCA Crim 2426.
R v Kay (2017) EWCA Crim 2214.
R v Mawji (Rizwan) (2003) EWCA Crim 3067.
R v Phillips (2020) EWCA Crim 126.
R v Skinner (2005) EWCA Crim Crim 1439, (2006) Crim. L.R. 56.
R v Spiby (1990) 91 Cr App R 186.
R v Thames Magistrates Court, ex parte Da Costa & Co (2002) EWHC 40.
R v Williams (2006) EWCA Crim 2148.
T v R (2012) EWCA Crim 2358.
The Bussey Law Firm PC & Timothy Raymond Bussey v Jason Page (2015) EWHC 563 QB.

United States of America

Tienda v State, 358 S.W.3d 633 Tex. Crim. App. (2012).
Griffin v State, 419 Md. 343, 19 A.3d 415 (2011).
Lorraine v Markel American Ins. Co. 241 F.R.D. 534 D. Md. (2007).
Noble Resources SA & Another v Gross (2009) EWHC 1435 (Comm).
People v Oyerinde (2011) Mich. Ct. App. No. 298199.
St. Clair v Johnny's Oyster & Shrimp, Inc. 76 F. Supp. 2d 773 S.D. Tex. (1999).
State of Connecticut v Robert Eleck 23 A.3d 818, 819 Conn. App. Ct. (2011).
The People v Albert Jerome Beckley JR, 110 Cal. Rptr. 3d 362 Ct. App. (2010).
The People v Valdez 135 Cal. Rptr. 3d 628 Ct. App. (2011).
United States District Court for the District of Columbia, Case No. AO 91 (Rev. 11/11).

Canada

R v Aslami (2021) ONCA 249.
R v Ball (2019) BCCA 32.
R v Bernard (2016) NSSC 358.

R v Durocher (2019) SKCA 97.
R v Hirsch (2017) SKCA 14.
R v JV (2015) ONCJ 837.
R v Khelawon (2006) SCC 57.
R v Martin (2021) NLCA 1.
R v Richardson (2020) NBCA 35.
R v Soh (2014) NBQB 20.
R v Starr (2000) 2 S.C.R. 144, 2000 SCC 40.
R. v Simpson (2007) ONCA 793, (2007) O.J. No. 4510.

Other Sources

The Association of Chief Police Officers (ACPO) Good Practice Guide for Digital Evidence, Version 5 (October 2011).

3 What Can Kenya Learn from International Case Law and the Practice of UN Human Rights Investigations to Date?

Introduction

This chapter examines international case law and the practice of UN human rights investigations to date in a bid to answer the research question, "what guidance is available on the use of open source evidence in legal processes from international practice?" This is done by looking at the legal framework and relevant decisions of international criminal courts and other international investigative mechanisms that arrive at findings through a quasi-judicial process such as UN-mandated human rights investigations. In examining these mechanisms, this chapter will draw upon not only decided cases but also various pieces of soft law such as the Commissions of Inquiry and Fact-Finding Missions on International Human Rights and Humanitarian Law: Guidance and Practice,[1] and the Berkeley Protocol on Digital Open Source Investigations (Berkeley Protocol).[2]

The overall aim of this chapter is to draw parallels between the discussed examples and consequently distil lessons that can inform the proposed framework for the litigation and judicial evaluation of open source evidence in Kenya. The guidance from international processes, while not binding within the Kenyan context, may nevertheless play an important role in shaping how litigants and judges interpret the law and rule on the admissibility of and the weight attributable to open source evidence in the future.

This assessment is also in line with the TWAIL framework and particularly the accepted recognition by TWAIL that international law is not always an instrument of colonial or post-colonial opposition. But it can, under certain circumstances, be an instrument for or a site of liberation such as enhancing accountability for human rights violations through setting standards for open source evidence. Accordingly, examining how international courts and tribunals, and UN human rights investigations have navigated the use of open

1 OHCHR, "Commissions of Inquiry and Fact-Finding Missions on International Human Rights and Humanitarian Law: Guidance and Practice," UN Doc HR/PUB/14/7, 2015.

2 Berkeley Protocol (n 4 above). It is important to note here that this is a co-authored document between the OHCHR and Berkeley.

DOI: 10.4324/9781003770343-3

source evidence in their processes can enhance the understanding of what a context-specific framework for Kenya can look like.

That being said, the analysis in this chapter will be conducted based on the following themes:

1. The first section analyses the legal framework and relevant decisions of international criminal courts and tribunals.
2. And the second part focuses on OHCHR official guidance and reports of UN-mandated human rights investigations.

Legal Framework and Relevant Decisions of International Criminal Courts and Tribunals

Due to the fact that the ICC has progressively developed detailed requirements for the admissibility of electronic evidence,[3] under which open source evidence generally falls, this section will focus on this Court by looking at how it has judicially analysed open source evidence.[4] It is important, however, to reiterate that the ICC favours the civil legal system due to its flexible approach to evidentiary processes in that "the compromise was to eschew generally the technical formalities of the common law system of admissibility of evidence in favour of the flexibility of the civil law system.[5] This is a limitation that will necessitate a cautious application of its approach on the evaluation of open source evidence in the consequent development of the proposed framework for Kenya as it is a common law system.

The evidentiary process at the ICC is governed by the Rome Statute, the Rules of Evidence and Procedure and the e-Protocol.[6] Due to its nature as an international court, the admissibility standard is generally low compared to a common law country like Kenya and the judges have significant discretion with respect to evidentiary matters.[7] Rule 63(2) of the Rules states: "a Chamber shall have the authority, in accordance with the discretion described in Article 64, paragraph 9, to assess freely all evidence submitted in order

3 It is important to mention here that a discussion of the legislation and decisions of regional bodies and their courts in this section would be desirable, but at the time of writing, there is no evidence that discloses the use of OSE within these courts. The closest example is the *Martha Wangari Karua v Attorney General of the Republic of Kenya* before the East African Court of Justice (EACJ) where video evidence was at play. Unfortunately, the question of the admissibility of this video evidence was not discussed by the EACJ.

4 Mehandru & Koenig (n 79 above).

5 *Prosecutor v Jean-Pierre Bemba Gombo*, Trial Chamber III, "Decision on the Admission into Evidence of Materials Contained in the Prosecution's List of Evidence," ICC-01/05-01/08, 19 November 2010, p 17.

6 Rules of Evidence & Procedure and the International Criminal Court e-Court Protocol.

7 KAA Khan, C Buisman & C Gosnell, *Principles of Evidence in International Criminal Justice*, Oxford University Press, (2010).

to determine its relevance or admissibility in accordance with Article 69."[8] Furthermore, Article 69(4) of the Rome Statute outlines that the Court may rule on the "relevance or admissibility of any evidence, taking into account, *inter alia*, the probative value of the evidence and any prejudice that such evidence may cause to a fair trial or to a fair evaluation of the testimony of a witness, in accordance with the Rules of Procedure and Evidence."[9]

Therefore, in order to understand how open source evidence has been judicially evaluated at the ICC, the starting point is to recognise that judges have discretion to determine issues of authentication and verification that may arise with respect to open source evidence. The Court set out a three-pronged test for an item to be admitted as evidence to include: relevance, probative value and the absence of prejudicial effect.[10] Articles 64(9)(a) and 69(4) of the Rome Statute as read together with the REP define relevance as denoting "existence of a fact at issue more or less probable."[11] This was the determination in *the Prosecutor v Thomas Lubanga* case where the Court noted that there must be *prima facie* relevance for the evidence to be considered.[12]

On the other hand, probative value has been defined as encompassing two aspects: the reliability of the item and the extent to which the item is likely to influence the determination of a particular issue.[13] Similarly, Article 69(4) of the Rome Statute requires that the probative value of an item is assessed before the same is admitted as evidence, and this assessment is based on "a number of considerations pertaining to the inherent characteristics of the evidence."[14] In *Prosecutor v Germain Katanga*, the Court linked the need to balance the probative value of the item against the potential prejudicial effect on the accused person.[15]

Due to the nature of open source evidence – that is, its ability to be manipulated and the potential prejudicial effect on the trier of facts, this linkage is very important as there is a need to ensure that the adducing of open source evidence does not interfere with the fair trial rights of the defending party. This

8 Rules of Procedure and Evidence, Rule 63(2).

9 UN General Assembly, Rome Statute of the International Criminal Court, ISBN No. 92-9227-227-6, 17 July 1998, Article 69(4).

10 See for example, *Prosecutor v Bemba*, ICC-01/05-01/08, Decision on the Admission into Evidence of Items Deferred in the Chamber's "Decision on the Prosecution's Application for Admission of Materials into Evidence Pursuant to Article 64(9) of the Rome Statute," 27 June 2013, p 9.

11 Mehandru & Koenig (n 63 above).

12 Trial Chamber I, "Decision on the Admissibility of Four Documents," ICC-01/04-01/06-1399, 16 June 2008, pp 27–32.

13 Mehandru & Koenig (n 79 above).

14 Rome Statute. See also, *Prosecutor v Germain Katanga and Mathieu Ngudjolo Chui*, Trial Chamber II, "Decision on the Prosecutor's Bar Table Motions," ICC-01/04-01/07, 19 December 2010, p 13.

15 Trial Chamber II, "Judgment pursuant to article 74 of the Statute," ICC-01/04-01/07, 07 March 2014, p 11.

is a requirement under Rules 69(4) and 63(2) which require that the adduced evidence must be "sufficiently relevant and probative to outweigh any prejudicial impact or effect its admission might cause."[16] It was emphasised by the Court in *Prosecutor v Jean-Pierre Bemba Gombo* where the majority noted that:

> the Chamber will evaluate, in accordance with Rule 63(2) of the Rules, the probative value and appropriate weight to be given to the evidence as a whole, at the end of the case when making its final judgement. The Chamber would then make the appropriate determinations on whether the probative value of the evidence is out-weighed by its prejudicial effect.[17]

There are various methods of determining reliability; the first method is by authentication, which has been defined as the process of proving that a digital file is genuine or not forged and that it has not been manipulated or altered.[18] The factors to consider under authentication include originality, integrity, and date/location of recording.[19] The second method is "other *indicia*," which has been held as including bias of the source, public or private nature of the information, testimonial nature of the information, purpose for which the information was created, *inter alia*.[20] Closely connected and equally necessary for the determination of the admissibility of open source evidence is the concept of verification, which has been defined as the process of ensuring that a claim or assertion statement in some medium of communication is reliable and/or true.[21]

Nonetheless, more recently, the ICC in the case of the *Prosecutor v Ali Muhammad Ali Abd-Al-Rahman ("Ali Kushayb")*, in the Situation in Darfur, Sudan, held, with respect to its approach on the submission of evidence, the Court ruled that the Chamber "will ultimately assess the relevance, probative value and potential prejudice of the evidence (the 'standard evidentiary criteria') as part of the holistic assessment of all evidence submitted when deciding on the guilt or innocence of the accused, in its judgment pursuant to Article 74 of the Statute."[22] In making this determination, the Chamber noted that

16 Rules of Procedure and Evidence.

17 Trial Chamber III, "Decision on the Admission into Evidence of Materials Contained in the Prosecution's List of Evidence," ICC-01/05-01/08, 19 November 2010, p 9.

18 S Dubberley, A Koenig & D Murray, "Introduction: The Emergence of Digital Witnesses," In *Digital Witness: Using Open Source Information for Human Rights Investigation, Documentation, and Accountability*, Oxford University Press (2020) 1st ed., pp 3–11.

19 Mehandru & Koenig (n 79 above).

20 Mehandru & Koenig (n 79 above).

21 Dubberley *et al.* (n 317 above).

22 ICC-02/05-01/20, 27 February 2023, para. 25. It should be noted that in this decision, when it refers to open source information, it refers to journalistic accounts, NGO reports, *inter alia*.

this is now an established practice of the Court.[23] This was in response to the document-specific objections that the Defence had raised while relying on the decisions in *Katanga and Ngudjolo*,[24] and *Ruto and Sang*.[25]

The Court stated, in response to these cases that, "these cases are not applicable *vis-à-vis* the present ruling, on the basis that in these cases the Chambers adopted a different approach to the reception of materials into evidence, i.e., that of 'admission' rather than 'submission'."[26] It seems that in instances where the Trial Chamber is following the "submission model," these factors will be taken into account at the deliberation stage, instead of at the judgment stage.[27] Regrettably, due to the flexible approach to evidence at the ICC, the standard is unpredictable and there is therefore not enough to be gleaned from this in so far as best practices are concerned.

On the issue of the determination of hearsay before the ICC, hearsay is admissible but it is apportioned lesser weight.[28] Unfortunately, due to the flexible approach to evidence at the ICC, the assessment and reliance on hearsay evidence is unpredictable and there is therefore not enough to be gleaned from this in so far as best practices are concerned. The best approach therefore, as noted by Freeman, is to ensure that open source investigators are well trained to identify hearsay to ensure that the necessary corroborative steps are taken.[29]

Having laid a foundation as to the general approach taken by judges when evaluating evidence at the ICC, this next section will analyse how the Court has specificalls evaluated open source evidence based on the said evidantiary

23 The Chamber made reference to the following Court documents and decisions in support of the fact that it is an established practice: See Chambers Manual, Sixth Edition, 24 November 2022, para. 84 and confidential annex. See also Trial Chamber IX, *The Prosecutor v Dominic Ongwen*, Decision on Prosecution's Request to Submit 1006 Items of Evidence, ICC-02/04-01/15-795 28 March 2017; Trial Chamber X, T*he Prosecutor v Al Hassan Ag Abdoul Aziz Ag Mohamed Ag Mahmoud*, Decision on the Prosecution's fourth, fifth and sixth requests for the admission of evidence from the bar table, ICC-01/12-01/18-2127, 23 February 2022; Trial Chamber V, *The Prosecutor v Alfred Yekatom and Patrice-Edouard Ngaïssona*, Decision on the First Prosecution Submission Request from the Bar Table, (Sexual and Gender Based Violence), ICC-01/14-01/18-1359, 12 April 2022.

24 Trial Chamber II, *The Prosecutor v Germain Katanga and Mathieu Ngudjolo Chui*, Decision on the Prosecutor's Bar Table Motions, ICC-01/04-01/07-2635, 17 December 2010, paras 12–13, 22–24, 27–35; Trial Chamber II, *The Prosecutor v Germain Katanga and Mathieu Ngudjolo Chui*, Decision on the Bar Table Motion of the Defence of Germain Katanga, ICC-01/04-01/07-3184, 21 October 2011, para. 17.

25 Trial Chamber V(A), *The Prosecutor v William Samoei Ruto and Joshua Arap Sang*, Decision on the Prosecution's Request for Admission of Documentary Evidence, ICC-01/09-01/11-1353, 10 June 2014, paras 44, 85–87.

26 *Prosecutor v Ali Muhammad Ali Abd-Al-Rahman* ("Ali Kushayb"), No: ICC-02/05-01/20, 27 February 2023, para. 26. See also, McDermott (n 92 above).

27 *Prosecutor v Ali Muhammad Ali Abd-Al-Rahman* ("Ali Kushayb"), ICC-02/05-01/20, 27 February 2023, para. 26.

28 Freeman (n 75 above) p 66.

29 Freeman (n 75 above) p 66.

considerations. It is noted that the ICC requires verifiable information that establishes where the item was obtained and/or the date and location of aquisition in the event that the information is no longer publicly available.

[30] In *Prosecutor v Katanga and Chui*, the Court noted the following with respect to videos, films, photographs and audio recordings:

> Before video or audio material can be admitted, the Chamber will require evidence of originality and integrity. However, once this has been established, this type of exhibit may often be admitted as evidence that speaks for itself and may be regarded, in this respect, as real evidence. Since the relevance of audio or video material depends on the date and/or location of recording, evidence must be provided in this regard.[31]

However, more recently, the court in the case *Prosecutor v Abd-Al-Rahman* has moved away from this authentication requirement in favour of a submission approach where it noted:

> However, in accordance with the Directions on the conduct of proceedings, and the now established practice of the Court, the Chamber "will ultimately assess the relevance, probative value and potential prejudice of the evidence (the 'standard evidentiary criteria') as part of the holistic assessment of all evidence submitted when deciding on the guilt or innocence of the accused, in its judgment pursuant to Article 74 of the Statute:"[32]

Further to the above, the e-Protocol requires the attachment of metadata that discloses the chain of custody in chronological order, the identity of the source of the item, the original author and recipient of the information, and the author and recipient's respective organisations.[33] Furthermore, the Court may require experts to provide more clarity on the adduced evidence, but the Court ultimately retains its discretion to exclude evidence that violates fair trial rights.[34]

When it comes to assessing how the Court has evaluated open source evidence, the first interaction of the Court with it was in the *Al Mahdi* case where the accused person was found guilty, as a co-perpetrator, for the "war crime of intentionally directing attacks against historic monuments and buildings dedicated to religion, including nine mausoleums and one mosque in Timbuktu,

30 Mehandru & Koenig (n 79 above).

31 Decision on the Prosecutor's Bar Table Motions, ICC-01/04-01/07, 17 December 2010, para 24(d).

32 Decision on the Prosecution's Bar Table Motion, ICC-02/05-01/20-885, 27 February 2023, para. 25. See also, McDermott (n 92 above).

33 International Criminal Court e-Court Protocol.

34 S Mason & D Seng, *Electronic Evidence* (2017) 21, 4th edn.

Mali, in June and July 2012."[35] As part of its evidence, the OTP introduced open source information, specifically videos from the internet and satellite imagery, through screenshots or downloads.[36] However, in light of the fact that Al Mahdi pleaded guilty, the authenticity of this open source evidence was not tested before this court.

Similarly, in the *Al-Werfalli* case, the Chamber issued a warrant of arrest based on, *inter alia*, social media posts, that is, videos that had been posted on Facebook.[37] In light of the fact that this case did not go to trial by virtue of Al-Werfalli's death, the Court did not pronounce itself conclusively and directly on the highlighted evidentiary considerations with respect to open source evidence. However, this being the first instance in which the Court relied heavily on open source evidence to issue a warrant of arrest further signalled this "court's willingness to evaluate digital evidence in substantially new ways."[38]

Most recently in the *Prosecutor v Al Hassan* case, relating to a charge of crimes against humanity and war crimes allegedly committed in Timbuktu, Mali, between 2012 and 2013, the OTP relied markedly on open source evidence to prove these charges.[39] The Prosecutor sought to admit 63 official documents published by United Nations bodies and specialised agencies that are available publicly.[40] The *Al Hassan* case is important in that both the Prosecutor and the Defence probed the admissibility of this open source evidence providing an insight into the different legal approaches that can be used by litigants in adducing and/or responding to the admission of such evidence in their pleadings.[41]

In its submission through a "bar table" motion,[42] it was argued *inter alia* that there is no "requirement that any documentary evidence should, where possible, be admitted through a witness."[43] In support of this admission, the

35 *Prosecutor v Ahmad Al-Faqi Al-Mahdi* (Judgment and Sentence) ICC-01/12-01/15, 25 February 2016. Al-Mahdi pleaded guilty, so this evidence was not tested in court.

36 *Prosecutor v Ahmad Al-Faqi Al-Mahdi* (Judgment and Sentence) ICC-01/12-01/15, 25 February 2016. Al-Mahdi pleaded guilty, so this evidence was not tested in court.

37 *Prosecutor v Mahmoud Mustafa Busayf Al-Werfalli* (Warrant for Arrest) ICC-01/11-01/17, 15 August 2017.

38 C Quilling, "The Future of Digital Evidence Authentication at the International Criminal Court," *Journal of Public & International Affairs*, Princeton University, 20 May 2022.

39 *The Prosecutor v Al Hassan Ag Abdoul Aziz Ag Mohamed Ag Mahmoud*, ICC-01/12-01/18, 27 March 2018.

40 Trial Chamber X, *Prosecutor v Al Hassan*, Prosecution's Second Request for the Admission of Documentary Evidence from the Bar Table, ICC-01/12-01/18-1412, 13 April 2021.

41 S Trevisan, "Open-source evidence at a crossroad: the (pending) case against Mr Hassan at the International Criminal Court and the fundamental right to a fair trial," Giurisprudenza Penale Web (2022) 1.

42 Pursuant to Articles 64(9), 69(3), 69(4) of the Rome Statute, and Rule 63(2) of the Rules of Procedure and Evidence and the Directions on the Conduct of Proceedings.

43 Trial Chamber X, *Prosecutor v Al Hassan*, Prosecution's Second Request for the Admission of Documentary evidence from the bar table, ICC-01/12-01/18-1412, 13 April 2021, para. 21.

Prosecutor argued that the material had *prima facie* probative value noting that it contained "sufficient *indicia* of reliability, including authenticity.[44] On authentication, it was argued that the items were self-authenticating given they were official documents that were available publicly from official sources,[45] and on reliability, it was argued that the material submitted contained other *indicia* of reliability such as logos and letterhead, dates of publication, authors and methodology or context of preparation.[46]

The legal reasoning on the issue of hearsay and open source evidence is another important aspect of the *Al Hassan* case. On this, the Prosecutor acknowledged the fact that due to the "non-attribution of the source of the information," anonymous hearsay concerns were triggered.[47] In relying on the *Bemba et al.* case and the Appeals Chamber decision in *Ngudjolo,* the Prosecutor however noted that:

> the fact that evidence is hearsay does not necessarily deprive it of probative value, and that the weight or probative value afforded to it will depend upon "the infinitely variable circumstances which surround hearsay evidence.[48]

Lastly, the Prosecutor also argued that information based on anonymous sources may be considered as corroboratory evidence.[49]

In its response, the Defence objected to the admission of this open source evidence based on various grounds. The first point of objection was directed at the fact that the open source evidence was not admitted through a witness, thereby denying the Defence a chance to proceed with in-court testimony to verify the reliability and authenticity of the adduced items, disadvantaging the

44 Trial Chamber X, *Prosecutor v Al Hassan*, Prosecution's Second Request for the Admission of Documentary Evidence from the Bar Table, ICC-01/12-01/18-1412, 13 April 2021, para. 14.

45 Trial Chamber X, *Prosecutor v Al Hassan*, Prosecution's Second Request for the Admission of Documentary Evidence from the Bar Table, ICC-01/12-01/18-1412, 13 April 2021, para. 15.

46 Trial Chamber X, *Prosecutor v Al Hassan*, Prosecution's Second Request for the Admission of Documentary Evidence from the Bar Table, ICC-01/12-01/18-1412, 13 April 2021, para. 19.

47 Trial Chamber X, *Prosecutor v Al Hassan*, Prosecution's Second Request for the Admission of Documentary Evidence from the Bar Table, ICC-01/12-01/18-1412, 13 April 2021, para. 19.

48 Trial Chamber X, *Prosecutor v Al Hassan*, Prosecution's Second Request for the Admission of Documentary Evidence from the Bar Table, ICC-01/12-01/18-1412, 13 April 2021, para. 19.

49 Trial Chamber X, *Prosecutor v Al Hassan*, Prosecution's Second Request for the Admission of Documentary Evidence from the Bar Table, ICC-01/12-01/18-1412, 13 April 2021, para. 19.

rights of the Accused.[50] The second point of contention was in relation to the issue of anonymous hearsay, in which the Defence argued that the prejudice occasioned by the open source evidence eclipsed its probative value, stating:

> it is nonetheless necessary to exercise "caution when items are submitted without any corresponding witness to comment on them." The prejudice caused through the inability to examine the source of information is particularly aggravated in the current instance as first, several items could and should have been submitted through a witness, and second, the majority of the tendered documents deny any assessment of the source/s of information. Without any means to verify even whether the hearsay is, for example, first-hand, third-hand, rumour circling in the civilian or military populations, a comment spreading on social media, or a government-promoted narrative fed to international agencies[.][51]

The third objection proffered by the Defence that relates to the issues this research probes was on authenticity concerns. It was submitted by the Defence that: "the Prosecution had adduced no evidence or information that would allow the Chamber to independently verify the originality, integrity and location of photographs included in the open source documents and relatedly argued that statements from the photographer would be required to authenticate these exhibits."[52]

Lastly, the open source evidence was objected to due to the lack of information relating to the methodology and sources on which point the Defence submitted that:

> Reliability must be demonstrated through … sufficient information to allow for a proper evaluation of sources, including whether the source was in a position to accurately and objectively record or recollect information concerning the facts and circumstances of the case, and the means used to compile the data or information in question.[53]

50 Trial Chamber X, *Prosecutor v Al Hassan*, Defence Response to Prosecution's Second Request for the Admission of Documentary Evidence from the Bar Table, ICC-01/12-01/18-1446, 28 April 2021.

51 Trial Chamber X, *Prosecutor v Al Hassan*, Defence Response to Prosecution's Second Request for the Admission of Documentary Evidence from the Bar Table, ICC-01/12-01/18- 1446, 26 April 2021, para. 9.

52 Trial Chamber X, *Prosecutor v Al Hassan*, Decision on Prosecution Application Submitting 63 Open Source Exhibits into Evidence, ICC-01/12-01/18-1514, 15 June 2021, para. 14.

53 Trial Chamber X, *Prosecutor v Al Hassan*, Defence Response to Prosecution's Second Request for the Admission of Documentary Evidence from the Bar Table, ICC-01/12-01/18- 1446, 26 April 2021, para. 5.

Yet again the ICC missed an opportunity to determine the admissibility of the open source evidence and similarly rule on the objections raised by the Defence in that matter. The Trial Chamber instead recognised the admission of this evidence without ruling on relevance and/or admissibility of the open source evidence and deferring this determination to "the part of the holistic assessment of all evidence submitted" in the final judgment.[54]

In critiquing the Chamber's approach, Trevisan observes that inasmuch as this approach is in line with the Court's RPE, it presents an extremely problematic precedent given the nature of open source evidence as more often than not the source of information cannot be identified.[55] This is an important observation, and one with which this research agrees, in that the Chamber's approach falls below international standards on open source verification. This is because these standards require that open source investigators verify open source information using different techniques such as those listed in the discussion of the Berkeley Protocol.[56] Trevisan argues further that by leaving this determination to the final judgment, the Defence is tasked with what she terms "an onerous burden to respond to all the submitted evidence regardless of its relevance or probative value escalating equality of arms challenges and affecting the rights of the accused person as a whole."[57]

In the Prosecution's Observations on the Agenda of the First Status Conference relating to the Situation in the Central African Republic II in the case of *Prosecutor v Alfred Yekatom and Patrice-Edouard Ngaïssona*, the Prosecution sought the admission of certain evidence *in limine* from the Bar Table including social media and other open source material.[58] This trial could provide further insight into the discussion on open source evidence at the ICC in light of the anticipated legal reasoning from both the Prosecution and Defence.

In sum, the jury is still out on how the ICC will evaluate open source evidence as this Court is yet to evaluate the admissibility of open source evidence in a final judgment.

The OTP has also used open source evidence in their investigations and/or to prove cases. For instance, in the *Jean-Pierre Bemba Gombo* case, the OTP used evidence from Facebook to support its case,[59] and in the *Al Werfalli* case,

54 Trial Chamber X, *Prosecutor v Al Hassan*, Decision on Prosecution Application Submitting 63 Open Source Exhibits into Evidence, ICC-01/12-01/18-1514, 15 June 2021, para. 4.

55 Trevisan (n 340 above) p 8.

56 Trevisan (n 340 above) p 8. These include, for example, geolocation, chronolocation, source analysis and triangulating documentary, physical and testimonial evidence.

57 Trevisan (n 340 above) p 8.

58 ICC-01/14-01/18-474-Conf, 10 June 2020, para. 18.

59 *Prosecutor v Bemba*, Prosecution's Third Request for the Admission of Evidence from the Bar Table, ICC-01/05-01/13-1170, 9 October 2015, para. 49-53; *Prosecutor v Bemba*, Public Redacted Version of Defence Response to Prosecution's Third Request for the Admission of Evidence from the Bar Table, ICC-01/05-01/13-1245, 09 October 2015, para. 83.

the OTP relied on social media posts, resulting in the Chamber issuing a warrant of arrest, as discussed in the foregoing.[60]

In its investigation that involves open sources, the OTP follows a consistent methodology based on the following criteria as seen in the *Situation in the Islamic Republic of Afghanistan*:[61]

i. Relevance – this is an assessment of how useful the open source information is for the determination of the points at issue;
ii. Reliability – an assessment of the veracity of the originator of the open source information;
iii. Credibility – an assessment of the quality of open source information that looks at the immediacy, internal consistency, and the presence of external verification;
iv. Completeness – an assessment of "the extent of the source's knowledge or coverage *vis-à-vis* the whole scope of relevant facts."

In concurrence, these criteria largely reflect those set out by the Berkeley Protocol in the foregoing.

OHCHR Official Guidance and Reports of UN-Mandated Human Rights Investigations

In order to harness the full capabilities of open source evidence, it is important that investigators and persons engaged in evidence collection consider both evidentiary and procedural issues to ensure reliability once this information is adduced in court. This is because they are legally required to disclose the methods used in the investigation/evidence collection together with the requirement to disclose sources to the defence based on the right to confront one's accuser.[62] This requirement of source evaluation in criminal law indicates the need for an identifiable source, which is not always possible due to the special nature of open source evidence where more often than not, the source is unknown.[63] This therefore requires a 'dual-source consideration' in that the investigator must evaluate both the platform's and the user's reliability.[64]

Another special consideration that ought to be made during an open source investigation/evidence collection process is the rights that need to be protected during this process. These rights include: ensuring that victims and

60 Warrant of Arrest, Al-Werfalli. See also, L Freeman & Vazquez Llorente, "Finding the Signal in the Noise: International Criminal Evidence and Procedure in the Digital Age," *Journal of International Criminal Justice* (2021) Vol. 19, 1, p 179.
61 Para. 29; Freeman (n 75 above) p 64.
62 See Article 50 (1) (k) of the Constitution of Kenya on the right to confront witnesses, for instance.
63 Freeman (n 75 above) p 65.
64 Freeman (n 75 above) p 65.

witnesses whose information may be disclosed by the open source information are protected; respecting the rights of an accused person; and ensuring that the principles of fairness are generally upheld during the proceedings.[65]

Closely tied to these rights is the requirement in criminal law that "he who alleges must prove" their case beyond reasonable doubt.[66] The only way to ensure that this standard has been discharged is by safeguarding the entire process, starting with the investigation/evidence collection stage. An equally important concern is that which relates to limitations that may be occasioned by technical and cognitive biases.[67]

The criteria used in determining admissibility that need to be considered during the investigatory process are: the relevance of the open source information to the case; the probative value of the open source information; and that the open source information be sufficiently relevant and probative to "outweigh any prejudicial effect its admission may cause."[68] Due to the fact that open source evidence is largely considered to fall under documentary evidence, the ICC assesses the weight as seen in *Prosecutor v Jean-Pierre Bemba Gombo* based on:

> provenance, source or author, as well as their role in the relevant events, the chain of custody from the time of the item's creation until its submission to the Chamber, and any other relevant information.[69]

An extensive discussion on how the Court evaluates these issues is provided in the section which focuses on judicial evaluation; the standard is only set out here in so far as it should underpin any investigation's methodology together with those set out in the Berkeley Protocol. This is discussed in the following section that focuses on the OHCHR official guidance.

Commissions of Inquiry and Fact-Finding Missions on International Human Rights and Humanitarian Law: Guidance and Practice

The OHCHR in its "Commissions of Inquiry and Fact-Finding Missions on International Human Rights and Humanitarian Law: Guidance and Practice" document has noted the importance of social media in providing an insight into modern conflicts and thereby supporting human rights investigations and thus enhancing accountability for human rights violations.[70]

65 See, Rome Statute, Articles 54–69; Article 50, Constitution of Kenya.
66 See, section 107(1) Evidence Act, Laws of Kenya; *R v Israili Epuku s/o Achietu*.
67 Y McDermott, A Koenig & D Murray, "Open Source Information's Blind Spot: Human and Machine Bias in International Criminal Investigations," *Journal of International Criminal Justice* (2021) Vol. 19, 1, p 91.
68 Freeman (n 75 above) p 64.
69 Freeman (n 75 above) p 64.
70 (2015) UN Doc HR/PUB/14/7.

The OHCHR Guidance and Practice does not provide guidance on how to particularly deal with open source material, but it provides a generalised approach from whence we can deduct some standards. For instance, in so far as the gathering and assessing of material is concerned, the importance of noting the collection details is noted. The OHCHR Guidance and Practice states that regardless of who, where, or how the information is collected, there is a minimum standard that is required. The provision of the following information, as relating to the collection of material, is important at the evaluation and analysis stages. That is:

i. Time, date and place obtained;
ii. From whom it was obtained;
iii. Who received it;
iv. Notes regarding origin and validity.[71]

Specifically for video material and photographs, the OHCHR Guidance and Practice requires that there be expert analysis in order to establish their authenticity and veracity.[72] The expert analysis would be looking to determine issues such as: whether the images were altered, whether the incident under investigation actually occurred, whether those depicted in the images actually committed the acts portrayed, *inter alia*.[73] Furthermore, the OHCHR Guidance and Practice notes that as far as open source material is concerned, independent corroboration of the material is essential.[74] The preferred standard of corroboration is by "obtaining concurring information from two other independent and reliable sources."[75] However, it is noted that this is not always possible.[76]

71 OHCHR, Commissions of Inquiry and Fact-Finding Missions on International Human Rights and Humanitarian Law: Guidance and Practice," UN Doc HR/PUB/14/7, 2015, p 40.
72 OHCHR, "Commissions of Inquiry and Fact-Finding Missions on International Human Rights and Humanitarian Law: Guidance and Practice," UN Doc HR/PUB/14/7, 2015, p 44. It is important to draw attention to the fact that here, the OHCHR appears to be using variants of the terms authenticity and veracity in conjunction to suggest they have separate but equally important meanings, which aligns with the Berkeley Protocol definitional approach that this research has adopted.
73 OHCHR, "Commissions of Inquiry and Fact-Finding Missions on International Human Rights and Humanitarian Law: Guidance and Practice," UN Doc HR/PUB/14/7, 2015, p 44.
74 OHCHR, "Commissions of Inquiry and Fact-Finding Missions on International Human Rights and Humanitarian Law: Guidance and Practice," UN Doc HR/PUB/14/7, 2015, p 44.
75 OHCHR, "Commissions of Inquiry and Fact-Finding Missions on International Human Rights and Humanitarian Law: Guidance and Practice," UN Doc HR/PUB/14/7, 2015, p 44.
76 OHCHR, "Commissions of Inquiry and Fact-Finding Missions on International Human Rights and Humanitarian Law: Guidance and Practice," UN Doc HR/PUB/14/7, 2015, p

Insofar as the evaluation and analysis of information is concerned, the OHCHR Guidance and Practice asserts that the evaluation process should consider: the relevance of the information to the subject matter of the investigation, the reliability of the source and the validity of the information.[77] It is important to note here that even at this level the source of the open source material is deemed very essential and denotes the fact that, should independent corroboration be absent, such material's admissibility capabilities would be detrimentally impacted. The evaluation process should also test the probity of the investigation, which entails the assessment of the integrity of the information collection process.[78] This confirms the importance of the minimum standard relating to the gathering and assessing of material as discussed in the foregoing.

The analysis of this information has been noted as being necessary as it provides an opportunity for the identification and correction of any weaknesses in the investigation methodology before the value of the collected information is compromised.[79] The OHCHR Guidance and Practice provides that this analysis should occur at three levels, that is, the factual analysis which aims to establish "whether the incident or event under investigation occurred and what happened, according to the information gathered," the legal analysis which connects the "facts to specific provisions of the law to determine whether the facts established constitute violations," and lastly, the analysis should establish the individuals or entities who are responsible for the violation under investigation.[80]

The OHCHR Guidance and Practice therefore provides that in order to authenticate open source information in the context of investigative bodies, the bare minimum requirements are the identification of the source, ascertaining their reliability and validating the information through independent corroboration.[81] It is clear that the OHCHR Guidance and Practice does not make provision for the authentication of anonymously posted open source

44. Regrettably, the document does not provide further guidance relating to the corroboration of secondary sources under which category video materials and photography have been placed.

77 OHCHR, "Commissions of Inquiry and Fact-Finding Missions on International Human Rights and Humanitarian Law: Guidance and Practice," UN Doc HR/PUB/14/7, 2015, p 59.

78 OHCHR, "Commissions of Inquiry and Fact-Finding Missions on International Human Rights and Humanitarian Law: Guidance and Practice," UN Doc HR/PUB/14/7, 2015, p 59.

79 OHCHR, "Commissions of Inquiry and Fact-Finding Missions on International Human Rights and Humanitarian Law: Guidance and Practice," UN Doc HR/PUB/14/7, 2015, p 59.

80 OHCHR, "Commissions of Inquiry and Fact-Finding Missions on International Human Rights and Humanitarian Law: Guidance and Practice," UN Doc HR/PUB/14/7, 2015, p 60.

81 OHCHR, "Commissions of Inquiry and Fact-Finding Missions on International Human Rights and Humanitarian Law: Guidance and Practice," UN Doc HR/PUB/14/7, 2015, p 42.

information, leaving the question as to what would happen to this type of evidence unanswered.

The Berkeley Protocol on Digital Open Source Investigations

On the collection, processing, preservation and forensic analysis of open source information, the Berkeley Protocol, a co-authored document between the Berkeley Human Rights Center and the OHCHR, is the appropriate starting point.[82] This is because it is a practical guide on the effective use of digital open source information in investigating violations of, among other things, human rights law.[83] The Berkeley Protocol is recognised as an international standard that guides the effective use of digital open source information for investigating violations; providing guidance on methodologies and procedures for gathering, analysing, and preserving digital information in a professional, legal and ethical manner; and sets out measures that online investigators can and should take to ensure victim and witness protection.

The Berkeley Protocol states that the investigation phase contains six main stages, and these include:

i. Online inquiry – which refers to the processes for discovering open source information;
ii. Preliminary assessment – processes for determining whether to collect a particular open source information;
iii. Collection – processes for capturing digital items from the internet;
iv. Preservation – processes for ensuring that the open source information collected is stored and retrievable;
v. Verification – processes for evaluating the reliability of sources and content; and
vi. Investigative analysis – processes for interpreting data, drawing conclusions and identifying gaps for further investigation.

In line with the focus of this research, and to avoid the regurgitation of the provisions of the Protocol, this part will only address the following aspects of the six investigation phases: relevance and reliability under preliminary assessment; collection; authenticity and chain of custody under preservation; verification as a whole; and some aspects of investigative analysis.

On the issue of preliminary assessment, the Berkeley Protocol notes that open source investigations should at the first instance determine whether a digital item is *prima facie* relevant to a digital investigation.[84] To this end, it is observed that the relevance of any open source item depends on its content

82 Berkeley Protocol (n 4 above).
83 Berkeley Protocol (n 4 above).
84 Para. 148.

and source together with the objectives of an investigation and the available knowledge of a situation.[85]

On the issue of reliability, the Protocol calls for open source investigators to determine whether the information or claims in digital content are *prima facie* reliable by "reviewing and evaluating the content as well as the contextual information contained in the file."[86] The process of establishing *prima facie* reliability can then comprise investigating embedded metadata,[87] linked information and the source.[88] The process of determining reliability should thus focus on efforts that are geared towards the identification of the original source of the open source material, necessitating the tracing of the data's online provenance, uploader or author.[89]

Another important factor to safeguard against during the preliminary assessment is the possibility of the removal from the Internet or from public access of the content. The Berkeley Protocol advises that when content removal is likely, "the most reliable known version of the content should be collected, even while further verification and investigation regarding earlier or better versions are conducted."[90] Lastly, there is an emphasis on the need for an open source investigator to pay attention to any legal duties that may arise upon taking custody of such a digital item. A good example is the duty arising from data protection laws that require the preservation of the content in a secure manner.[91]

With respect to the collection of open source digital items, which issue goes to the heart of the form of open source information and its consequent admissibility in judicial processes,[92] the Berkeley Protocol indicates that once the above considerations on preliminary assessment have been made, an open source investigator must determine the proper method of collection. This determination is based on three factors: whether the online content has potential evidentiary value in judicial processes; if it will be used or relied upon for decision-making purposes; or if it will contribute to internal work product only.

Where content has potential probative value, the Berkeley Protocol indicates that the collection may require a more thorough and sound method

85 Para. 148.
86 Para. 149.
87 Where metadata are data that describe and give information about other data. Metadata are relevant in describing an item and the circumstances of its generation, dissemination or alteration. Metadata might include the creator of a file, its date of creation, upload date, modifications, file size and geodata.
88 Para. 149.
89 Para. 149.
90 Para. 150.
91 Para. 150.
92 Collection is the act of gaining possession of online information through a screenshot, conversion to PDF, forensic download or other forms of capture.

of capture and it provides guidance on what to collect and how to collect the said item. The Berkeley Protocol sets out a bare minimum standard for providing evidence in court to include three items: uniform resource locator (URL), Hypertext Markup Language (HTML) source code and full-page capture.[93] Furthermore, it notes that the provision of the following information will strengthen the foundation of any open source information and thus its inclusion should be a matter of best practice in any context:

i. Target web address: the web address of the collected content, also known as the uniform resource locator (URL) or identifier (URI), should be recorded.
ii. Source code: investigators must capture the HTML source code of the web page, if applicable. HTML source code includes a lot more information than the visible portion of the website. The HTML source code will contribute to the authentication of the material collected.
iii. Full-page capture: investigators should first take a screen capture of the target web page with the date and time indicated. The reason for this process is to have the best possible representation of what was seen at the time of collection.
iv. Embedded media files: if downloading a web page with videos or images, for example, those specific items should also be extracted and collected from the web page.
v. Embedded metadata: investigators should collect the additional metadata of the digital item, if available and applicable. Metadata can vary depending on the sources, but common metadata includes uploader user identifier; post, picture or video identifier; upload date and time; geotag; hashtag; comments; and annotation.
vi. Contextual data: contextual content should also be collected if it is relevant to understanding the digital item. This may include comments on a video, image or post; upload information; and/or uploader/user information, such as a username, real name or biography. Whether surrounding information should be collected needs to be determined based on the specifics of the case and the digital item.
vii. Collection data: open source investigators must record all relevant data pertaining to the collection, such as the name of the collector, the IP address of the machine used to collect the information, the virtual identity used, if any, and a time stamp. Investigators should make sure that the system clock is accurate, preferably by synchronising it with a Network Time Protocol server. The reason for this step is to ensure time-related metadata are accurately represented in the files collected. If a virtual identity is used to access the information collected, that should be noted.

93 Para. 155.

viii. Hash value: hash values are a unique form of digital identification that confirm, through the use of cryptography, that the content collected is unique and has not been modified since the time of collection. At the point of collection, open source investigators should manually add – or the collection tool should automatically add – a hash value. There are many different types of hashes to choose from and the standards have evolved over time. Investigators should evaluate which hash to use based on the currently accepted standard.

As to standards of preservation, which connects to the question of authenticity and chain of custody, the Berkeley Protocol states that in order for digital material to remain accessible and usable for the purposes of ensuring legal accountability, there is a need to preserve it for both the short and long term.[94] The Berkeley Protocol notes further that when engaging in digital preservation for the purposes of ensuring legal accountability, "the goal is to manage and maintain digital material in a manner that helps ensure their accessibility, authenticity and potential use by accountability mechanisms, including their admissibility in legal proceedings." Open source investigators should therefore heed the call to ensure that the digital material that is collected should remain independently understandable to its intended users, in this case judicial actors, with sufficient confirmation of its authenticity.

As to the matter of chain of custody, which has been defined as referring to the chronological documentation of the sequence of custodians of a piece of information or evidence, and documentation of the control, date and time, transfer, analysis and disposition of any such evidence, the Berkeley Protocol provides that a digital item's chain of custody should be maintained at all times and that this can be achieved by putting in place a proper digital preservation system.[95] When considering the preservation system and particularly the question of the choice of storage, the Berkeley Protocol states that regard must be had to storage capacity; access and control; backups; relevant law; and information security and data protection.[96]

It is also important for the open source investigator to maintain an evidentiary copy of the collected material, that is, the digital item collected by an open source investigator in its original form should not be altered or changed but be stored in their original form.[97] For purposes of their investigative analysis, the investigator should instead use a working copy resulting in minimal handling of the original and less risk of its being compromised or altered, *ergo* increasing its chances of admissibility in evidentiary processes.[98]

94 Para. 157.
95 Para. 167.
96 Para. 170.
97 Para. 168.
98 Para. 169.

Verification, on the other hand, has been defined as the process of establishing the accuracy or validity of information that has been collected online and can be broken down into three separate steps: verification of the source, the digital item or file, and the content.[99] Due to the challenge of the anonymity of the sources or the use of pseudonyms, the Berkeley Protocol recommends that attribution analysis should always be done in the first instance, where possible. Where attribution analysis has been defined as "determining the source of the digital information, which might be a specific website, subscriber or user of a given account or platform, or the identity of the persons who authored, created or uploaded certain content."[100]

In a clarification that seems to point to the common law right of a defendant to confront their accuser, the Berkeley Protocol observes that a lack of identification of an author of an open source information is not necessarily detrimental as the same is not generally critical for establishing an online item's authenticity and this is due to the availability of other ways to authenticate open source information.[101]

Technical analysis, on the other hand, relates to the analysis of a digital item itself, to test the integrity of a file to determine whether it has been digitally altered, manipulated, or modified.[102] The Berkeley Protocol asserts that it is important for open source investigators to subject the file to digital forensic examination, which process can also be referred to as digital investigative analysis.[103] Conversely, content analysis has been defined as the process through which the information contained within a video, image, document or statement is assessed for its authenticity and veracity.[104] The Berkeley Protocol notes that content analysis is also a multifaceted process in that it involves analysing visual clues and/or corroborating the image with the metadata.

This has been necessitated by the characteristics of the online environment and the numerous issues that can affect the actual or perceived validity or veracity of information from online open sources.[105] Some of these issues that an open source investigator needs to be aware of during content analysis are: circular reporting, decontextualisation of information and misinterpretation. The Berkeley Protocol then proceeds to outline a list of factors that an open source investigator can look at as they engage in content analysis for purposes of proving the authenticity and veracity of the open source information. These include: looking for unique identifiers, identifying objectively verifiable

99 Para. 176.
100 Para. 177.
101 Para. 177.
102 Para. 183.
103 Para. 183.
104 Para. 187.
105 Para. 187.

information, geolocation,[106] chronolocation,[107] completeness, internal consistency and external corroboration.[108]

Lastly, on the issue of investigative analysis, the Berkeley Protocol formulates that due to the volume and varying quality of open source information, an open source investigation needs to take a well-structured approach to analysis. Therefore, during the investigative analysis, which has been defined as the practice of reviewing and interpreting factual information to develop substantive findings relevant to decision-making or case-building.[109] The Berkeley Protocol reiterates the fact that any such analysis should be done on the working copy as opposed to the original copy as discussed in the foregoing.

Having set out the available guidance from the OHCHR, a discussion of the next section will look at the reports of UN-mandated human rights investigations in a bid to distil lessons from these processes that can inform the proposed framework for the use of open source evidence within legal proceedings in Kenya.

Reports of UN-Mandated Human Rights Investigations

UN-mandated human rights investigations have used open source evidence in their investigations to document violations of international law in conflict situations, and their findings have fed into various judicial processes or have been used to support legal findings.[110] It has been noted that open source evidence "has emerged as a significant source of information for human rights fact-finding missions and those working in accountability generally."[111]

The United Nations Human Rights Council established the Independent International Fact-Finding Mission on Myanmar (FMM) to establish the facts and circumstances of the alleged human rights violations by military and security forces, and abuses, in Myanmar in 2017.[112] As part of this mandate, the FFM collects material through open source investigations and acknowledges

106 Identification or estimation of the location of an object, an activity or the location from which an item was generated.

107 Corroboration of the dates and times of the events depicted in a piece of information, usually visual imagery.

108 Para. 188–194.

109 Para. 195.

110 It is critical to highlight here that these are non-judicial investigations and, as will be seen in the ensuing discussions, a different standard of proof from that of judicial investigations is applied.

111 Leiden University, "Report on Digitally Derived Evidence used in UN Human Rights Fact-Finding Missions: Approaches and Standards of Proof," December 2020.

112 The United Nations Human Rights Council, the Independent International Fact-Finding Mission on Myanmar (IIFFMM). Available: https://www.ohchr.org/en/hr-bodies/hrc/myanmar-ffm/index, accessed 11 November 2023.

the critical need to collect open source information such as videos, photographs and geospatial imagery publicly available on the internet or social media.[113]

The collected material is then "analysed based on reliability and probative value, taking into account evidentiary and methodological standards and principles applicable in relevant national and international legal systems."[114] The Mechanism then uses this analysis to prepare case files on individuals who have allegedly committed serious international crimes and violations of international law in Myanmar since 2011.[115] In its report before the UN GA, the FFM noted that when open source information "is collected in line with international best practices, verified and analysed by experts, it is increasingly recognised as a probative form of evidence in criminal proceedings."[116]

Based on the Human Rights Council resolution 43/26, the FFM is allowed to share information in relation to ICJ proceedings and to this end, it shared information with The Gambia as part of the *Gambia v Myanmar* case before the International Court of Justice (ICJ) in which case the ICJ issued, *inter alia*, an order directing Myanmar to "take all measures within its powers" to prevent the commission of acts defined in the Genocide Convention.[117] In addition, Resolution 43/26 called "for close and timely cooperation between the Mechanism and any future investigations by national, regional or international courts or tribunals, including by the International Criminal Court[.]"[118] In light of the authorisation that the ICC OTP has received to investigate the alleged violation of crimes in the Situation of Bangladesh/Myanmar, it is noted that the FFM has continued to share information with the OTP that is relevant to its investigation into alleged crimes against the Rohingya and open source information is inevitably included.[119]

There is therefore a significant use and reliance on open source information by this Mechanism which, as indicated above, has consequently fed into judicial processes both before the ICJ and the ICC as part of the OTP's investigatory process. Unfortunately, the Mechanism's reports do not disclose the steps that were followed in authenticating this open source material beyond noting the use of technology in its analysis. For instance, in its 2022 report, it

113 United Nations General Assembly, "Report of the Independent Investigative Mechanism for Myanmar," A/HRC/48/18, 5 July 2021.

114 Independent Investigative Mechanism for Myanmar, "Evidence Collection and Case Building." Available: https://iimm.un.org/en, accessed 11 November 2023.

115 Independent Investigative Mechanism for Myanmar (n 412 above).

116 United Nations General Assembly, "Report of the Independent Investigative Mechanism for Myanmar," A/HRC/51/4, 12 July 2022.

117 Independent Investigative Mechanism for Myanmar, "ICJ – The Gambia v Myanmar." Available: https://iimm.un.org/en, accessed 11 November 2023.

118 UN HRC in Resolution 43/26, 3 July 2020.

119 United Nations General Assembly (n 415 above).

is noted that: "the Mechanism has invested in world-leading software capable of performing advanced analytics on organised data sets and is customising an in-house platform for evidence review, gap analysis and legal classification."

The Report of the detailed findings of the independent international Commission of inquiry on the protests in the Occupied Palestinian Territory (OPT Commission) showed extensive reliance on social media content such as videos and photos as it is noted that approximately 95% of the videos used were found on social media.[120] Furthermore, this Commission also made reference to official and unofficial Facebook pages and posts belonging to individual protesters to ascertain the character of the 'Great Return March' on whether it was a peaceful demonstration or not.[121] The OPT Commission relied further on video evidence to prove that Palestinian demonstrators and journalists wearing PRESS jackets did not pose a threat to the Israeli Security Forces (ISF) and that their consequent targeting was unlawful as it violated international human rights law.[122] This Commission also used open source evidence in a different way, that is, using video evidence to discredit a false narrative that had been presented by the ISF pertaining to a 16-year-old that they had killed.[123] This was done by relying on a "clip that surfaced showing a man in close proximity to him 'exhorting the crowd', thereby presenting an alternative narrative that this man was the intended target."[124]

Similarly, the OPT Commission's report does not disclose in detail what steps were followed in authenticating the said videos and photos. It is, however, important to note that authenticated video and photographic material, satellite imagery, and documents were categorised as direct information.[125] In order for this direct information to meet the Commission's standard of proof, it had to have been independently corroborated by "at least one or more additional credible sources of information."[126] In assessing the reliability and credibility of each source, the Commission considered *inter alia* where and how the information was obtained and the reasons for which it was provided.[127] In assessing the validity of the information, the following issues were considered:

120 A/HRC/40/CRP.2, 18 March 2019.
121 "Report of the Detailed Findings of the Independent International Commission of Inquiry on the Protests in the Occupied Palestinian Territory," (OPT Report) (Fortieth session) UN Doc A/HRC/40/CRP.2, 18 March 2019, para. 195–211.
122 OPT Report (n 420 above).
123 OPT Report (n 420 above) para. 123–124.
124 Leiden University (n 410 above) p 10. Based on the fact that it relates to the same conflict, it is important to highlight here that South Africa relied on open source evidence, such as tweets, in its legal intervention against the state of Israel before the ICJ regarding the conflict in Gaza, and this is part of the evidence that the ICJ relied on to indicate provisional measures.
125 OPT Report (n 420 above) para. 19.
126 OPT Report (n 420 above) para. 18.
127 OPT Report (n 420 above) para. 20.

"its relevance to the inquiry, its internal consistency and coherence, its logic, and its consistency with and corroboration by other information."[128]

And lastly, a very critical distinction the Commission made in its assessment was to distinguish "between the reliability and credibility of the source and the validity of the information provided."[129] This distinction is important as it potentially provides support for the admissibility of open source evidence when the source is anonymous as long as all the other considerations, that is the requirement for authentication and relevance, are met. The various Commissions of Inquiry into the Syrian Arab Republic, the Inquiry in Libya, Sri Lanka and Yemen have also extensively made use of open source evidence including video and photo materials from social media and satellite imagery.[130]

With respect to the African region, the investigations in Burundi revealed the use of video and photo materials from social media platforms. For instance, in 2018, the Commission in Burundi used a video posted on social media in support of findings that a violation had occurred at a location that was alleged to be a secret detention and this was based on the presence of blood stains outside this location.[131] The legal issues in question here related to the right to life as a result of arbitrary executions and other deprivations.[132]

In South Sudan, video and photo material from social media and satellite imagery were used to prove various violations.[133] For instance, in 2019, photos that showed the aftermath of a school that had been ransacked were considered alongside witness statements and satellite imagery to "assess that approximately 7,345 structures were damaged or destroyed over a given time period in areas of Unity State."[134]

There is however no explicit mention of the process followed in authenticating the video and photo material but some inferences can be made. At the information gathering stage, there is a need to maintain a clear chain of

128 OPT Report (n 420 above) para. 22.

129 OPT Report (n 420 above) para. 23.

130 See for instance, Report of the Independent International Commission of Inquiry on the Syrian Arab Republic, A/HRC/44/61, 2 July 2020 and the Report of the Independent International Commission of Inquiry on the Syrian Arab Republic, A/HRC/34/64, 2 February 2017; Investigation by the Office of the United Nations High Commissioner for Human Rights on Libya: Detailed Findings, A/HRC/31/CRP.3, 23 February 2016; Report of the OHCHR Investigation on Sri Lanka, A/HRC/30/CRP.2, 16 September 2015; Report of the Group of Eminent International and Regional Experts as submitted to the United Nations High Commissioner for Human Rights, A/HRC/42/17, 9 August 2019; Comprehensive Report of the Group of Eminent International and Regional Experts on Yemen, A/HRC/45/6, 14 September 2020.

131 "Rapport Final Détaillé de la Commission d'enquête sur le Burundi" (Thirty-ninth session) UN Doc A/HRC/39/CRP.1, 12 September 2018, para. 257.

132 Leiden University (n 410 above) p 9.

133 Report of the Commission on Human Rights in South Sudan, A/HRC/40/CRP.1, 21 February 2019.

134 Leiden University (n 410 above) p 12 & 14.

custody which entails cataloguing and organising evidence in a database as this would directly impact any criminal investigations that aim to ensure accountability.[135] Another important step of note, which aligns with the OHCHR Guidance and Practice, is the requirement for independent corroboration by "at least one or more credible source(s) of information."[136]

The determination of the reliability and credibility of the source was also deemed an important step and in ascertaining this, the Commission took into account, amongst other considerations, where and how the information was obtained, and the reason for which the information was provided.[137] Other factors that were considered in the assessment which would consequently impact the admissibility of the open source information are a determination of: the material's relevance to the subject matter, the material's internal consistency and coherence, "its logic, and its consistency with and corroboration by other information."[138] A critical practice is revealed here, that is, "assessments of the reliability and credibility of the source were separated from assessments of the validity of the information."[139] This is critical because it is the closest standard that would support the admission of open source evidence from an anonymous source provided all other authenticating factors stay constant.

In its 2023 Report, the Commission provided a bit more information as to how it went about authenticating video and photographic material. The extrajudicial killings had been circulating on social media depicting one man being burnt alive in a hut and three men being killed by a firing squad.[140] In making a finding that these extrajudicial killings had been committed by the state, the Commission used chronolocation, geolocation and extensive advanced open source analysis of the material.[141] It is further noted that, "although metadata was not available in the video recordings received by the Commission because it had been stripped by the social media platforms used to share them, through an extensive open source review, and the use of trigonometry and calculation software, the approximate location could be established."[142]

Having discussed the instances in which these investigations have resulted in legal findings, a consideration of how these investigative bodies dealt with this research's questions is important. First, these investigative bodies apply a

135 Report of the Commission on Human Rights in South Sudan (n 432 above) para. 13.
136 Report of the Commission on Human Rights in South Sudan (n 432 above) para. 15.
137 Report of the Commission on Human Rights in South Sudan (n 432 above) para. 19.
138 Report of the Commission on Human Rights in South Sudan (n 432 above) para. 20.
139 Report of the Commission on Human Rights in South Sudan (n 432 above) para. 21.
140 'Unity State Orders Violent Extra-judicial Killing of Suspects Accused of Murdering Mayom County's Former Commissioner, Nyamilepedia, 8 August 2022. Available at: https://www.nyamile.com/, accessed 11 November 2023.
141 Report of the Commission on Human Rights in South Sudan (n 432 above) para. 139. Unfortunately, the Commission does not actually define these terms or provide details as to what is entailed in each process.
142 Report of the Commission on Human Rights in South Sudan (n 432 above) p 40.

different standard of proof which is the "reasonable grounds to believe" standard.[143] It is noted that the "reasonable grounds to believe" standard is one which has become a consistent practice of UN fact-finding bodies.[144]

It has further been noted that open source evidence has been considered primary information as long as the open source evidence has been authenticated.[145] This means that open source evidence has been given the same weight as evidence derived from victim interviews and evidence from eye witnesses.[146] It is important to point out here that this seems to be a departure from the provisions of the OHCHR Guidance and Practice which categorises video material and photography as secondary evidence.

In determining how these investigative bodies have gone about authenticating open source information, regrettably most investigative bodies do not elaborate on what is entailed in the process of authentication.[147] For the Commissions that have provided this information, the authentication of video and photographic material has been done by way of corroborating this material with other credible and reliable information.[148] This was a deduction from the processes of the Commission in Myanmar in 2019, for instance.[149]

Conclusion

There is a steady development of international practice from various legal, policy and investigative processes that can be studied comparatively in order to distil best practices. As to approaches from international and regional processes, the ICC emerged as the best source of judicial best practice due to its substantial interaction with open source evidence in both the OTP investigations and judicial evaluation. However, the Court is yet to pronounce itself conclusively and directly on the highlighted evidentiary considerations with respect to open source evidence. This is due to the fact that, thus far, no case that is seeking to probe these issues has progressed to the hearing and judgment stages.

On approaches relating to open source investigations/evidence collection, the Berkeley Protocol emerged as the accepted source of best practice as it is a practical guide on the effective use of digital open source information in

143 Leiden University (n 410 above) p 7.
144 Leiden University (n 410 above) p 7. As a demonstration of this, the Reports by the Commissions in Burundi, South Sudan and Palestine have expressly made reference to this standard. This is a limitation that has to be noted in the sense that this standard falls short of the judicial 'beyond reasonable doubt' standard.
145 Leiden University (n 410 above) p 10.
146 Leiden University (n 410 above) p 10.
147 Leiden University (n 410 above) p 10.
148 Leiden University (n 410 above) p 11.
149 "Report of the Detailed Findings of the Independent International Fact-Finding Mission on Myanmar," (Thirty-ninth session) UN Doc A/HRC/39/CRP.2, 17 September 2018, para. 306–309.

investigating violations of, among other things, human rights law. It was also noted that the OTP's methodology seems to follow that which has been enunciated in the Berkeley Protocol and primarily focuses on relevance, reliability, credibility and completeness of the open source item.

Non-judicial investigative bodies mandated by UN organs such as the Independent International Fact-Finding Mission on Myanmar, the independent international Commission of inquiry on the protests in the Occupied Palestinian Territory, Commissions of Inquiry into the Syrian Arab Republic, Libya, Sri Lanka, Yemen, Burundi and South Sudan have been shown to also use open source information and evidence in their investigations. This has consequently fed into judicial processes as in the investigation in Myanmar and the ensuing case before the ICJ. Conversely, this evidence has been used by these investigative bodies to make legal findings, for instance, the substantiation of the violation of international human rights by the IFS as determined by the Commission of Inquiry in the Occupied Palestinian Territory. Unfortunately, these reports have not extensively revealed the steps that were followed by the investigative bodies to authenticate the open source material to enable further discussion on the same.

The OHCHR has also recognised the emergence and importance of this type of evidence, noting its importance in providing an insight into modern conflicts. Accordingly, open source evidence has been included in the OHCHR's "Commissions of Inquiry and Fact-Finding Missions on International Human Rights and Humanitarian Law: Guidance and Practice" document.

To sum up, this chapter has demonstrated the various significant uses of open source evidence that, in the first instance, confirm the presence of this type of evidence before international and regional judicial bodies. Secondly, the discussions have shown the use of open source evidence to support various investigative processes, be they judicial or non-judicial. Beyond the best practice that can be gleaned from these discussions, it also supports one of this research's contentions that open source evidence is a type of evidence that the Kenyan legal system will have to contend with imminently necessitating a framework for its use in legal proceedings as proposed by this research.

Bibliography

Books

Khan, KAA, Buisman, C & Gosnell, C *Principles of evidence in International criminal justice* (Oxford University Press 2010).

Mason, S & Seng, D *Electronic evidence* (Institute of Advanced Legal Studies 2017).

Book Chapters

Dubberley, S, Koenig, A & Murray, D 'Introduction: The emergence of digital witnesses' in S Dubberley, A Koenig & D Murray (Eds) *Digital witness: Using open source information for human rights investigation, documentation, and accountability* (Oxford University Press 2020).

Journal Articles

Freeman, L 'Digital evidence and war crimes prosecutions: The impact of digital technologies on international criminal investigations and trials' (2018) 41(2) *Fordham International Law Journal* 283.

Freeman, L & Llorente V Finding the signal in the noise: International criminal evidence and procedure in the digital age' (2021) 19 *Journal of International Criminal Justice* 1.

McDermott, Y, Koenig, A & Murray, D 'Open source information's blind spot: Human and machine bias in international criminal investigations' (2021) 19(1) *Journal of International Criminal Justice* 85.

Mehandru, N & Koenig, A 'ICTS, social media, & the future of human rights' (2019) 17 *Duke Law & Technology Review* 129.

Quilling, C 'The future of digital evidence authentication at the international criminal court' (2022) *Journal of Public & International Affairs*, Princeton University.

International Instruments

Rome Statute of the International Criminal Court, adopted on 17 July 1998, entered into force on 1 July 2002.

United Nations Documents

Human Rights Council 'Report of the Independent International Commission of Inquiry on the Syrian Arab Republic' 2 February 2017 UN Doc A/HRC/34/64.

Human Rights Council 'Report of the Independent International Commission of Inquiry on the Syrian Arab Republic' 3 September 2020 UN Doc A/HRC/44/61.

Human Rights Council 'Report of the OHCHR investigation on Sri Lanka (OISL) 16 September 2015 UN Doc A/HRC/30/CRP2.

Human Rights Council 'Resolution adopted by the Human Rights Council on 22 June 2020 on the situation of human rights in Myanmar' 3 July 2020 UN Doc A/HRC/RES/43/26.

Human Rights Council, 'Report of the Commission on Human Rights in South Sudan' 21 February 2019, UN Doc A/HRC/40/CRP.1.

Human Rights Council, 'Report of the detailed findings of the independent international Commission of inquiry on the protests in the Occupied Palestinian Territory' 22 March 2019, UN Doc A/HRC/4.

Human Rights Council, 'Situation of human rights in Yemen, including violations and abuses since September 2014: Report of the Group of Eminent International and Regional Experts as submitted to the United Nations High Commissioner for Human Rights' 9 August 2019 UN Doc A/HRC/42/17.

Human Rights Council, 'Situation of human rights in Yemen, including violations and abuses since September 2014' 28 September 2020 UN Doc A/HRC/45/6.

OHCHR, 'Commissions of Inquiry and fact-finding missions on international human rights and humanitarian law: Guidance and practice' 2015 UN Doc HR/PUB/14/7.

OHCHR, 'Rapport final détaillé de la Commission d'enquête sur le Burundi' (Thirty-ninth session, 12 September 2018) UN Doc A/HRC/39/CRP.1.

OHCHR, 'Report of the detailed findings of the Independent International Fact-Finding Mission on Myanmar' (Thirty-ninth session, 17 September 2018) UN Doc A/HRC/39/CRP.2.

OHCHR & Human Rights Center UC Berkeley School of Law, 'Berkeley Protocol on Digital Open Source Investigations: A practical guide on the effective use of digital open source information in investigating violations of international criminal, human rights and humanitarian law' 2022 UN Doc HR/PUB/20/2.

United Nations General Assembly, 'Report of the Independent Investigative Mechanism for Myanmar' 5 July 2021 UN Doc A/HRC/48/18.

United Nations General Assembly, 'Report of the Independent Investigative Mechanism for Myanmar,' 12 July 2022 UN Doc A/HRC/51/4.

Other International and Regional Sources

Information in Electronic Form, ICC-01/04-01/10-87-Anx 30-03-2011.

International Criminal Court, Rules of Procedure and Evidence of the International Criminal Court, 2019.

Unified Technical Protocol ("e-Court Protocol") for the Provisoin of Evidence, Witness and Victims.

National Legislation, Policies and Bills

Constitution of Kenya, 2010.

Evidence Act, Laws of Kenya, Cap 80.

Working Papers, Published Articles and Reports

Leiden University, 'Report on Digitally Derived Evidence used in UN Human Rights Fact-Finding Missions: Approaches and Standards of Proof' December 2020' https://leiden-guidelines.com/.

Internet Sources

Independent Investigative Mechanism for Myanmar, ICJ – The Gambia v Myanmar, https://iimm.un.org/en.

Nyamilepedia, 'Unity State orders violent extra-judicial killing of suspects accused of murdering Mayom county's former commissioner' 8 August 2022 https://www.nyamile.com/news/unity-state-ordersviolent-extra-judicial-killing-of-suspects-accused-of-murdering-mayom-countys-former-commissioner/.

Trevisan, S 'Open-source evidence at a crossroad: The (pending) case against Mr Hassan at the International Criminal Court and the fundamental right to fair trial,' Giurisprudenza Penale Web, 27 January 2022 https://www.giurisprudenzapenale.com/2022/01/27/open-source-evidence-at-a-crossroad-

the-pending-case-against-mr-hassan-at-the-international-criminal-court-and-the-fundamental-right-to-fair-trial/.
United Nations Human Rights Council, 'Independent International fact-finding mission on Myanmar' https://www.ohchr.org/en/hr-bodies/hrc/myanmar-ffm/index.

Table of Cases

International Criminal Court

The Prosecutor v Ahmad Al-Faqi Al-Mahdi, Trial Chamber VIII, ICC-01/12-01/15-171 25 February 2016.
The Prosecutor v Alfred Yekatom & Patrice-Edouard Ngaïssona, Trial Chamber V, ICC-01/14-01/18- 1359 12 April 2022.
The Prosecutor v Alfred Yekatom and Patrice-Edouard Ngaïssona, Office of the Prosecutor, ICC-01/14- 01/18-474-Conf, 24 April 2020.
The Prosecutor v Al Hassan Ag Abdoul Aziz Ag Mohamed Ag Mahmoud, Office of the Prosecutor, ICC 01/12-01/18-1412 13 April 2021.
The Prosecutor v Al Hassan, Defence Response to Prosecution's Second Request for the Admission of Documentary Evidence from the Bar Table, ICC 01/12-01/18-1446, 28 April 2021.
The Prosecutor v Ali Muhammad Ali Abd-Al-Rahman ("Ali Kushayb") Trial Chamber I, ICC-02/05- 01/20, 27 February 2023.
The Prosecutor v Dominic Ongwen, Trial Chamber IX, ICC-02/04-01/15-795 28 March 2017.
The Prosecutor v Germain Katanga, Trial Chamber II ICC-01/04-01/07-3436-tENG 07 March 2014.
The Prosecutor v Germain Katanga, Trial Chamber II, ICC-01/04-01/07-2635 19 December 2010.
The Prosecutor v Germain Katanga, Trial Chamber II, ICC-01/04-01/07-3184 21 October 2011.
The Prosecutor v Jean-Pierre Bemba Gombo, Aimé Kilolo Musamba, Jean-Jacques Mangenda Kabongo, Fidèle Babala Wandu and Narcisse Arido, Office of the Prosecutor, ICC-01/05-01/13-1170-Red 18 September 2015.
The Prosecutor v Jean-Pierre Bemba Gombo, Aimé Kilolo Musamba, Jean-Jacques Mangenda Kabongo, Fidèle Babala Wandu and Narcisse Arido, Defence / Response, ICC-01/05-01/13-1245 09 October 2015.
The Prosecutor v Jean-Pierre Bemba Gombo, Trial Chamber III, ICC-01/05-01/08 27 June 2013.
The Prosecutor v Jean-Pierre Bemba Gombo, Trial Chamber III, ICC-01/05-01/08-1022 19 November 2010.
The Prosecutor v Mahmoud Mustafa Busayf Al-Werfalli, Pre-Trial Chamber I, ICC-01/11-01/17 15 June 2022.
The Prosecutor v Thomas Lubanga Dyilo, Trial Chamber I, ICC-01/04-01/06-1399 16 June 2008.
The Prosecutor v William Samoei Ruto and Joshua Arap Sang, Trial Chamber V(a), ICC-01/09-01/11- 1353 10 June 2014.

East African Court of Justice

Martha Wangari Karua v The Attorney General of the Republic of Kenya & 2 others No. 20 of 2019.

4 Assessing the Suitability of Kenya's Legal Framework in Relation to Open Source Evidence

Introduction

This chapter seeks to assess whether Kenya's legal framework is suitable in relation to open source evidence or whether law reform is needed in order to harness the power of open source evidence. This is done by reviewing the ways in which open source evidence has been used in litigation and judicially evaluated in Kenya. The approaches taken in the collection, preservation and presentation of open source evidence in legal proceedings are equally assessed. Open source investigations within the Kenyan context are also discussed.

This chapter builds on the discussions in Chapter 1 by analysing the legal framework relating to evidentiary rules and procedures that may impact the use of open source evidence in Kenya. This chapter relies on primary data that was collected through the survey and the systematic case study. The survey was carried out through advanced questionnaires and key informant interviews while the systematic case study was conducted based on the research methodology as set out in Chapter 1.

Legal Framework for Electronic and Digital Evidence in Kenya

In Kenya, the evidentiary process is governed by the Kenyan Evidence Act of 1963 (the Act), which applies to all judicial proceedings in any court in Kenya.[1] The Act speaks of electronic and digital evidence, which is governed by its sections 78A and 106B. Therefore, within the Kenya-specific context, the discussions will reflect a reference to electronic and digital evidence. It is also important to reiterate the fact that this Act covers both civil and criminal cases in Kenya. For this reason, and as a result of the data from the survey, civil cases in which courts have interpreted the admissibility of electronic and digital evidence have been included in the analysis in this chapter. This is despite

1 Evidence Act, Laws of Kenya, CAP. 80. It is important to note that section 106B was added to the Evidence Act as an amendment in 2009 (Kenya Communications (Amendment) Act, 2009) and in 2014, the Evidence Act was further amended to include section 78A (by the Security Laws (Amendment) Act, 2014).

DOI: 10.4324/9781003770343-4

this research's overall focus on human rights violations, which focus rightly denotes that fact that this research's primary interest is on decisions from the Criminal and Constitutional and Human Rights Divisions.

Section 78A on admissibility of electronic and digital evidence provides that:

(1) In any legal proceedings, electronic messages and digital material shall be admissible as evidence.
(2) The court shall not deny admissibility of evidence under subsection (1) only on the ground that it is not in its original form.
(3) In estimating the weight, if any, to be attached to electronic and digital evidence, under subsection (1), regard shall be had to –
 (a) the reliability of the manner in which the electronic and digital evidence was generated, stored or communicated;
 (b) the reliability of the manner in which the integrity of the electronic and digital evidence was maintained;
 (c) the manner in which the originator of the electronic and digital evidence was identified; and,
 (d) any other relevant factor.
(4) Electronic and digital evidence generated by a person in the ordinary course of business, or a copy or printout of or an extract from the electronic and digital evidence certified to be correct by a person in the service of such person, is on its mere production in any civil, criminal, administrative or disciplinary proceedings under any law, the rules of a self-regulatory organization or any other law or the common law, admissible in evidence against any person and rebuttable proof of the facts contained in such record, copy, printout or extract.

Section 106B of the Act, which categorises electronic evidence as documentary evidence, then sets the standards of admissibility. The constituent elements of section 106B are discussed below.

Section 106B (1) provides that:

> Notwithstanding anything contained in this Act, any information contained in an electronic record which is printed on a paper, stored, recorded or copied on optical or electro-magnetic media produced by a computer (herein referred to as computer output) shall be deemed to be also a document, if the conditions mentioned in this section are satisfied in relation to the information and computer in question and shall be admissible in any proceedings, without further proof or production of the original, as evidence of any contents of the original or of any fact stated therein where direct evidence would be admissible.

This is therefore the operative section that brings open source evidence within the realm of the documentary evidence regime by virtue of the statement, "shall be deemed to be also a document" above.

Section 106B (2) and (3) provide the technical requirements that are necessary to enable the admissibility of electronic and digital evidence. The sections provide that:

(2) The conditions mentioned in subsection (1), in respect of a computer output, are the following –
   (a) the computer output containing the information was produced by the computer during the period over which the computer was used to store or process information for any activities regularly carried out over that period by a person having lawful control over the use of the computer;
   (b) during the said period, information of the kind contained in the electronic record or of the kind from which the information so contained is derived was regularly fed into the computer in the ordinary course of the said activities;
   (c) throughout the material part of the said period, the computer was operating properly or, if not, then in respect of any period in which it was not operating properly or was out of operation during that part of the period, was not such as to affect the electronic record or the accuracy of its content; and
   (d) the information contained in the electronic record reproduces or is derived from such information fed into the computer in the ordinary course of the said activities.

(3) Where over any period, the function of storing or processing information for the purposes of any activities regularly carried on over that period as mentioned in paragraph (a) of sub-section (2) was regularly performed by computers, whether –
   (a) by a combination of computers operating in succession over that period; or
   (b) by different computers operating in succession over that period; or
   (c) in any manner involving the successive operation over that period, in whatever order, of one or more computers and one or more combinations of computers,

then all computers used for that purpose during that period shall be treated for the purposes of this section to constitute a single computer and references in this section to a computer shall be construed accordingly.

Lastly, section 106B (4) and (5) provide the procedural requirements that should be followed in the process of adducing electronic and digital evidence in court. The sections provide that:

(4) In any proceedings where it is desired to give a statement in evidence by virtue of this section, a certificate doing any of the following –
   (a) identifying the electronic record containing the statement and describing the manner in which it was produced;
   (b) giving such particulars of any device involved in the production of that electronic record as may be appropriate for the purpose of showing that the electronic record was produced by a computer;
   (c) dealing with any matters to which conditions mentioned in sub-section (2) relate; and
   (d) purporting to be signed by a person occupying a responsible position in relation to the operation of the relevant device or the management of the relevant activities (whichever is appropriate),

shall be evidence of any matter stated in the certificate and for the purpose of this sub-section it shall be sufficient for a matter to be stated to the best of the knowledge of the person stating it.

(5) For the purpose of this section, information is supplied to a computer if it is supplied thereto in any appropriate form and whether it is so supplied directly or (with or without human intervention) by means of appropriate equipment, whether in the course of activities carried on by any official, information is supplied with a view to its being stored or processed for the purpose of those activities, that information, if duly supplied to that computer, shall be taken to be supplied to it in the course of those activities.

However, the operative law is plagued with various gaps that directly impact the feasibility of it being the legal framework for determining the admissibility of open source evidence in Kenya. The first major challenge is that sections 78A and 106B of the Act relate to digital and not open source evidence. Secondly, this challenge may be a direct result of the first challenge; the conditions set out in the operative section primarily relate to the computer system from which the electronic evidence was derived and whether the said computer was performing its regular functions. This is in variance with the fundamental nature of open source information – publicly available information in which the source may or may not be known.

The third challenge goes beyond the foregoing and, as noted by Rutenberg *et al.*, the sections only set out the considerations in estimating the probative value of the evidence without setting out the conditions preceding admissibility.[2] By offering little guidance to investigators and actors with respect to the admission of digital evidence, there is a resultant grey area on how to address

2 Rutenberg *et al.* (n 86 above) p 37.

issues such as the right to privacy – a constitutionally mandated right – and ensuring the sanctity of such investigations.[3]

Lastly, there exists a contradiction between section 78A and section 106B on the requirement to adduce a certificate to, *inter alia,* prove the provenance of the e-evidence, the integrity of the system, or its functionality.[4] That is, section 78A of the Act does not make any requirement for a certificate whereas section 106B has a certificate requirement. Courts have addressed this uncertainty by treating the requirement for a certificate under section 106B as being mandatory despite the fact that the wording of the Act does not disclose such a precondition, essentially disregarding the blanket declaration of admissibility under section 78A.[5] An interpretation by the courts that does not reflect the wording of the Act further complicates the admissibility of open source evidence in Kenya in that, if there are discrepancies between the operative law and how it has been judicially interpreted, then the entire system becomes flawed.

Review of Any Other Legislations/Policies That May Impact the Use of Open Source Evidence in Kenya

The Kenya Information and Communication Act, No. of 2 of 1998 and The Kenya Information and Communication (Amendment) Bill, 2022

Other than the Evidence Act, the Kenya Information and Communication Act No. 2 of 1998 (KICA) and its amendments have an impact on the admissibility of open source evidence in Kenya.[6] Generally, KICA gives legal recognition to electronic records at section 83G. Section 83H of KICA provides for the retention of electronic records and requires that such records remain accessible in the format they were originally generated. KICA also requires that details facilitating the identification of the original destination, date, and time of dispatch or receipt of such electronic record are available in the electronic record.

However, the proposed amendments to KICA in the form of the Kenya Information and Communication (Amendment) Bill, 2022 (commonly

3 P Chepkemoi, "A Comparative Study on the Admissibility of Digital Evidence in Criminal Courts in Kenya," 2017. Available: https://su-plus.strathmore.edu/handle/11071/5242?show=full, accessed 11 November 2023. The right to privacy is provided for under Article 31 of the Constitution of Kenya.

4 Rutenberg *et al.* (n 86 above) p 37.

5 See for instance, *County Assembly of Kisumu & 2 others v Kisumu County Assembly Service Board & 6 others* [2015] eKLR; and *Idris Abdi Abdullahi v Ahmed Bashane & 2 others,* [2018] eKLR; and, *Mable Muruli v Wycliffe Oparanya & 3 others,* [2013] eKLR.

6 Other legislation that relates generally to the use of open source evidence in Kenya include: Computer Misuse and Cybercrime Act of 2018; Kenya Copyright Act, Kenya National Cohesion and Integrity Act, Penal Code (section 66), Sexual Offences Act, Cybercrime Standard Operating Procedure Manual of 2018, Data Protection Bill, Central Bank of Kenya Guidelines, National Cybersecurity Strategy of 2018. Refer to Figure 4.1. for other legislations as underscored by the findings from the data collection process.

dubbed "the Social Media Bill") are one which will specifically have far-reaching consequences on open source evidence in Kenya. This is because, as will be discussed, if these amendments are passed, they will have the effect of limiting the freedom of expression that is currently enjoyed on social media platforms.

The Bill, which was first tabled before the Parliament of Kenya on 2 October 2019 for its first reading, seeks to amend the provisions of KICA by introducing stringent regulations on the use of social media in Kenya. The most pertinent concern is the regulation of social media platforms under section 84IA as the Bill, among other things, introduces the requirement for a social media licence. This licence must be obtained, in respect of a social media platform which is accessible in Kenya, by the social media platform operator in question.

Furthermore, there is a requirement for social media platforms to keep all data relating to users of their platform and submit this data to the Communications Authority of Kenya on request, effectively raising adverse data privacy concerns.[7] Specifically, this requirement will impact anonymous posting on social media platforms, thus directly affecting the aspect of open source evidence that this research focuses on.

Additionally, the Bill seeks to regulate the conduct of social media users through responsibilities as envisioned under its section 84IC. It provides that: a social media user shall ensure that any content published, written or shared through the social media platform –

a) does not degrade or intimidate a recipient of the content;
b) is not prejudicial against a person or group of people[;]
c) is fair, accurate and unbiased.

In addition to this, the Bill under section 81IC (2) requires an administrator of a group on a social media platform to approve the content being published on that platform. The contravention of these requirements is an offence.[8]

The Bill similarly seeks to regulate online content by requiring the licensing of bloggers under section 84ID while providing a very wide and ambiguous definition of blogging under its section 2 to include: collecting, writing, editing and presenting of news or news articles on social media platforms or on the internet. There is concern that due to the Bill's wide and ambiguous definitions, its provisions are broad enough to include ordinary users of social media platforms such as Twitter, Facebook and YouTube.[9] This will have an impact on open source evidence in Kenya, specifically its availability.

7 The Kenya Information and Communication (KICA) (Amendment) Bill, 2019, National Assembly Bills, 2019.

8 Section 84IC (3), KICA (Amendment) Bill, 2019.

9 D Mwathe, "Highlights on Proposed Law Introducing Strict Regulation of Social Media," *Bowmans Law*, 16 October 2019. Available: https://www.bowmanslaw.com/insights/intel-

Despite the discussed far-reaching impact that these amendments would have on the freedom of expression generally, the Bill is still on track to be passed as a law.

Other than the KICA, a number of pieces of legislation were also mentioned in the survey by the respondents, which in their opinion related to the use of open source evidence in practice in Kenya. However, these legislations do not affect the substantive aspects of the admissibility of open source evidence in Kenya. As such, an in-depth analysis of these Acts falls outside the scope of this research. They are, however, highlighted in Table 4.1 for the sake of rigor.[10]

Open Source Evidence in Kenyan Courts

As mentioned in the foregoing, this section draws from primary data from a systematic case study of the Kenya Law database that sought to assess the use of open source evidence in legal proceedings in Kenya. More specifically, the assessment sought to ascertain the types of open source evidence that are generally accepted and the extent to which they have been used. The systematic case study focused on cases from the Criminal and the Constitutional & Human Rights Divisions in line with the research topic. The assessment was based on set parameters that include the year, key words and subject matter, as elaborated in the research methodology section in Chapter 1. Furthermore, cases that were highlighted by respondents during the data collection process have also been discussed.

As a classic testimony to the challenges of admission of open source information as evidence, Kenyan courts have had a topsy-turvy interaction with it thus far, as illustrated by the findings from the systematic case study.[11] The most relevant and illustrative case that probes the aims and objectives of this research, and on which the hypothetical case contained in the data collection tools is based, is the case of *Ndwiga Steve Mbogo v Independent Electoral and Boundaries Commission & 2 others*.[12] The facts of the case were that:

> The petitioner sought to submit six videos that had been downloaded from YouTube and Facebook as evidence in support of his election petition and called two witnesses, plaintiff witness 7 (PW7) and plaintiff witness 8 (PW8) to persuade the court that the videos were admissible in

lectual-property/highlights-on-proposed-law-introducing-strict-regulation-of-social-media/, accessed 11 November 2023.

10 Some guidelines were also mentioned, and these are the Central Bank of Kenya Guidelines and the National Cybersecurity Strategy of 2018.

11 See for instance, *Martha Wangari Karua v Independent Electoral & Boundaries Commission & 3 others*; *William Odhiambo Oduol v Independent Electoral and Boundaries Commission & 2 others*; and, *Raila Amolo Odinga & another v Independent Electoral and Boundaries Commission & 2 others*.

12 [2017] eKLR.

Table 4.1 Pieces of legislation highlighted by respondents as relating to open source evidence in Kenya

Name of legislation	*Description*
The Computer Misuse and Cybercrimes Act, No.5 of 2018, Laws of Kenya	AN ACT of Parliament to provide for offences relating to computer systems; to enable timely and effective detection, prohibition, prevention, response, investigation and prosecution of computer and cybercrimes; to facilitate international co-operation in dealing with computer and cybercrime matters; and for connected purposes.
The Kenya Copyright Act, Chapter 130, Laws of Kenya	An Act of Parliament to make provision for copyright in literary, musical and artistic works, audio-visual works, sound recordings, broadcasts and for connected purposes.
The Kenya National Cohesion and Integrity Act, No. 12 of 2008, Laws of Kenya	An Act of Parliament to encourage national cohesion and integration by outlawing discrimination on ethnic grounds; to provide for the establishment, powers and functions of the National Cohesion and Integration Commission, and for connected purposes.
The Penal Code, Chapter 63, Laws of Kenya	An Act of Parliament to establish a code of criminal law (section 66 was specifically mentioned).
The Sexual Offences Act, No. 3 of 2006, Laws of Kenya	An Act of Parliament to make provision about sexual offences, their definition, prevention and the protection of all persons from harm from unlawful sexual acts, and for connected purposes.
The Cybercrime Standard Operating Procedure Manual of 2018	An Act of Parliament to give effect to Article 31(c) and (d) of the Constitution; to establish the Office of the Data Protection Commissioner; to make provision for the regulation of the processing of personal data; to provide for the rights of data subjects and obligations of data controllers and processors; and for connected purposes.
The Data Protection Act, No. 24 of 2019, Laws of Kenya	An Act of Parliament to give effect to Article 31(c) and (d) of the Constitution; to establish the Office of the Data Protection Commissioner; to make provision for the regulation of the processing of personal data; to provide for the rights of data subjects and obligations of data controllers and processors; and for connected purposes.

evidence, pursuant to the provisions of the Evidence Act. The petitioner also provided the court with links to the said videos.

PW7, who is a law student, signed a certificate on 5th September 2017, indicating that the videos in question were downloaded by her and that she had made both the hard-disc and the transcript available

> to the court. PW 7 also provided the particulars of the laptop which she used to download the videos. During cross-examination, PW7 informed the court: that she had downloaded the videos from YouTube and Facebook; that the videos had not been recorded by her, nor was she present when the videos were being recorded; that she did not know when the videos were recorded; that she would be unable to confirm whether or not the contents of the videos had been stage-managed; that she was unaware of the identity of the persons who had shot the videos; and, that she had no way of confirming whether or not the events captured actually occurred.
>
> PW8 identified himself as an ICT expert who had completed a degree course on computer science and was yet to graduate. PW 8 obtained videos from PW7, but the said PW7 neither disclosed to PW8 the identity of the person who shot the videos nor the identity of the person who had posted the videos on YouTube and Facebook. PW8 told the court that it was possible to identify the person who had posted the videos on YouTube and Facebook, however in this case he did not identify the person who had uploaded the videos. According to PW8, he could not tell either the time when, nor the location where the videos were taken. PW8 further informed the court that he had the ability to verify whether or not the contents of the video were an act or a play stating that there is software which could enable him to determine the authenticity of the videos concluding that the said videos had not been edited. PW8 did not identify the equipment which had been used to shoot the videos.[13]

The court ruled that video evidence from social media was inadmissible due to the fact that, among other things, downloading social media videos did not constitute part of the responsible person's 'ordinary activities' as required by section 106B (2) of the Evidence Act. The implication being that, for a litigant to adduce evidence obtained from social media, they would have to procure the services of an individual whose ordinary activities entail downloading media from these platforms.

From this ruling, the Court did not interact with the technical questions surrounding the use of social media evidence due largely to procedural considerations. However, in order to more specifically probe the research questions posed by this thesis, a hypothetical case that is based on this case is presented by curing the procedural considerations as below:

> the said six videos had been posted anonymously on Facebook and YouTube; the videos were downloaded by an investigator thereby constituting their "ordinary activities;" they were adduced in court by a

13 [2017] eKLR.

prosecutor or a human rights actor as corroborative evidence in a human rights violations case.

The *Ndwiga Steve Mbogo* case is an exemplification of the challenges that surround the use of open source evidence in legal proceedings in Kenya. It is also indicative of the challenges that actors who are looking to deploy open source information as evidence in Kenyan courts encounter due to the lack of established standards on authentication of open source evidence in Kenya. This discloses a need for a standardised framework that would, in the first place, provide a standard for the authentication of open source evidence in Kenya. Secondly, the standardised framework would assist by addressing the challenges that currently surround this process.

Having analysed the case on which the hypothetical case that underpins this research is based, the other cases will be discussed based on the themes that emerged from the analysis. These themes include: admissibility of evidence from social media platforms, determination of relevance, authentication of the said evidence and the consequent determination of reliability and weight to be apportioned.

The first point that needs to be underscored from the findings is that Kenyan courts have accepted the admission of open source information as evidence in court. This was evidenced, for instance, by the case of *Kakuta Maimai Hamisi v Peris Pesi Tobiko & 2 others*, where social media excerpts were relied on as evidence.[14] The findings established that the legal basis for this admission is section 78(1)A of the Evidence Act. Accordingly, in *Idris Abdi Abdullahi v Ahmed Bashane & 2 others*, it was noted that in addressing the admissibility of the video recording that "in any legal proceedings electronic messages and digital material shall be admissible as evidence."[15] It was further noted that "in section 78(2)B of the Act, it prescribes that the Court shall not deny admissibility of evidence under sub-section(1) only on the ground that it is not in its original form."[16]

The said social media evidence has been admitted by categorising it as documents by virtue of section 106B (1) of the Evidence Act which states that any computer output will be deemed a document. Indeed in the *Idris Abdi Abdullahi v Ahmed Bashane & 2 others* the court was called upon to determine the admissibility of a video recording that had been derived from a social media platform and it was held admissible pursuant to section 106B(1).[17] Based on this decision, it can be concluded that the admissibility of electronic records or evidence, under which open source evidence falls, is treated like documentary evidence as espoused by the Act.

14 [2013] eKLR.
15 [2018] eKLR.
16 [2018] eKLR.
17 [2018] eKLR.

This position was affirmed by the Court of Appeal in *John Lokitare Lodinyo v Independent Electoral and Boundaries Commission & 2 others* where the court, having quoted section 106B (1) *verbatim*, held that "essentially, the sections provide that electronic evidence which is printed out shall be treated like documentary evidence and will be admissible without production of the computer used to generate the information."[18]

This categorisation of open source evidence as documentary evidence conforms the Kenyan approach to the prevailing practice in other leading common law jurisdictions such as England and Wales, as discussed in the comparative chapter.

Furthermore, on the issue of categorisation, it is important to note that case law reveals that material that has been downloaded from social media platforms such as YouTube is categorised as secondary sources. This was the position of the court in *Francis Wambugu Mureithi v Owino Paul Ongili Babu & 2 others.*[19] Here too, exists a consistency in the approach by Kenyan courts as the court in this case was reiterating the sentiments of Ochieng, J in the *Steve Ndwiga Mbogo* case discussed above.

This categorisation is presumably due to the fact that this evidence is assessed under the domain of documentary evidence. Here too exists a commonality with the England and Wales approach. But of more importance is that this further categorisation of open source evidence will subsequently affect the determination of the weight to be attached to it. This is a critical point to underscore as it will influence one of this research's consequent proposals that, instead of taking an approach that focuses on inclusion or exclusion discourses, Kenya should employ an approach that is dependent on an assessment of the weight of the open source material.

The analysis of the case law also discloses a consensus that any consideration of the admissibility of electronic records requires a conjunctive reading of sections 78A and 106B of the Evidence Act. This is because section 78A provides that "the contents of electronic records may be proved in accordance with the provisions of section 106B."[20] Inasmuch as the operative word in this section is "may," it seems that courts have interpreted it to mean "must." This is because it is only through such an interpretation that the requirement of production of a certificate accompanying any electronic records can be considered as being mandatory. As a plain reading of the section does not explicitly disclose the mandatory aspect, as is the standpoint in the analysed cases.

This was, for instance, the holding in the *Hassan Ahmed Ibrahim v Kenya National Bureau of Statistics & 2 others* case which considered the use of

18 [2018] eKLR, para. 54.
19 [2018] eKLR.
20 Evidence Act, Laws of Kenya, CAP. 80.

printouts of conversations on Facebook as evidence.[21] It can therefore be concluded that there is consistency in case law to the effect that courts in Kenya have interpreted the requirement for a certificate of authentication as being mandatory for the admissibility of open source evidence. This is an important revelation as it addresses the challenge that Rutenberg *et al.* had highlighted of the existing contradiction between section 78A and section 106B on the requirement to adduce a certificate, as aforementioned.

As to how Kenyan courts assess the authenticity of electronic evidence and consequently evaluate its probative value, the assessed case law shows that this is done by means of the said certificate of authentication as provided for by section 106B of the Evidence Act – which section sets out the requirements for the admissibility of electronic records. To this end, the court in *Idris Abdi Abdullahi v Ahmed Bashane & 2 others* reiterated the principle that, through the certificate "the Court will be able to examine the evidence and evaluate the probative value … as well as authenticity."[22] The court further elaborated on the importance of this certificate, observing that:

> the certificate shall contain information that complies with section 78A(3) of the Act. The certificate shall provide vital information as to the source, process and delivery of the electronic record or evidence to the Court and parties so as to enable admission of the electronic record as evidence. The content of the certificate would aid and satisfy the court as to reliability of generation of the electronic record/evidence; the integrity of the process and the origin of the content.[23]

This enables a segue into a discussion of the source of electronic evidence which relates to the crux of this research, that is, the position of anonymously posted open source evidence in Kenya. The *Idris Abdi Abdullahi* case confirms the Kenyan position regarding the source as the court stated "before the Court can admit electronic records/evidence a certificate is mandatory to confirm source, process, custody and delivery of the said electronic record before admission so as to preempt manipulation of the record."

A similar position was held in *Francis Wambugu Mureithi v Owino Paul Ongili Babu & 2 others* where the Court held video evidence from a social media platform as being inadmissible on the basis that there was a failure of the source of the videos to testify rendering the same as hearsay.[24] The Court, stating that it was persuaded by the decision of Ochieng, J in the case of

21 [2019] eKLR. See also, *Idris Abdi Abdullahi v Ahmed Bashane & 2 others* [2018] eKLR; *John Lokitare Lodinyo v Independent Electoral and Boundaries Commission & 2 others* [2018] eKLR.

22 [2018] eKLR.

23 Of importance is that, despite the certificate being a procedural and technical matter, it has been noted that it cannot be ousted by Article 159 (2) of the Constitution of Kenya.

24 [2018] eKLR.

Ndwiga Steve Mbogo v I.E.B.C & 2 others held *inter alia* that "the person who produced the original record would be the most appropriate person to produce the record in evidence … I hereby decline to admit the video evidence presented by the petitioner."[25]

The requirement for a source of the electronic material to be available as a witness to testify is thus a consistent approach in Kenya. In as far as this approach is an interpretation of the requirements of the Evidence Act, then this means that the Evidence Act is not fit for purpose, that is, this Act cannot adequately support the assessment of the admissibility of open source evidence. This is because most iterations of open source information nowadays do not disclose its source. Insisting on the presence of such a source as a means of determining the admissibility of open source evidence is therefore akin to outrightly rejecting its applicability in legal proceedings in Kenya.

Another important consideration that also affects the admissibility of open source evidence is the requirement for verification. In *Abdikheir Abdullahi Dubow v Independent Electoral and Boundaries Commission & 2 others,* the petitioner had attached Facebook printouts but did not name the device used for generating the evidence, did not provide a certificate which described how the evidence was generated, stored and communicated and how its integrity was maintained.[26] The court noted, "by merely looking at the annexed Facebook printouts one cannot tell what was taking place on the ground. Without verification, the certificate and cogent evidence, this court cannot rely on the annexed Facebook printouts." This is an approach that aligns with prevailing approaches to assessing the admissibility of open source evidence, as seen in Chapter 2 discussions.

Another theme that has been revealed in the case analysis relates to the challenges of using this type of evidence. In *Kakuta Maimai Hamisi v Peris Pesi Tobiko & 2 others,* which related to the reliance on an excerpt of a social media page, the court held that "the document has obvious alterations on the first paragraph. It has explanatory or additional text. The font size in that paragraph is different from the rest of the document."[27] For these reasons, the Court held that "being secondary evidence from an electronic site, it is capable of electronic manipulation and is unreliable evidence."[28]

In *John Lokitare Lodinyo v Independent Electoral and Boundaries Commission & 2 others* which related to the use of screenshots of social media messages from WhatsApp and Facebook, it was stated that:

> We agree with the observations of the … court that various factors come into play when proceeding to admit such evidence as electronic evidence

25 [2018] eKLR, para. 60.
26 [2018] eKLR.
27 [2013] eKLR, para. 90.
28 [2013] eKLR, para. 90.

> due to the vulnerability and easy manipulation of electronic evidence and the ease with which such evidence can be modified during the collection of the evidence. The evidence may also be easily tampered with making it more difficult to detect any signs of manipulation of documents.[29]

The issue of hearsay and whether open source evidence amounts to hearsay was also brought out in the findings. The *Abdullahi v Independent Electoral & Boundaries Commission & 3 others* case related to evidence that contained information from undisclosed sources and from Facebook accounts.[30] The question before the court was whether this information amounted to hearsay evidence. The court did not, however, make a determination on this issue due to the fact that the said averments, in their opinion, did not go to the crux of the matter and it would therefore not matter whether or not it amounted to hearsay evidence.

However, in *Clement Kungu Waibara v Annie Wanjiku Kibeh & another*, the court held, in relation to evidence that was derived from social media including Facebook and WhatsApp that:

> I do not think they amount to hearsay evidence if read in the sense in which they are offered: not to prove the veracity of the matters asserted in those statements but to prove that the Petitioner did actually become aware of the existence of the statements or the social media accounts.[31]

The case of *Martha Wangari Karua v Independent Electoral and Boundaries Commission & 3 others* addressed the fair trial rights discourse in relation to open source evidence.[32] The applicant in this case alleged the violation of her right to fair trial on the basis that electronic evidence, video evidence, filed together with her petition, disappeared/was stolen from court – an issue which was confirmed by the Court of Appeal as a matter of fact. The applicant subsequently brought this case before the East African Court of Justice, which found that the Government of Kenya violated her right to fair trial.

Beyond bringing out the fair trial discourse, the *Martha Wangari Karua* case is also important as it provides a good example of the fact that there are other important considerations that impact the admissibility of open source evidence in Kenya beyond the assessment of the capacity of the legal framework. As this case clearly demonstrates the presence of an infrastructural challenge and brings out the question of whether the Kenyan judiciary has sufficient checks and balances to ensure the sanctity of open source evidence once it has been filed.

29 [2018] eKLR, para. 56.
30 Election Petition E006 of 2022 [2022] KEHC 15079 (KLR) (2 November 2022) (Ruling).
31 [2017] eKLR.
32 [2019] eKLR.

Having analysed the cases from the systematic study, the ensuing discussions will focus on the cases that were highlighted by the respondents from the survey. These are critical to this research in the sense that they were not divulged by the systematic study, as a result of the scope of the search, but they provide an avenue through which a discussion of how other Kenyan courts, outside of the Criminal and the Constitutional and Human Rights Divisions, have interpreted issues relating to the admissibility of electronic evidence. This is critical given that, despite this research's scope, the Evidence Act of Kenya covers both criminal and civil matters as highlighted in preceding discussions. For these reasons, some of these cases will be civil suits.

The first case, and one which is considered a case *classicus* on admissibility of electronic evidence in Kenya, is the case of *Republic v Barisa Wayu Matriguda* whereby the main evidence related to a compact disc (CD) which was made from CCTV footage.[33] By relying on section 106B(1) and observing that "whereas formerly the Evidence Act did not specifically cover the question of the admissibility of such electronic evidence, following great advances in this field, the courts could not continue to ignore the great impact which modern technology plays in the world in all spheres up to and including the collection and storage of evidence," the court held that:

> What this provision therefore means is that any information stored in a computer (such as a CCTV camera) which is then printed or copied to optical media (such as a CD) shall be treated just like documentary evidence and will be admissible as evidence without production of the original. Thus the CD made by PW11 is *prima facie* admissible evidence, without necessarily having to produce the original CCTV footage. However section 106B also provides that such electronic evidence will only be admissible if the conditions laid out in that provision are satisfied.[34]

The court further noted on section 106B(4) that:

> This provision makes it abundantly clear that for electronic evidence to be deemed admissible it must be accompanied by a certificate in terms of section 106B(4) ... Such a certificate must in terms of section 106B(4) (d) be signed by a person holding a responsible position with respect to the management of the device... who would sign to certify the validity and correctness.[35]

33 [2011] eKLR.
34 [2011] eKLR.
35 [2011] eKLR.

The rest of the cases follow the same curve and draw heavily from the *Barisa Wayu Matriguda* case. In *MNN v ENK*, a civil suit, the issue related to the admissibility of an audio record, specifically an electronic record of a conversation, where the court while quoting the *Barisa* case held that:

> The material sought to be relied on was an electronic recording of a conversation. It is not indicated how the recording was done, who and how the same was transcribed. The telephone numbers of the persons engaged in the alleged communication are also not identified. A mobile phone is an electronic device, and it is one of the devices envisaged in section 106B of the Evidence Act. The recording must be accompanied by a certificate by a person who occupied a responsible position in relation to the operation of the recording device or the management surrounding the recording and transcription thereof. A certificate which defines and describes the production and history of the recording up to the moment of production in court. To that extent the recoding is inadmissible.[36]

In *Jackline Vusevwa Selenge v Olivier Guiguemde*, a case before the Employment and Labour Relations Court, the case related to the issue of admissibility of electronic evidence, specifically audio recording.[37] This case highlighted some of the challenges that would have to be contended with in determining whether Kenyan courts have the infrastructural capacity to admit all forms of open source evidence. And it reinforces the foregoing discussions under the analysis of the *Wangari Maathai Karua* case. In this case, the respondent had submitted that the Judiciary e-filing platform did not allow for the uploading of the audio recording as the reason why the audio recording was not availed together with the other documents in support of the respondent's case. This explanation was accepted by the court where it noted:

> No doubt, the e-filing platform is technology based and it is not lost to me that such technology may have certain unforeseen limitations. The uploading of an audio recording may be such one limitation. It is therefore plausible that the Applicant was not able to upload the audio recording at the time he filed his documents.[38]

On the question of the admissibility of the audio recording, this court relied on the same reasoning as in the *Barisa* case and held that:

36 [2017] eKLR.
37 [2021] eKLR.
38 [2021] eKLR.

> the Applicant has filed a certificate of authenticity … wherein he confirms the authenticity of the recording. The certificate has identified the electronic record contained in the statement, described the manner in which it was produced and given particulars of the device involved in the production of the electronic record (CD). The certificate has also been signed by the said Moses Alango upon confirming that he is the person responsible in respect of the management of the computer which was used in the reproduction of the CD. In the foregoing circumstances, I find that the electronic evidence contained in the CD and which the Applicant seeks to adduce, has also met the legal threshold set out under section 106B (4) hence is admissible as evidence in these proceedings.[39]

The *Peter Ngethe Ngari t/a PNN Funeral Services v Standard Group Limited PLC & another* case concerned objections raised by the plaintiff over the production of documents by the defence. Specifically the objection was on the grounds that one document was a photograph of writings and needed to have the author for examination whilethe other document was about a tweet by the ombudsman, who was not available for examination."[40] The court similarly relied on the *Barisa* case in arriving at its decision.

The *Republic v Mark Lloyd Steveson* case, on the other hand, related to the question of whether an email was properly excluded for lack of authentication.[41] It is noted that this is the case *classicus* on the issue of authentication of electronic evidence. The court stated generally that "it is incumbent upon a party who wishes to proffer evidence to lay the foundation for it and properly identify the item of evidence sufficiently to support a finding that the item is what the party wishing to proffer the evidence claims it is."[42] The court held further that:

> For avoidance of doubt and for future guidance, it is important to point out that authentication is required where any "real" evidence (as opposed to testimonial evidence) is sought to be adduced at trial. This applies both to e-evidence as well as other documents or items sought to be admitted into evidence. Authentication of proposed evidence is a crucial step in its admission – one which reliance on section 78A of the Evidence Act (or even section 106B) does not obviate.

The court then set out four steps to be considered in the authentication process and these are:

39 [2021] eKLR.
40 [2020] eKLR.
41 [2016] eKLR.
42 [2016] eKLR.

i. First, the Court determines if the proposed evidence is relevant. Here, the Court simply determines the probative value of the proposed evidence: whether the proposed evidence has a tendency to make the existence of any fact that is of consequence to the determination of a fact in issue more or less probable than it would be without the evidence. If the proposed evidence passes the Relevancy Test, it proceeds to the second step.
ii. Second, in the case of tangible exhibits (like the two documents in this case), the proponent for the evidence authenticates the proposed piece of evidence; that is, the proponent must prove that the evidence is what the proponent claims it to be. The court only proceeds to the third step if the proposed evidence passes muster under the Authentication Test. It is important to explain here that the term "authentication," though the technically correct word which is widely used for this step, can be misleading. In fact, what is meant by "authentication" at this stage is merely that a proper foundation for admission of the document or exhibit has been laid. It does not, at all, mean that the exhibit must now be accepted and believed. The trial court, as the fact finder, must ultimately weigh (in step 4 below) the admitted evidence in light of all the circumstances. The weighing can only happen after the foundation for the proposed evidence has been laid.
iii. Third, the Court, at the urging of the parties or on its own motion, determines if there is any other rule of evidence that excludes the proposed evidence. Here is where the Court considers whether the evidence is excluded by the Constitution (for example, the right against self-incrimination discussed above, prohibition against hearsay evidence, or whether the proposed evidence would lead to unfair prejudice with its probative value substantially outweighed by the danger of unfair prejudice). If the proposed evidence survives this Exclusion Test, then the proposed evidence is admitted into evidence and the Court proceeds to the fourth step.
iv. Fourth, the Court considers the weight to be accorded to the admitted evidence. At this stage, the opponent may still bring to the Court's attention evidence opposing the authenticity of the evidence, thereby allowing the Court to give less weight to the evidence or no weight at all.

The court then proceeded to apply this standard to the particular facts and outlined what a proper authentication would look like when dealing with an email printout.

> First, it is important to reiterate that the purpose of authentication is to demonstrate to the Court that there is a reasonable probability that the proposed evidence is what the proponent claims it is. For example, the Trial Court must be put in a place where it can determine that it is reasonably probable that there was no material alteration of the evidence

after it came into the custody of the proponent. This requirement is no less true for email print-outs sought to be introduced under section 78A of the Evidence Act as in the present trial.

The court listed the following as ways of authentication:

i. For email print-outs (as well as other printed electronic messages), the most convenient authentication technique would be circumstantial. Elsewhere, this is defined as "evidence of its distinctive characteristics and the like – including appearance, contents, substance, internal patterns, or other distinctive characteristics, taken in conjunction with circumstances." (US Federal Rule of Evidence 901(b)(4)).
ii. An email may also be authenticated through testimony by the recipient that the sender closed with a nickname known only to the recipient.
iii. Emails can also be authenticated through technological footprints such as internet protocol addresses or an IP address. Since an IP address identifies which computer sent an email, the Service Provider can be called to testify that the IP address from where the email was sent is the residence or business premises of the opponent. Similarly, an expert can also testify that a particular email was retrieved from an author's email hard drive. In this case, it would have been appropriate for this expert to lay the foundation by authenticating it through the email's technological footprint.

The court further pronounced itself on the issue of section 78A where it noted that:

> My understanding of this section is that it makes explicit that electronic messages are admissible as evidence in Kenya provided that they satisfy the other requirements for such admission. This section does not obviate the need for establishing the relevance of the proposed evidence in the same way it does not excuse the need for authentication of the proposed evidence. This section is also helpful in codifying the factors to be taken into account in assessing the weight to be given to an authenticated and admitted electronic message … This section, in essence, provides for a route for print-outs of electronic documents to be admitted as evidence where such documents are produced in the course of business and are accompanied by certification by a person in the employ of the business in question that the document was, indeed, generated in the course of business.

The court further connected section 106B to authentication by noting that the required certificate served the authenticating purpose. The court clarified the issue of the presumption under 106(I) of the Evidence Act which provides that

> a court may presume that an electronic message forwarded by the originator through an electronic mail server to the addressee to whom the message purports to be addressed corresponds with the message as fed into his computer for transmission, but the court shall not make any presumption as to the person by whom such a message was sent.

The court interpreted this section to mean that:

> The presumption goes to the authenticity of the electronic message as produced by the addressee by permitting the Court to assume that there was no manipulation of the contents of the message between the sending and the reception of the message … It is important to note that this section applies to situations where the addressee produces the electronic message and seeks its admission as proof that it was the same message sent to him or her. The section is categorical on two things: First, it is expressly categorical that the presumption does not extend to the identity of the author of the message. Hence, a proponent of such evidence would have to introduce some other evidence to link the message with its alleged author. Second, the section does not obviate the need for authenticating the proposed evidence (electronic message). Indeed, the section is a substantive instruction to the trial court on what to do with an admitted piece of evidence. It does gives no guidance whatsoever to the process of admission of such a piece of evidence. Differently put, such a piece of proposed evidence must, first, be admitted in the usual way described above.

A good question at this point is whether such a presumption can apply to open source evidence in Kenya.

The *Republic v Edward Kirui* case tested the admissibility of video evidence in relation to a police shooting during the post-election violence in 2008 in a murder charge.[43] Since the case has been appealed, this research will analyse the appellate court's decision due to its authoritative precedential value. The Court of Appeal summarised the facts of the case in relation to the video evidence as:

> There was no doubt at all that there was a shooting incident at Kondele, a fact proved by the prosecution through what the judge called 'a very rare kind of evidence; a video caption, in which the incident was captured. The video caption was played before the court. The learned Judge then directed that there be produced a slow motion version of the caption … Having watched the video caption, I saw a man dressed in a jungle jacket and also wearing a helmet. He was carrying a gun in his hands.

43 [2010] eKLR.

> He appeared from behind some make-shift structures. The words of PW 12, Lucy Hannan, perhaps best describe the scene captured on the video caption. This is what she said;
>
> "I saw one officer in camouflage, with helmet, running- stalking with his gun, ready to fire. He was of average height not heavy built. I was watching him as he moved towards his target. We filmed him coming, then he shot. I saw 2 young men who were laughing and taunting. I was focusing on the Police Officer. He then shot the two young men. Then he went and booted one of them when he was on the ground. The young man he kicked was still alive." PW 12 noted that the two young men were not armed. That fact comes out very clearly in the video footage.

On assessing the reliability of the video evidence, the Court of Appeal noted that, "it appears that the said video was not apportioned sufficient weight, if at all, by the court."[44] The higher court based this conclusion on the fact that the lower court had categorically noted that the accused person had been captured on film appearing to shoot the two victims.[45] The Court of Appeal further observed that, "this conclusion is interesting because in the ruling to determine whether the accused had a case to answer, the court had noted, in relation to the video evidence that, "from the video clips it appears that it was not easy to identify the particular police officer who shot the victims. But it is also on record that at some point, the police officer concerned, raised the helmet, exposing his face. From that evidence, it would appear that the accused was placed squarely at the scene of crime."[46] The Court of Appeal, in stating that "we have no hesitation to state that the case of *Republic v Edward Kirui* occasioned great miscarriage of justice" was similarly struck by the trial court's departure from its earlier ruling and the disregard for the video evidence.[47]

Two other cases were mentioned in the responses, but the decisions have not been analysed here for various reasons. The first case is the *Chief Magistrates Case Number 1765/2014*, where Nicholas Mwangi and Meshack Mburu were charged with sexually assaulting a female passenger in a public transport bus that was headed to an area in Nairobi known as Githurai 44. Anonymously posted video evidence, as corroborated by material that was retrieved from a physical search of the accused person's houses, was part of the evidence that the prosecution used, resulting in a death sentence (which was commuted to life imprisonment for the accused persons). Regrettably, being a chief magistrate's case, the same is unreported and can therefore not be adequately analysed herein.

44 [2010] eKLR.
45 [2010] eKLR.
46 [2010] eKLR.
47 [2010] eKLR.

The second case was mentioned by both the Chief Investigator and the Senior Prosecutor, where Dr Mohamed Ali Abdi also known as Abu Fida'a was charged with a terrorism-related charge based on the evidence deriving from an open source investigation. This led to the arrest and institution of criminal charges against the said Dr Mohamed Ali Abdi. Regrettably, at the time of writing, the case was still at the preliminary stages and the respondents were not at liberty to disclose any material information such as the Prosecution's Submissions, as these had not yet been filed in court and did not form official court records.

From the foregoing analysis of the legal framework that governs the admissibility of electronic and digital evidence and the consequent case analysis that has shown how Kenyan courts have interpreted these provisions, it is clear that there is no distinct admissibility regime for audio-visual evidence, which reflects a departure from the approach taken by the international comparators as enunciated in Chapter 3. Nevertheless, the inference is that the assessment of the admissibility of all open source evidence, as defined in this research, is by dint of the provisions for electronic and digital evidence as elaborated in the foregoing. Accordingly, the proposed framework that is provided in Chapter 5 hinges on this inference.

Furthermore, from the case analysis, there seems to be a tension, from the perspective of the pursuit of "justice" in applying the same standard to human rights cases as is applied in criminal cases. That is, while in criminal cases multiple corroborating pieces of open source evidence alone might not be sufficient to discharge the "beyond reasonable doubt" standard and consequently convict an accused person and potentially deprive them of their liberty, it is this research's contention that the same standard should not apply to a determination of whether the state is responsible for a violation of rights. Rather, the standard of "a balance of probabilities" should be applied. This militates towards finding that to the extent that a proposal on the application of an evidentiary rule is needed, this research proposes that the focus in determining the admissibility of open source evidence should not lean towards inclusion or exclusion, but rather towards appropriate weight.

Admissibility of Open Source Evidence in Kenya Based on the Responses of Litigants and Judicial Actors

In order to assess the admissibility of open source evidence in Kenya, various questions were posited to the respondents. This was done through a set of preliminary and substantive questions. The preliminary questions leaned towards a quantitative assessment whereas the substantive questions leaned towards a qualitative assessment. The substantive questions were based on a hypothetical case fashioned after the *Steve Ndwiga Mbogo* case, as aforementioned. However, the hypothetical case was variated to cater to the idiosyncrasies of the different respondent groups. The hypothetical cases are listed as Annexure 5.

How has Open Source Evidence Been Categorised in Kenya?

The data from the survey discloses that the surveyed legal professionals have a standard understanding of the concept of open source evidence as defined in this research, as 70% of the respondents had adduced social media evidence in legal proceedings.[48] Most of the respondents conceptualised open source evidence as being synonymous with social media evidence, and thus these terms will be used interchangeably, especially in the forthcoming discussions in this chapter.

A reading of section 78A and section 106B of the Evidence Act, as seen in the foregoing discussions, discloses an interpretation that open source evidence has been categorised as a sub-set of digital and electronic evidence in Kenya. Interestingly, a majority of the respondents were of the opinion that there was a difference between 'digital evidence' and 'social media evidence' as categories of evidence.[49] One respondent gave a very in-depth response by differentiating between the terms based on the medium of the evidence, the issue of the standard of proof and the 'reasonable man' test. They noted:

> I think there is a difference between digital evidence and social media evidence for various reasons but more so because of the nature of social media and the medium. I will use the example of Twitter. Social media forums like Twitter are conversational, transitory, and temporal. The standard to be used in determining whether a tweet posted is for example defamatory is that of an average Twitter user. It might be difficult to collect evidence of a Twitter user as the scope is extremely wide, thus

48 For the defence counsel questionnaire, open source evidence was synonymised with social media evidence as this would be the term that most of them would have interacted with in practice and so there was no question that asked for the direct definition of open source evidence.

49 12 out of 20 respondents. The sum of their responses were: i) Digital evidence is information stored in electronic or binary form that can be adduced in court as part of testimony. Social media evidence is data contained in social media platforms that has evidential value in a court of law, ii) Social media evidence is a type of digital evidence obtained from social media platforms. Digital evidence is the broader category of evidence retrieved from electronic devices, for example, text messages, call logs, images. Both are usually in electronic formats but social media evidence must have been obtained from social media platforms for it to qualify as such. iii) Digital evidence refers to any electronic evidence which could be in the form of an email, website, text message or any other electronic media both offline and online. Social media evidence, on the other hand, refers to evidence obtained specifically from social media. This would include Twitter, WhatsApp, Facebook, among others, iv) Digital evidence is evidence transmitted through an electronic device. It includes emails, text messages, files and documents extracted from computers, audio files, among others. Social media evidence is evidence stored on a social media platform, v) Digital evidence is any type of electronic data or information used as evidence in court such as emails, photographs, while social media evidence refers to information or data that is collected from social media platforms and used as evidence, vi) Digital evidence is gathered from electronic devices; social media evidence is gathered from social media platforms.

> the probative value is questionable. Twitter users can have distinct or contrasting views and may or may not agree with one's statement. The importance of this is that it will determine the meaning attributed to a tweet by a potential plaintiff or complainant in the circumstances. Social media evidence, in my view ought to be contextualised in line with how the medium is built and its purpose. There is lack of permanency when it comes to social media platforms and publications and therefore difficult to assess a "reasonable man."

A few of the respondents were of the opinion that there is no distinction between digital evidence and social media evidence as categories.[50] Both the judges who were interviewed fell within this minority. They were of the opinion that there was no difference between the terms and that social media evidence is a sub-set of digital evidence. One judge observed:

> In my mind, I doubt that there is a difference between the two of them. As to how they relate in law, I think it cannot be anything outside the framework of the Evidence Act. It has to do with electronic evidence and thus section 78A of the Evidence Act is operable.

This approach taken by these judges, in categorising open source evidence as a sub-set of digital and electronic evidence, is consistent with case law. For instance, the court in the *Steve Mbogo* case analysed the videos from Facebook under the framework of sections 78A and 106B of the Evidence Act, the operative laws that guide the admissibility of digital and electronic evidence in Kenya. It is also important to highlight that this position tracks with the general categorisation of open source evidence even in the surveyed common law jurisdictions as discussed in Chapter 2 above.

In that sense, there then seems to be a disparity in definitional approach between the Bench and a majority of the members of the Bar who were surveyed.[51] A disparity that would have to be bridged if open source evidence is going to be an established practice within legal proceedings in Kenya.

Notwithstanding, this research's categorisation is that open source evidence is a sub-set of digital and electronic evidence and thus, there ought to be no

50 They justified their responses as: i) Social media evidence is a facet of digital evidence. Digital evidence may be broader than just social media evidence, but that would not mean there is a difference between the two, ii) I believe social media evidence falls under digital evidence. Social media evidence just signifies that the evidence is hoisted on a particular social media platform. However, it is captured and stored in digital media, iii) I think digital evidence is the genus while social media evidence is the species, iv) I believe social media evidence arguably forms part of digital evidence, v) Social media evidence is part and parcel of digital evidence.

51 For the purposes of this research, the Bar is construed as consisting of litigators, that is defence counsel but excluding prosecutors due to their special role as state counsel.

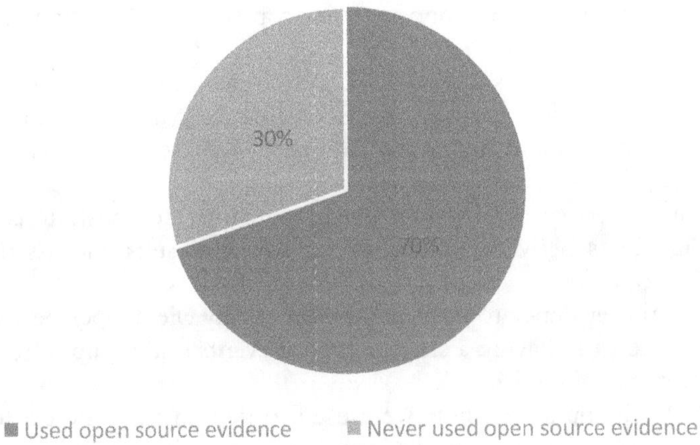

Figure 4.1 Percentage of respondents who have adduced open source evidence

difference between the way they are treated (as evidence) because one is a subset of the other.

How has Open Source Evidence Been Used in Litigation and Judicially Evaluated in Kenya?

In order to assess the suitability of the legal framework for the use of open source evidence in Kenya, it is prudent to determine how this evidence has been used in legal proceedings in Kenya, if at all. Equally important is an understanding of how it has been judicially evaluated. The data showed that most of the respondents had interacted with open source evidence in court and Figure 4.1 is a representative demonstration of the percentage of respondents who had adduced open source evidence in court.

The types of evidence listed by the respondents included: printouts of digital newspaper articles, links to YouTube videos containing news articles, photographs, Facebook posts, extracts/hyperlinks from X (formerly Twitter), WhatsApp, text and email correspondence, website links, images uploaded on social media, social media screenshots, WhatsApp screenshots and video. The following were the noted usages of this evidence:[52]

52 Three of the respondents provided usages that related to civil litigation and not the Criminal and the Constitutional & Human Rights Divisions as instructed. The civil usages that were found were primarily relating to defamation suits and the responses are: I used this evidence to demonstrate that the defendant had indeed published said defamatory words which caused reputational loss to my client; It was used to show publication of a defamatory statement made by a client; and to prove defamation.

i. In support of and in opposition to constitutional petitions in various courts.
ii. I have used printouts of Facebook posts in various cases. An example was in defending my client who had been charged with the criminal offence of cyber harassment under the Computer Misuse and Cyber Crime Act (Kenya).
iii. To prove service of pleadings and documents, demonstrate contractual engagements between parties, prove abuses, insults and assault, fraud, among others.
iv. I used this evidence to shed more light on my client's perspective and to aid the court in having a clear picture of events leading up to the suit.
v. As evidence of service.
vi. The WhatsApp screenshots were used to demonstrate the existence of a verbal agreement between the complainant and the accused, hence negating the fraudulent element in obtaining by false pretences.
vii. To prove murder charges while representing the victim's family.[53]
viii. To establish an alibi.
ix. It was a Judicial Review Application against a Cabinet Ministry and a State Department who through their official Twitter accounts made remarks about the closure of my client's establishment for flaunting environmental rules. This evidence was produced to show the imminent danger and threat that the client was facing.

From this list, only the last usage, that is, number (ix), reflects an open source. This shows that even though the respondents have a general understanding of open source evidence, it is not necessarily one that matches the definition of open source evidence as conceived in this research. This underscores a need for initiatives that will raise awareness about the intricacies of open source evidence within the legal profession in Kenya, as such an understanding by the litigators and adjudicators is crucial for the mainstreaming of its use within legal proceedings.

Authentication of Open Source Evidence in Kenya

As discussed in the foregoing, the data shows that the admissibility of open source evidence is governed by sections 78A and 106B of the Evidence Act. The main point of note from these sections, as regards authentication, is the fact that open source evidence is admissible within this legal framework and that there is a requirement of a certificate of authenticity. Simply put, authentication of open source evidence in Kenya is based on the requirement for

53 It is supposed that this is under the context of watching brief, as in Kenya, prosecutions are conducted by the DPP as a general rule, and private prosecutions are very rare.

a certificate of authenticity, which requirement has become settled law and practice as underscored by the findings from the survey.

This position was reiterated by a respondent who quoted a court decision and noted:

> Sections 106A and B of the Evidence Act provides for the conditions for admissibility of electronic records including that a certificate of electronic records as under section 106B is mandatory. In the absence of certificates of electronic records for the six videos downloaded from YouTube, these videos ought to be expunged from the record. I rely on the case of *Republic v Barisa Wayu Matuguda [2011] eKLR*, where the court held that the provision is clear that for electronic evidence to be deemed admissible, it must be accompanied by a certificate in terms of section 106B(4)(d) signed by a person holding a responsible position with respect to the management of the device and that the evidence is inadmissible without the required certificate.[54]

This certificate is essentially the avenue through which the determination of the reliability of the material would be conducted. As it will disclose, *inter alia*, the manner in which the integrity of the electronic and digital evidence was maintained, thus speaking to the chain of custody.

Beyond the certificate of authenticity, the existence of corroborative material was shown to be a means of authenticating the open source evidence. The respondents provided a range of ways in which they would corroborate open source evidence. Accordingly, bringing a witness who would testify and thus provide corroboration of the events captured by the material was one of the most common methods of corroboration. This was based on the fact that a witness testimony would provide confirmation of "what had taken place in the video even if it was posted anonymously."[55] This respondent further noted that they would be guided by the holding of the court in the case of *MNN v ENK (2017)*, which has been analysed in the foregoing discussions.[56]

Requiring the investigator to testify to the methodology and results of their investigation is another way through which the authenticity of the open source evidence would be ascertained as demonstrated by the findings.[57] This type of corroboration is important as it is an avenue through which any potential fallout brought about by reliance on anonymous open source evidence can be mitigated. The main reason that was given for requiring such testimony

54 This respondent was reflecting on the authenticity of the videos in the hypothetical case.

55 Respondent from the survey.

56 This is a civil case that discusses the issue of the admissibility of an audio record, specifically an electronic record of a conversation; it is discussed extensively in the first part of this chapter.

57 This was in response to question 11: Would you still require the ODPP to call the investigator to testify in relation to the methodology and results of their investigation? If yes, why? If no, why?

was to provide the defence with an avenue to cross-examine the investigator on the integrity of the videos for information that would, as noted by one respondent, "satisfy the court that the investigator complied with the strict legal requirements for the collection, storing, handling and presentation of the evidence adduced."[58]

The use of cross-examination as an authentication tool was further emphasised as linking to the constitutional right of an accused to a fair trial. Specifically, it was lauded for being the most effective tool through which to query an open source investigator on the "methodology and results of their investigation."[59] One respondent posited that:

> Calling the investigator would allow me to cross-examine them on the methodology and results of their investigation. This is a cardinal right of every accused person under Article 50(2)(k) of the Constitution of Kenya to adduce and challenge evidence.

This response brings to the fore a potential challenge to the use of anonymous open source evidence in Kenyan courts. As far as the said Article 50(2)(k) of the Constitution is concerned, one is guaranteed the right to confront their accuser. This means that the unavailability of the source to be 'confronted' would directly impact the realisation of this constitutional right and consequently affect the admissibility of this evidence.

The need for the presence of the source to be cross-examined as an aspect of authentication was further stressed, and one respondent, speaking in the context of the hypothetical case noted that

> the video evidence does not meet the legal threshold of veracity and authenticity due to the following: the originator of the videos is unidentified and therefore the source of the videos cannot be established nor verified; the reliability of the manner in which the videos were generated, stored or communicated cannot be established nor verified; the reliability of the manner in which the integrity of the videos was maintained cannot be established nor verified.

To that extent, it can be deduced that the requirement for the source of the open source evidence to be availed for cross-examination purposes is held in high regard as a form of authentication in Kenya.

It can therefore be concluded that for anonymously posted open source evidence to be admissible, the existing authentication process, by virtue of section 106B of the Evidence Act, requires either the presence of author of the material or the computer which produced the output, as the means of

58 Respondent from the survey.
59 Respondent from the survey.

authentication. One defence counsel summarised this position very aptly, and noted that:

> Section 78A(3) requires the court to consider the manner in which the evidence was generated, stored, and communicated, and the manner in which it was identified. Since the videos were uploaded anonymously, the prosecution cannot explain the chain of custody or produce the maker for cross-examination.

The findings further showed an apparent recurrent emphasis on the need to verify the evidence through the source. Due to the nature of open source evidence, in order for this legal framework to be fit for purpose, it needs to reflect the fact that authenticity can be tested through other ways beyond the requirement of the source and the computer which produced the output.

To this end, one defence counsel gave an alternative approach that underscores the need to avoid an authentication test that focuses on "inclusion" and "exclusion" but rather focuses on the weight to be apportioned to the open source material. The counsel noted that they would not argue against the admission of the evidence "because section 78A(2) states that *the court shall not deny admissibility of evidence under subsection (1) only on the ground that it is not in its original form*. But rather, they would argue against the evidence on the basis of its reliability." This research agrees with this approach because ultimately, and as far as the law is concerned, this type of evidence is admissible. Thus, the only relevant questions should go to its reliability and probative value.

At this juncture, it is important to assess how then judges would evaluate such reliability and probative value of open source evidence. Two approaches that would be used to make this determination were revealed by the judges who were interviewed. One judge employed a conservative approach which they justified as being warranted because reliance on anonymous open source evidence is, by its very essence, fraught with credibility issues. For this reason, this judge set a high standard for assessment. They noted that "there must be independent corroboration: independent of the material itself" in order for them to apportion any weight to the open source evidence. They gave an example of such independent material and stated that:

> If you can show that the open source evidence you are seeking to rely on is a result of an automated process, with no direct human input, this can enhance the credibility of the source and consequently make it more reliable thus increasing the weight that I will apportion to the said material when writing my judgment.

On the other hand, the second judge took a much more relaxed approach and noted that, in light of the fact that evidence falls into different categories, and since this evidence is being adduced by means other than through the original source, they would categorise it as secondary evidence and assess its admissibility based on that regime, that is section 66 of the Evidence Act.

The two positions therefore seem to be different as one judge appears to be wary of open source evidence whereas the other one seems to be comfortable with it. Such a difference in approach by the Bench means that there would be confusion among practitioners as to how exactly the Bench would assess the admissibility of open source evidence in Kenya. This provides further proof of the need for a standardised approach to guide such an assessment.

The pertinent question then is, what sort of authentication test would bring the Kenyan legal framework to a point where open source evidence can be authenticated, without a mandatory requirement of the presence of the source of the material and a heightened focus on the computer that produced the output? Several of the respondents discussed the need to use circumstantial evidence as an alternative means through which to authenticate open source evidence, noting that the use of several pieces of circumstantial evidence can be sufficient to discharge the burden of proof.

The provision of such circumstantial evidence would entail laying a good foundation for why the adducing party believes the open source evidence to be critical. This includes asking questions such as: "who is the author of the evidence? Can the author be found? If they cannot be found, is there evidence that the information is not manipulated?"[60]

Another important aspect of proving the circumstantial aspect of the material is to ensure that the chain of custody is proved, that the material was sufficiently authenticated and providing the court with an explanation as to "why it was difficult to get the original author."[61] Once these explanations have been provided satisfactorily, courts would regard this open source evidence as secondary evidence. Such categorisation would thus mean that the procedure that was followed in retrieving and authenticating this material becomes critical.

Lastly, one of the judges who was interviewed provided another alternative approach that can be employed in authenticating anonymously posted open source evidence. The judge provided a unique interpretation of section 78A (3) (d) of the Evidence Act. The section provides that "in estimating the weight, if any, to be attached to electronic and digital evidence, under subsection (1), regard shall be had to *any other relevant factors.*" It was this judge's opinion that this sub-section provides judicial officers with a wide berth of discretion to consider any other relevant factors that may be necessary to determine the admissibility of open source evidence.

She noted that because each case turns on its facts, this sub-section provides leeway through which one can argue against a mandatory requirement for a

60 Respondent from the Office of the Director of Public Prosecutions.
61 Respondent from the Office of the Director of Public Prosecutions.

source of the material to authenticate it through cross-examination. She was of the position that this part of the law can therefore be used as the foundation through which other 'non-traditional' means of authentication can be accepted by the court, especially for a novel issue such as open source evidence.

Having set out the existing legislative framework, assessing how it has been categorised and ascertaining the existing authentication procedures for open source evidence in Kenya, the next section seeks to gauge the suitability of this framework to enable the use of this evidence in legal proceedings in Kenya.

Adequacy of the Legislative Framework in Kenya

Having set out the legal framework that guides the admissibility of open source evidence in Kenya, the next level of assessment is determining whether this legal framework is suitable to support the use of open source evidence in legal proceedings in Kenya. The specific question that this section seeks to answer is whether open source evidence can adequately be adduced within the parameters of the current legislative framework or whether there is a need for some reforms. This assessment is based on the views of the practitioners and judicial officers who were interviewed.

The findings show that a majority of the respondents are of the opinion that the legal framework is not sufficient to support the use of open source evidence in Kenya. Various reasons were proffered for this position. One counsel noted, for instance, that:

> When section 78A and section 106B were enacted (both before 2014), it may not have anticipated the impact that social media evidence would have on the process of adducing evidence and could therefore not make any provisions to that effect.

It was reasoned further that this insufficiency derived largely from the issue of the source of the material. They observed that, as seen in the foregoing discussions, the current legal framework places significant emphasis on admissibility through a source. This means that a practitioner would be at a loss when dealing with anonymously posted open source evidence. They stated:

> The current legal framework does not take into account the nuances presented by evidence obtained from social media platforms as set out herein. It is extremely difficult to authenticate the authorship of social media evidence and to have the proof of that authenticity and integrity presented to court in a manner that satisfies the requirements of section 78A, 106B and 107 of the Evidence Act.

Another respondent measured the inadequacy based on the fact that, in their opinion, the existing framework does not provide sufficient safeguards against the highly manipulable nature of open source evidence. They posited:

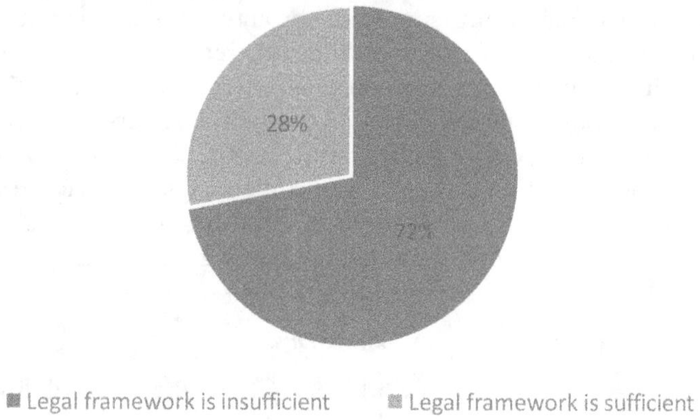

Figure 4.2 Representation of the views of respondents on the adequacy of the legal framework

> The requirement of a certificate of authenticity does not really provide sufficient safeguards in as far as open source evidence is concerned. This is because there have been significant technological developments such as artificial intelligence. The impact of these advancements on open source evidence can be very adverse if left unchecked. The law therefore needs to be adapted to incorporate more safeguards and to be able to predict any level of manipulation to this type of evidence.

On the other hand, a smaller number of the respondents were of the opinion that the legal framework is sufficient. Their reasoning was based on the understanding that section 106B(4) of the Evidence Act was sufficient to cater for this type of evidence. Figure 4.2, provides a visual representation of the views of the respondents on the sufficiency of this legal framework.

From the analysis of the operative legal provisions, this research agrees with the position taken by the majority of the respondents that the legal framework is not suitable, as is, to support the use of open source evidence in legal proceedings in Kenya. This is due to the shortcomings that encumber sections 78A and 106B of the Evidence Act, as discussed extensively in Chapter 1 and in the foregoing discussions in this chapter. In order to realise the full potential of open source evidence within the Kenyan legal space, various reforms need to be made to the existing legal framework.

Relatedly, the adequacy of the Kenya Information and Communication (Amendment) Bill, 2022, which is being drafted and proposes to make further amendments to the KICA, as at the time of writing, to form a regulatory regime for social media in Kenya was also discussed. Specifically, this assessment sought to ascertain whether the respondents thought this Bill would ultimately impact the use of evidence derived from social media in Kenya. A majority of the respondents rightly recognised the potential of the KICA

(Amendment) Bill to impact the use of social media evidence in legal proceedings. Various reasons were proffered to justify this position.[62]

The reason why this research agrees that the KICA (Amendment) Bill will impact the use of open source evidence is due to the fact that, even if this impact will not go to the substance of the determination of the admissibility of this evidence, it will ultimately impact related rights. For instance, section 84IC of the Bill provides for regulations on the use of social media platforms and the penalties for breaching them.[63] Such regulations will certainly have the effect of limiting the existing freedoms on these platforms directly impacting the availability of open source information.

A potential positive impact of this Bill was highlighted by one of the interviewed judges. This judge was of the opinion that due to the fact that the KICA (Amendment) Bill is being drafted at a time when significant technological developments have already taken place, it is an opportune moment for the drafters. That is, they could take advantage of this contemporary knowledge to plug the existing gaps in the Evidence Act insofar as digital and electronic evidence is concerned. In which case, the determination of admissibility of evidence such as those that have been derived from open sources can be done through an interpretation that sees the Evidence Act read together with the KICA (Amendment) Bill. Indeed, this is an ingenious way of addressing the gaps that exist in the Evidence Act insofar as open source evidence is concerned.

Supplemental Issues

As stated in the introduction to this chapter, there are additional themes that were established by the findings which have not been covered in previous chapters. These additional themes are fair trial considerations and challenges that actors within the Kenyan legal space have to contend with in relation to using open source evidence. Since ultimately the objective of this research is to propose a framework for the use of open source evidence in Kenya, it is

62 The reasons proffered for this positive response can be summarised within the following responses: i) The Kenya Information Communication (Amendment) Bill, 2022 provides that all social media users in Kenya will need to have a social media licence. This would result in information obtained from social media being more easily verifiable by enhancing the chances of tracking the source, ii) To some extent, yes. The Bill attempts to regulate social media activities to rein in on misinformation, abuse and fraud. To that limited extent, the evidence from social media is likely to gain some level of credibility, iii) The Bill proposes the licensing of social media. One of the terms and conditions for licensing includes the requirement to register all users of the social media platform using legal documents, thereby enabling the identification of the user/maker. Additionally, the licencee would be required to submit all the users' data to the Commission when required. The proposed section 841B provides that the licencee may collect, use, preserve and share information of its user where it is reasonably necessary to respond to a legal process.

63 Kenya Information and Communication (Amendment) Bill, 2022.

prudent that these issues are similarly canvassed as they will have significant implications on the substantive applicability of the proposed framework.

Fair Trial Rights and Open Source Evidence

In the context of open source evidence, an assessment of whether the admission of this evidence would interfere with the right to a fair trial is very relevant. Accordingly, the findings revealed that a majority of the respondents were of the opinion that the admission of open source evidence would indeed interfere with the right to fair trial.[64] The key component of the fair trial discourse that would be impacted is the right to fair hearing as guaranteed under Article 50(2) – specifically (2)(b) and (2)(k) of the Constitution of Kenya. The reason that underpinned this opinion was mainly focused on the fact that the defence would be denied an opportunity to challenge the originator of the open source evidence through cross-examination.

One counsel adeptly summarised the issue and noted that:

> Article 50(2)(k) of the Constitution of Kenya provides for the right to challenge the evidence in a criminal proceeding by way of cross-examination. In the absence of the maker of the evidence, the accused person cannot exercise this right. Further, Article 50(2)(b) of the Constitution provides for the right to be informed of the charge, with sufficient detail to answer it. By failing to provide sufficient detail in respect of the evidence sought to be relied upon, which evidence forms part of the charge, the accused's ability to answer to the charge is impeded.

Emphasising the need for cross-examination and the surety that this provides, another respondent noted:

> The right to a fair trial generally includes the opportunity for the accused to cross-examine witnesses and challenge the evidence presented against them. Regarding the admissibility of evidence, including videos, the rules of evidence require that evidence be relevant, reliable, and subject to challenge or scrutiny. This includes the right to cross-examine witnesses who provide evidence against the accused. Cross-examination allows the defense to question the credibility and accuracy of the evidence and challenge the statements made by the witness. If a video is presented as evidence, and the maker of the video is not available for cross-examination, it could potentially raise concerns about the accused's ability to challenge and question the evidence effectively.

64 A majority of 17 out of the 20 respondents.

Additionally, it was noted that reliance on anonymously posted evidence without the presence of the source would:

> Interfere with an accused person's right under Article 50(2)(j) of the Constitution of Kenya to be informed in advance of the evidence the prosecution intends to rely on, and to have reasonable access to that evidence. It also infringes on Article 50(4) which provides that evidence obtained in a manner that violates any right or fundamental freedom in the Bill of Rights shall be excluded if the admission of that evidence would render the trial unfair, or would otherwise be detrimental to the administration of justice.

Furthermore, it is of the essence to reiterate here that Kenyan courts have interpreted Article 50 (2) of the Constitution of Kenya as a cluster of rights that guarantee a fair trial for an accused person. The import of such an interpretation is that these rights are read together as a whole and not in isolation. This was the decision of the court in the persuasive authority of *Dennis Edmond Apaa & Others v Ethics & Anti-Corruption Commission*, where Justice Majanja held that "this right is to be read together with other rights to fair trial."[65] The significance of this, therefore, is that even if the use of open source evidence will limit only one aspect of the cluster of rights under Article 50 (2), this will be sufficient grounds for a holding that fair trial rights as guaranteed by the Constitution have been violated.

Since they are the final arbiters, it is rational to pay a bit more attention to the responses of the judges on this issue. One judge gave an interesting response as they noted that the presence of any such violations would simply be resolved in favour of the accused person based on the maxim that the accused person is "innocent until proven guilty." And that it is the onus of the adducer of this type of evidence to ensure that the constitutional rights of an accused person are not violated. This approach appears to be strict as it does not provide much leeway for the adducer of the open source evidence.

On the contrary, the second judge gave a response that was equally compelling. In this judge's estimation, the older generation of judges would be more likely to reject the admission of open source evidence on the grounds that it violates fair trial considerations. They seemed to imply that generational differences within the Bench would impact the consequent interaction that an arbiter would have with open source evidence. In expounding on this point, the judge noted that:

> As an adjudicator, you have to determine whether your assessment is for justice or technical considerations. Of course we know that the principle for the administration of justice under the Constitution of Kenya is

65 [2012] eKLR. See also, *Ahmed Abdullahi Maalim v Republic* [2022] eKLR.

> that justice shall be administered without undue regard to technicalities. However, for the older generation of advocates – who of course then become judges – practice was hinged on technicality.

This is a fair representation of the situation as during the course of the interviews, it was clear that the senior judge took a more conservative approach whereas the younger judge gave a more flexible approach.

Another notable issue from the above quote is that it appears that this judge is of the opinion that the technical requirements of section 78A of the Evidence Act could be dispensed with under the current constitutional dispensation, unlike in the former one. However, the court expressly stated in *Idris Abdi Abdullahi v Ahmed Bashane & 2 others*, that despite the fact that the requirement for the production of a certificate of authenticity is a procedural and technical issue, this requirement cannot be ousted by Article 159(2)(d) of the Constitution of Kenya.[66]

Having ascertained that within Kenya, anonymously posted open source evidence would potentially violate the right to fair trial, it is essential to similarly discuss approaches for the rectification of such violation. Due to the position of power assigned to the Office of the Director of Public Prosecutions (ODPP), as they ultimately make the decision to press charges or not, the prosecutors were specifically asked questions relating to the inequality of arms discourse and the related rights. The main thrust of the findings is that in order to mitigate inequality of arms concerns, it is crucial to ensure that open source evidence is authenticated and there is independent corroboration.[67]

Additionally, it was underscored that observing the rules of disclosure of evidence would not only mitigate inequality of arms, but it would also ensure that the right to fair trial is upheld. To this end, a Senior Prosecutor noted that:

> Disclosure of prosecution evidence, that is, the requirement to disclose everything that the prosecution intends to rely on during the trial is the main guarantee of a fair trial. And if such disclosure occurs in advance, then the defence should be in a position to be able to prepare adequately. So providing the defence with advance notice during disclosure would cure majority of the fair trial issues.

66 [2018] eKLR.

67 The respondents from the Office of the Director of Public Prosecutions also reiterated their obligation under Article 157(11) of the Constitution of Kenya to ensure that all the rules of evidence are observed. They noted that they have a duty as prosecutors to prevent abuse of the process and thus ensure that all fair trial rights are upheld. They remain bound by these duties even when dealing with open source evidence.

The findings similarly showed that another important aspect of this right as provided under Article 50(2) of the Constitution of Kenya is that, to ensure the fairness of proceedings, it is essential for the prosecution to involve the defence early on in the processing and analysis of raw data as required by rules of disclosure.

The court expounded on the parameters of the prosecution's duty of disclosure in *Dennis Edmond Apaa & Others v Ethics & Anti-Corruption Commission*, noting that it is a continuing obligation where it was stated that:

> The duty imposed on the court is to ensure a fair trial for the accused person and this right of disclosure is protected by the accused being informed of the evidence before it is produced and the accused having reasonable access to it. This right is to be read together with other rights to fair trial. Article 50(2)(c) guarantees the accused the right to have adequate facilities to prepare a defence. This means the duty is cast on the prosecution to disclose all evidence, trial materials and witnesses to the defence during the pre-trial stage and throughout the trial. Whenever a disclosure is made during the trial the accused must be given adequate facilities to prepare his/her defence. The obligation to disclose was a continuing one and was to be updated when additional information was received.[68]

Nevertheless, it is paramount to place emphasis on the fact that the accused's right to a fair trial is not an absolute right.[69] This signifies that the right must be balanced with other "equally fundamental societal interests in bringing those accused of crime to stand trial and account for their actions."[70]

Given the nature of open source evidence, the research operated on the hypothesis that there is a potential risk that open source evidence could be interfered with by the defence team as a result of this duty of disclosure. However, this hypothesis was disproved by the respondents from the ODPP. One prosecutor asserted, for instance, that discharging the duty of disclosure is not synonymous with risking interference of the evidence by the defence. This is because the ODPP does not disclose the original material in its raw form.

It was also revealed that even though prosecutors have a duty to disclose all the evidence that they seek to rely on at the beginning of a trial, they have the discretion to determine how exactly to conduct such a disclosure. The Senior Prosecutor gave an example of a highly sensitive terrorist case in which open source evidence was used. Due to the sensitivity of the evidence in question, the defence counsel was only allowed to view the evidence on a "for your eyes

68 [2012] eKLR.

69 *Kamau Mbugua v Republic* [2010] eKLR.

70 *Kamau Mbugua v Republic* [2010] eKLR.

only" basis at the Anti-Terrorism Police Unit Headquarters. The prosecutor proposed that a similar strategy can be developed for open source evidence that may be risked by the requirement for early disclosure.

This position is in consonance with case law in that courts have held that "the right of an accused person to a fair trial must be balanced with the victim of the offence's right to access justice and the public interest generally."[71] For that reason, it can be concluded that there is room for different strategies, such as the one proposed above by the Senior Prosecutor, that would allow the prosecution to discharge their duty of disclosure without necessarily risking potential interference with the open source evidence by the defence upon disclosure.

This provides a segue to a finding that revealed that the ODPP routinely conducts comparative analysis with other countries to ascertain the best practice on how to handle some contemporary issues. It is through one such analysis that the UK was seen as having a good model. One prosecutor noted accordingly that:

> The UK has a good model of dealing with this issue by involving defence counsel (special advocates) who have been vetted and can handle high risk cases such as national security cases. So that when there is any sensitive material that might jeopardise the security of the state, these particular defense counsel are not required to disclose sensitive material to their client.

This prosecutor further observed that:

> This is a practice that we may think of using in these highly scientific modes of investigations, such as open source investigations. So that the defence counsels are able to understand the case from the beginning hence upholding the right to fair trial but because of the special commitment made, they would not disclose and jeopardise the investigation. We may therefore consider having a vetting system whereby the aim is not to violate the attorney-client privilege but safeguarding the rights of all parties.

This revelation that the ODPP frequently conducts comparative analysis with other national jurisdictions to glean best practices to influence their prosecution techniques is also a crucial finding as it provides further validation to this research's choice of engaging in a comparative study to glean best practices from other national jurisdictions as has been done in Chapter 2.

In conclusion, even though it is anecdotal evidence, these responses clearly demonstrate that fair trial considerations pose a significant challenge that may

71 *Ahmed Abdullahi Maalim v Republic* [2022] eKLR.

impede the consequent applicability of open source evidence in Kenya. In accordance with Article 25 of the Constitution of Kenya, the right to a fair trial under Article 50 of the Constitution is a non-derogable right and, as such, cannot be limited under any circumstances. Therefore, any proposed framework for the use of open source evidence in legal proceedings in Kenya has to directly propose a way through which the rectification of such violation and/or a counterbalance can be achieved.

Challenges of Using Open Source Evidence in Kenya

One of the main challenges faced when using open source evidence in Kenya relates to the issue of the capacity of actors to engage with this type of evidence, given its technical nature. This is because of the recognition that the mere substantive existence of an enabling legal environment does not necessarily translate to a practical realisation of such a provision. That is, just because the laws provide for its use does not necessarily ensure the capability or willingness of legal practitioners to interact with this type of evidence.

To this end, most of the respondents were of the opinion that they would not have been in a position to interpret the data that would have been necessary to authenticate the open source evidence in the hypothetical case. They noted that they would have sought the services of an expert to provide such interpretation. The deference to an expert is important as it ensures that evidence is handled expertly. However, it raises questions of access to justice and primarily the affordability of such experts and whether the average court user would be able to afford such services. This is based on the fact that only 4 out of the 20 defence counsel who were interviewed would be able to interpret such data without the support of an expert. This is contrasted with the ability of an average court user in Kenya to pay legal fees in the first place, let alone the added costs of retaining the services of such an expert. Accordingly, questions relating to access to justice and whether this type of evidence will enhance this access or impede it will ultimately be raised.

The other challenge relates to the capacity of the judicial system and physical infrastructure to support the use of this type of evidence. This issue was discussed during the interviews with the judges who were asked about the challenges that the courts would face in analysing evidence that has been derived from social media platforms. The first challenge that was brought out by the respondents appertained to the problems attributable to the physical infrastructure. Both judges observed that not all courts are equipped with the necessary physical infrastructure to enable the courts to receive/allow litigants to present some open source material in court.

A practical example that clearly highlights this challenge is the case of *Jackline Vusevwa Selenge v Olivier Guiguemde*, which was referenced by one of the respondents and concerned the admissibility of an audio recording.[72] The adducing party submitted that "the judiciary e-filing platform did not allow for the uploading of the audio recording hence the reason the same was not availed together with the other documents in support of the Applicant's case." In accepting this submission, the court stated:

> No doubt, the e-filing platform is technology based and it is not lost to me that such technology may have certain unforeseen limitations. The uploading of an audio recording may be one such limitation. It is therefore plausible that the Applicant was not able to upload the audio recording at the time he filed his documents.[73]

The other challenge that was brought out by the judges was the level of tech-savviness among the Bench members and what impact this would have on the admissibility of open source evidence. Both judges were cognisant of the reality that younger judges were more tech-savvy and would therefore be generally more open to this type of evidence as compared to the older generation of judges. But they also agreed on the fact that this scale would be balanced regardless, as the latter group has the benefit of extensive judicial experience; hence, they are still capable of assessing such evidence. In conclusion, it was surmised that:

> So this is, I suppose, both a positive and a negative aspect and in the long run, how the open source evidence is presented in court will ultimately make all the difference.

It was also noted that questions relating to the ease of manipulation of this evidence would remain a big obstacle which would constantly necessitate the need for the source to present this evidence in court. Additionally, owing to the adversarial nature of the Kenyan judicial system which limits judges from descending into the arena of the dispute and/or moving *suo moto* to seek clarifications, especially in criminal cases, one judge noted that it would be up to the litigants to help the court by ensuring that this evidence is presented in a way that addresses all the relevant technical and procedural requirements.

On the other hand, the findings demonstrated that legal practitioners, that is, defence counsel and prosecutors, are encumbered by a host of challenges. In order to propose an adequate and context-specific framework for these practitioners, it is crucial to appreciate the full extent of the possible complexities brought about by open source evidence, as perceived by them. It is for this reason that the challenges that were highlighted by the said legal practitioners during the survey are set out in their entirety in Box 4.1.

72 [2021] eKLR.
73 [2021] eKLR.

Box 4.1 Challenges faced by defence counsel when using open source evidence in Kenya

I. Capacity to ascertain from end to end that the evidence is original material which was captured by some equipment and was uploaded on social media as it is, without any editing and has been downloaded as is. That requires expert evidence, and not every accused person would be able to afford access to that sort of expertise.

II. Authenticating the evidence would be a challenge because it would require ensuring the accuracy of the time stamps and metadata; balancing between adhering to privacy protection and the need for evidence can be difficult; it would be an expensive exercise because digital forensic experts would be required to extract, analyse and interpret the data.

III. The challenge would be that it would be difficult to verify the evidence obtained from social media. In Kenya, there are also no specific laws governing the production of evidence obtained from social media.

IV. There is no clarity as to what is admissible or not when it comes to digital/electronic evidence. This is considering the provisions under section 78A and 106B, having been enacted at different points in time, and which arguably create an interpretation gap, as it is not clear if the later provision, section 78A, ought to be read together with section 106B or independent of it. However, the courts have from time to time come to a similar conclusion as to the admissibility of digital/electronic evidence, as requiring that this evidence be analysed through the lens of both provisions of the Evidence Act, that is, Jackline Vusevwa Selenge v Olivier Guiguemde (2021, Peter Ngethe Ngari t/a PNN Funeral Services v Standard Group Limited PLC & another (2020) and Republic v Barisa Wayu Matuguda (2011).

V. Lack of funds to remunerate experts in the digital space - most of the criminal law clients are indigent and can barely afford legal services let alone additional experts; and inconsistency in jurisprudence on the requirement of a certificate under section 106(B)(4) of the Evidence Act.

VI. The biggest challenge will be the verification of the metadata of the evidence adduced. With the advent of Photoshop and video and photo editing tools, most of which are easily and freely accessible, anyone can edit this type of evidence. Furthermore, legal practitioners are trained in the law and are not technical persons. While they would ably adduce such evidence in court, there will always be serious underlying technical questions regarding the reliability of the evidence if they do not get the input of an expert in this field.

VII. Inability to trace the source/maker of the evidence from social media platforms, particularly since the use of fake profiles, pseudo accounts and impersonation is prevalent; the majority of the social media companies are located in other jurisdictions, thereby confounding practitioners' ability to address the cross-jurisdictional complexities of such legal proceedings; inadequate resourcing, that is, forensic tools required for examination of evidence derived from social media platforms, are often resource-intensive.

VIII. Proving the credibility of the source; identifying the original author; integrity of the evidence; maintenance or storage of the evidence remain a big challenge.

IX. Authenticating such evidence, ensuring its admissibility, coupled with the courts' failure to properly interpret that evidence, remains a main challenge; the Evidence Act has not been amended to include evidence from emerging trends such as social media. The constitutional loopholes created by such evidence, as it would limit certain rights such as freedom of speech, are another challenge.

The challenges posed by the prosecutors were to a large extent similar to those reflected by the defence counsel above. However, there were a few that were outstanding, and these are enumerated in Box 4.2.

Box 4.2 Challenges faced by prosecutors when using open source evidence in Kenya

I. Getting the original video would require involving the social media platform administrators, which would require working collaboratively with the social media platforms. But this involves very many challenges, such as jurisdictional issues, as most social media companies are headquartered and have their servers outside Kenya. So when a request for information is made, it becomes a jurisdictional issue necessitating Mutual Legal Assistance (MLA), and this process takes a lot of time – an aspect that does not bode very well with social media evidence, which can disappear very quickly.

II. Some actors within the criminal justice system, especially the senior ones, do not appreciate the benefit of digital information. This attitude impedes the ability to take advantage of the rich source of evidence that these platforms provide.

III. The ability of the ordinary police to effectively collect this type of evidence is also a big problem. As in most instances, they do not follow the process that has been elucidated by the Evidence Act on the collection of digital and electronic evidence. Making such evidence unreliable, the result being that the case is lost on a technicality. Another challenge with the police is the issue of preservation of this evidence. For example, when they confiscate a digital device – a phone or tablet, they do not switch it off or disconnect it from the internet, and we have had instances where such devices are accessed remotely, through hacking, say the police station's WIFI, and all the evidence is wiped out from the device. So we need measures to safeguard against such complexities. And we also need to raise awareness, sensitisation, and capacity building within the entire criminal justice system.

IV. More judicial officers appreciate computers and digital evidence. However, a number of them are still clueless as there are some judges who until now cannot access their emails without assistance. So imagine how difficult it would be to appear before this particular judge and attempt to adduce open source evidence before them.

Based on the foregoing, it is evident that the challenges as perceived by the respondents are quite diverse and this further justifies a need for a standardised system for determining admissibility of open source evidence in legal proceedings in Kenya.

Open Source Investigations in Kenya

How has Open Source Investigations Been Utilised in Kenya?

The findings showed that investigators have become aware of the effectiveness of social media as a source of information during the conduct of their investigations. This is based on the realisation, rightly, that technology has taken centre stage in society given that everybody interacts with a mobile phone and social media platforms. The investigators thus noted that, even though they still employ traditional means to conduct investigations, the use of technology and specifically the use of evidence from social media platforms has taken centre stage in their investigations. Specifically, it was established that there now exist teams within the Department of Criminal Investigations that conduct open source investigations.

In order to assess how open source evidence has been used in investigations in Kenya, it is prudent to first assess what such an investigation looks like within the Kenyan context. This primarily involves a determination of the sequence of an investigation that involves using open source information. The next level of inquiry, after this determination, is to assess how this open source information is authenticated in order for it to consequently be used in legal proceedings as evidence. The analysis in this section will then be concluded with a determination of the challenges that open source investigators face when conducting investigations in Kenya.

The Sequence of an Open Source Investigation in Kenya

The first step of an open source investigation is conducting chatter mining by collecting comments from social media users.[74] This preliminary stage entails an assessment of how a user has interacted with social media and the internet generally, and it was based on the realisation that a lot of background information can be retrieved from social media platforms.[75] The preliminary stage is conducted informally, and the process is then formalised once the preliminary search has revealed reliable information.[76] The Chief Investigator spoke to the process of formalisation as including an application for a court order – as the manner in which this information is acquired must be credible and must also be repeatable by the defence counsel. The court order is then served upon the said social media platform requesting this information, at which point it of course ceases to be open source.

Therefore, from the findings, it is clear that social media platforms are used especially in preliminary investigations. It is, however, important to highlight here that the formalisation process, in the form of a court order, and the consequent receipt of information from the social media systems administrator already lends credibility to the provenance of this information.

The evidentiary rules and standards that are required to be observed in the process of conducting such an investigation were also cited as a crucial aspect of this sequence.[77] It was noted that in the first instance, the person who is conducting the data mining has to be qualified to do so.[78] They must have an information technology background and must have been trained and certified to conduct such an action, as without the relevant certification and educational background, the evidence will be challenged.[79] This points to an alignment between the legal requirements under section 106B of the Evidence Act and the prevailing investigatory practices.

The other aspects of standards that need to be upheld in the conduct of an open source investigation appertain to the tools and software that are used in the investigations. Accordingly, in order for the product of an open source investigation to be reliable in legal proceedings, the tools and software that were used must be validated.[80] This denotes the requirement of valid licences. The Chief Investigator noted, for instance, that these licences are important

74 Interview with a Chief Investigator from the Department of Criminal Investigations.
75 Interview with a Chief Investigator from the Department of Criminal Investigations.
76 Interview with a Chief Investigator from the Department of Criminal Investigations.
77 Interview with a Chief Investigator from the Department of Criminal Investigations.
78 Interview with a Chief Investigator from the Department of Criminal Investigations.
79 Interview with a Chief Investigator from the Department of Criminal Investigations.
80 Interview with a Chief Investigator from the Department of Criminal Investigations.

as they are the channel through which the integrity of such tools becomes unquestionable.

Similarly, there are rules that should be followed in the process of analysing this evidence. It was noted that the relevant legal framework that governs the forensics analysis would be determined by the subject matter of the investigation.[81] However, the legislation listed in Table 4.1 were noted as being the general operative legal framework.[82]

That being said, the findings showed that one of the most critical rules that need to be observed during the forensics analysis of the open source evidence is upholding the chain of custody requirements.[83] It was noted that this is maintained through a document known as the Exhibit Memo Form, which will consequently be filed in court alongside the open source evidence. This emphasis on ensuring the chain of custody is unassailable aligns with the findings from the interviews with the legal practitioners and judges as being a pivotal issue in determining the authenticity of the open source evidence.

The forensics analyst also emphasised the need to ensure that the analysis of the open source information is based only on the aspects of the exhibit that were explicitly requested by the investigator. The analyst noted that it is through honouring such specificity that the violation of the right to privacy is avoided. Furthermore, the specificity was also noted as being key in ensuring that forensic analysts are not overwhelmed by the sheer volumes of open source information.[84]

Ensuring Authenticity of Open Source Evidence during Investigations

Having set out the sequence of an open source investigation in Kenya in the foregoing, as demonstrated by the respondents, it is vital, in line with the themes of this research, to categorically outline how the authenticity of open source evidence is ensured during the course of an open source investigation. Hence, this section seeks to answer the question as to how open source investigators ensure that open source information is authentic and can withstand any scrutiny once adduced as evidence in legal proceedings.

From the findings, it is evident that the process of ensuring that open source evidence is authentic during the investigation process in Kenya reflects the same common themes that manifest in open source investigations as brought out in the discussions in Chapter 2. These themes include issues of chain of custody, preservation of the open source information, the management of the vast amount of open source information and how to persuade the court on the reliability of open source material, even in instances where it has been posted

81 Interview with a Forensics Analyst from the Department of Criminal Investigations.
82 See Table 4.1 above.
83 Interview with a Forensics Analyst from the Department of Criminal Investigations.
84 Interview with a Forensics Analyst from the Department of Criminal Investigations.

anonymously. The forthcoming discussions will therefore be an analysis of these themes from the perspective of the respondents from the Department of Criminal Investigations.

As far as chain of custody is concerned, it was noted that it is important to document each and every step that was taken during the process. The forensic analysis would accordingly entail:

> the investigating officer filling out a request form in which they provide all the relevant information, that is, setting out the parameters of the analysis; listing down the exact hardware and software equipment that are used to conduct the data extraction and analysis; providing the licensing details of this software; and noting down every step that is taken when conducting an analysis to authenticate the information.[85]

The respondents also noted that the way in which the evidence is preserved will consequently impact its authenticity. Hence, it was observed that once information has been found during the preliminary stage, as discussed above, it is important to request social media platforms to preserve the content through legal authorisation. This authorisation is in the form of a court order and will not only ensure that the provenance of the information is upheld but will also guarantee that social media platforms will preserve the evidence, thus safeguarding against the risk of the material being lost as a result of deletion.

Regarding the physical preservation aspects, the respondents indicated that the information is stored on a clean and sterile hard drive whereby, after extracting information from, say, social media, the information is placed in a master copy and then two or three duplicate copies are also kept.[86] It was additionally pointed out that screenshots are equally an important way to preserve the information.[87] This elicits a conclusion that screenshots are a form through which open source evidence can be provided in legal proceedings in Kenya. It further reflects the practice in the studied common law jurisdictions as discussed in Chapter 2, thus aligning this aspect of the open source investigation process in Kenya to the prevailing practices.

As regards the issue of reliability within the context of anonymously posted open source evidence, the Chief Investigator indicated that the most important factor is to ensure that there is linkage between the accused person and the open source evidence. He further observed that without this linkage, "the open source information will have no probative value as it remains speculative

85 Interview with a Forensics Analyst from the Department of Criminal Investigations.
86 Interview with a Forensics Analyst from the Department of Criminal Investigations.
87 Interview with a Forensics Analyst from the Department of Criminal Investigations.

as there is no direct link between the information online and the accused person."[88]

It was observed further that, in some instances, external corroboration of the information received from the social media platforms is needed to enhance its reliability.[89] And this would be dependent on the quality of information retrieved from the preliminary analysis.[90] This external corroboration could, for instance,

> entail connecting the information that was retrieved from online sources to the information that was found on the accused upon arrest. That is, matching the open source evidence to information that was extracted from the accused person's mobile phone or other devices.[91]

Challenges That Investigators Face while Conducting Open Source Investigations

As reiterated throughout this chapter, and in line with this research's theoretical framework, in order to propose a context-specific framework to enhance the effectiveness of open source investigations in Kenya, it is critical to understand the prevailing challenges. To this end, this section addresses three challenges that were brought out by the findings.

The first challenge that was underscored by the findings was the disparity in competences within the criminal justice system. The respondents intimated that more often than not, investigators are usually very highly trained in investigation techniques such as open source investigations, while the other actors within the criminal justice sector do not receive equivalent training. The consequence is that there is a disconnect between the investigators and the prosecutors in the first instance, and then between the defence counsel and the court once this open source information is adduced as evidence in court.

It was, however, observed that there have been a lot of improvement in terms of the multi-agency approach to issues in Kenya. Here, reference was made to the presence of specialised prosecutors and courts that are dedicated to technical cases, such as human trafficking and organised crime. However, this discloses a gap in the existing practice in that it appears only a select section of actors within this system possess the relevant expertise to adequately interact with open source evidence. Therefore, there is a need to ensure that other actors within the entire legal system in Kenya also possess this expertise.

88 Other than this linkage, the Chief Investigator reiterated the importance of ensuring that only authenticated open source evidence is adduced in court. The reasoning for this emphasis was that "using unauthenticated videos may prejudice the Department of Criminal Investigations as whole and impact other investigations."

89 Interview with a Chief Investigator from the Department of Criminal Investigations.

90 Interview with a Chief Investigator from the Department of Criminal Investigations.

91 Interview with a Chief Investigator from the Department of Criminal Investigations.

The second challenge appertained to the financial cost of accessing licenses and software updates. As at the time of the interview for instance, there were some software that the analysts did not have access to as the licences had expired and were yet to be renewed. This obviously impacts their ability to effectively analyse open source information. Relatedly, the need for increased manpower to manage the large volumes of data that need to be analysed following an open source investigation, and the potential risk of overloading investigative resources due to an unmanageable digital evidence backlog was highlighted.[92]

It was however noted that various mechanisms have been put in place to try and manage these large volumes. These include the use of keywords to sift through large volumes of open source information during the investigation process discussed above. Secondly, with respect to the evidence analysis, investigators cannot give open-ended requests to the forensics analysts; instead, they are required to specify the exact aspects of the open source material that need to be analysed, making the process more manageable.

Conclusion

In conclusion, the findings disclose that legal practitioners and judicial actors possess a good grasp of the concept of open source evidence as conceived by this research. It is also clear that the same standards apply when adducing "normal" digital evidence and open source evidence in Kenya. This means that the admissibility of the latter is currently governed by sections 78A and 106B of the Evidence Act. So in general, the weight to be attached to open source evidence would be dependent on the fulfilling of the threshold set out in section 78A as read together with section 106B. However, challenges arise when adducing anonymously posted open source evidence as this legal framework does not fully provide for the idiosyncrasies of open source evidence as discussed in the foregoing discussions.

In order for open source evidence to be admissible and relied upon, the importance of authentication was highlighted and the need to have the original author of the open source material to adduce it in court was emphasised. The existence of expert evidence and other independent corroboration to confirm the open source evidence was also deemed crucial. Requiring the investigator to testify to the methodology and results of their investigation is another way through which open source evidence can be authenticated in court. This level of corroboration was deemed important as it would provide an avenue to possibly mitigate any potential fallout brought about by reliance on anonymous open source evidence. The main reason that was given for requiring such testimony was to provide the defence with an avenue to cross-examine the investigator on the integrity of the videos for information.

92 Interview with a Forensics Analyst from the Department of Criminal Investigations.

Therefore, the important considerations in authenticating open source evidence relate to ensuring the integrity of the material, the underlying chain of custody and providing an opportunity for the open source evidence to be tested through cross-examination.

On the sufficiency of the legal framework to support the use of open source evidence in legal proceedings in Kenya, the findings established that a majority of the respondents were of the opinion that this legal framework is not sufficient. Therefore, a need for a legal framework that specifically provides guidance on the admissibility of open source evidence and provides clarity on how this evidence can be authenticated and how the probative value of this type of evidence can be assessed was demonstrated.

Other supplemental issues relating to the use of open source evidence in legal proceedings in Kenya were highlighted by the respondents. These included its potential to impact the right to fair trial, particularly the right to fair hearing as guaranteed under Article 50(2) of the Constitution of Kenya. The reasoning was mainly focused on the fact that the defence would be denied an opportunity to challenge the originator of the videos through cross-examination.

As far as the use of open source evidence in investigations is concerned, it is clear that social media is used especially in preliminary investigations but that such information has to be supplemented by independent corroboration.

The challenges that arise from the use of open source evidence in Kenya were also a supplemental issue that was highlighted by the respondents, ranging from the insufficiency of the legal framework to support this evidence, to the technical capacity of legal practitioners and adjudicators to interact with this evidence, to the capacity of the physical infrastructure of the judiciary to admit this evidence. The challenges that encumber open source investigations in Kenya largely related to disparity in competences within the criminal justice system, financial challenges resulting from the cost of accessing licenses and software updates, and the need for increased manpower to manage the large volumes of data that are derived from open source investigations.

Bibliography

National Legislation, Policies and Bills

Central Bank of Kenya Guidelines.
Computer Misuse and Cybercrime Act of 2018.
Copyright Act.
Cybercrime Standard Operating Procedure Manual of 2018.
Data Protection Bill.
Evidence Act, Laws of Kenya, CAP. 80.
National Assembly Bills, 2019.
National Cohesion and Integrity Act.
National Cybersecurity Strategy of 2018.
Penal Code.
Sexual Offences Act.
The Kenya Information and Communication (KICA) (Amendment) Bill, 2019.

Table of Cases

National Case Law

Ahmed Abdullahi Maalim v Republic [2022] eKLR.
County Assembly of Kisumu & 2 others v Kisumu County Assembly Service Board & 6 others [2015] eKLR.
Election Petition E006 of 2022 [2022] KEHC 15079 (KLR) (2 November 2022) (Ruling).
John Lokitare Lodinyo v Independent Electoral and Boundaries Commission & 2 others [2018] eKLR.
Kamau Mbugua v Republic [2010] eKLR.
Idris Abdi Abdullahi v Ahmed Bashane & 2 others, [2018] eKLR.
Mable Muruli v Wycliffe Oparanya & 3 others, [2013] eKLR.
Martha Wangari Karua v Independent Electoral & Boundaries Commission & 3 others.
Raila Amolo Odinga & another v Independent Electoral and Boundaries Commission & 2 others.
William Odhiambo Oduol v Independent Electoral And Boundaries Commission & 2 others.

Internet Sources

D Mwathe, 'Highlights on Proposed Law Introducing Strict Regulation of Social Media,' *Bowmans Law*, 16 October 2019. Available: https://www.bowmanslaw.com/insights/intellectual-property/highlights-on-proposedlaw-introducing-strict-regulation-of-social-media/, accessed 11 November 2023.

Other Sources

Interview with a Chief Investigator from the Department of Criminal Investigations.
Interview with a Forensics Analyst from the Department of Criminal Investigations.
Respondent from the Office of the Director of Public Prosecutions.

5 Proposed Framework for the Use of Open Source Evidence in Kenyan Courts

Introduction

Existing evidential rules in Kenya provide general procedures and requirements for dealing with open source evidence by virtue of sections 78A and 106B of the Evidence Act. However, they are not sufficient to support the use of evidence that has been gathered from open sources within circumstances such as in the hypothetical case. That is, instances where open source evidence has been posted anonymously and the source of such material is not able to adduce the said material as a witness in court. This is due to the fact that there are very many challenges that arise as a result of using open source evidence within the current legal framework.

These challenges mainly relate to: the fact that technological advancements make it easier for digital information to be manipulated, resulting in questions about its credibility and authenticity; the lack of common standards regarding the collection and analysis of open source evidence; and common law rules and legislative provisions embody guidelines that were developed around paper documents – and open source evidence is accordingly categorised as documentary evidence – as opposed to electronic documents, thereby making it unfit for purpose, especially in relation to the peculiarities of open source evidence.[1]

There is, therefore, a need for the legal framework that governs the use of digital evidence in criminal and human rights violation cases to keep pace with digital developments and thus generally remain fit-for-purpose.[2] The meaning accorded to "fit for purpose" is that the authentication standard for open source evidence should be high enough to safeguard against the risks associated with open source evidence, particularly the fact that it is highly susceptible to manipulation, but not too high a standard to dissuade its use.[3]

Therefore, this chapter proposes a framework that seeks to answer the question: how should open source evidence be litigated and judicially evaluated in

1 Mason & Stanfield (n 120 above) pp 193–260.
2 Goldstraw-White (n 113 above).
3 O'Floinn & Ormerod (n 114 above) pp 486–512.

DOI: 10.4324/9781003770343-5

Kenyan courts? The objective of this proposed framework is thus to answer the question "when authentication of open source evidence arises as an issue in a Kenyan court, of what must the judge be satisfied to admit the evidence?" This is done by providing a standardised and reproducible framework that provides litigators, court users and the judiciary with a foundation for the determination of the admissibility of open source evidence in legal proceedings in Kenya. The proposed framework thus covers both the legal and technical requirements for the determination of the admissibility of open source evidence in legal proceedings in Kenya.

In order to achieve this, the structure of the framework is based on the overarching themes of this research, that is, a proposal for an adequate legal framework that can support the use of open source evidence in legal proceedings in Kenya even in instances where this material is posted anonymously. The second part of the framework focuses on an authentication test which incorporates steps that can be followed to systematically adduce and admit open source evidence in a court.

Legal Requirements for the Determination of the Admissibility of Open Source Evidence in Legal Proceedings in Kenya

Introduction

As discussed in Chapter 1, Kenya has a legal framework that provides for the admissibility of electronic and digital evidence, the primary law being sections 78A and 106B of the Evidence Act.[4] Section 78A provides that electronic and digital evidence is admissible in legal proceedings while section 106B provides for the 'how' by categorising electronic and digital evidence as documentary evidence thus setting out the admissibility standard.[5] Open source evidence falls within the purview of electronic and digital evidence, as discussed in Chapter 4, and this is settled law and practice in Kenya. This was seen through the court's analysis and determination of the *Steve Ndwiga Mbogo* case. It was also established from the feedback from the data collection, specifically the responses to the question that sought to assess whether there was a difference between "digital evidence" and 'social media evidence' and the question that addressed the categorisation of open source evidence in Kenya.

However, this legal regime is saddled with various challenges that make it less effective as the primary and only law that regulates the admissibility of open source evidence in legal proceedings in Kenya.

4 The Kenya Information and Communication (Amendment) Bill, 2022 (commonly dubbed "the Social Media Bill") would also be relevant as it seeks to regulate the conduct of social media users through responsibilities as envisioned under its section 84IC.

5 It is important to highlight here, as discussed in Chapter 3, that evidence from social media platforms has similarly been categorised as documentary evidence in England & Wales and Canada thereby aligning Kenya with the prevalent practice with other common law jurisdictions.

The first challenge, as discussed in Chapter 1, is that the conditions set out in the operative section primarily relate to the computer system where the electronic evidence was derived and whether the said computer was performing its regular functions. As discussed before, section 106B of the Evidence Act which sets out the admissibility of electronic evidence, makes provisions that primarily target the computer system as a means of assessing the provenance of the electronic and digital evidence.[6]

6 Section 106B provides that: (1) Notwithstanding anything contained in this Act, any information contained in an electronic record which is printed on paper, stored, recorded or copied on optical or electro-magnetic media produced by a computer (herein referred to as computer output) shall be deemed to be also a document, if the conditions mentioned in this section are satisfied in relation to the information and computer in question and shall be admissible in any proceedings, without further proof or production of the original, as evidence of any contents of the original or of any fact stated therein where direct evidence would be admissible.

(2) The conditions mentioned in subsection (1), in respect of a computer output, are the following –

(a) the computer output containing the information was produced by the computer during the period over which the computer was used to store or process information for any activities regularly carried out over that period by a person having lawful control over the use of the computer;

(b) during the said period, information of the kind contained in the electronic record or of the kind from which the information so contained is derived was regularly fed into the computer in the ordinary course of the said activities;

(c) throughout the material part of the said period, the computer was operating properly or, if not, then in respect of any period in which it was not operating properly or was out of operation during that part of the period, was not such as to affect the electronic record or the accuracy of its content; and

(d) the information contained in the electronic record reproduces or is derived from such information fed into the computer in the ordinary course of the said activities.

(3) Where over any period, the function of storing or processing information for the purposes of any activities regularly carried on over that period as mentioned in paragraph (a) of sub-section (2) was regularly performed by computers, whether –

(a) by a combination of computers operating in succession over that period; or

(b) by different computers operating in succession over that period; or

(c) in any manner involving the successive operation over that period, in whatever order, of one or more computers and one or more combinations of computers,

then all computers used for that purpose during that period shall be treated for the purposes of this section as constituting a single computer and references in this section to a computer shall be construed accordingly.

(4) In any proceedings where it is desired to give a statement in evidence by virtue of this section, a certificate doing any of the following –

(a) identifying the electronic record containing the statement and describing the manner in which it was produced;

(b) giving such particulars of any device involved in the production of that electronic record as may be appropriate for the purpose of showing that the electronic record was produced by a computer;

(c) dealing with any matters to which conditions mentioned in sub-section (2) relate; and

(d) purporting to be signed by a person occupying a responsible position in relation to the operation of the relevant device or the management of the relevant activities (whichever is appropriate),

This is the section of the law that is intended to set out the admissibility standard, which would ideally regulate the use of open source evidence in legal proceedings in Kenya. However, it is at variance with the fundamental nature of open source information, that is, publicly available information whose source may or may not be known. Subjecting this type of evidence to a standard that predominantly focuses on regulating the computer system where this information was derived does not provide much assistance in terms of guidance.

Secondly, and as discussed in Chapter 1, this section only sets out the considerations to be taken in estimating the probative value of the evidence without setting out the conditions preceding admissibility. This offers little guidance to investigators, litigants and the judiciary, for that matter, on the standards to be followed prior to the arrival of this information as evidence in court.

The third challenge relates to the contradiction between section 78A and section 106B on the requirement to adduce a certificate that, *inter alia*, proves the provenance of the e-evidence, the integrity of the system, or its functionality. However, both the systematic case study and feedback from the data collection process revealed that the requirement for a certificate of authenticity has become settled law and practice despite this contradiction. For instance, in *Idris Abdi Abdullahi v Ahmed Bashane & 2 others*, the court held that "before the Court can admit electronic records/evidence a certificate is mandatory to confirm source, process, custody and delivery of the said electronic record before admission so as to preempt manipulation of the record."[7]

Beyond these challenges, it is also important to highlight here that an overwhelming majority of the respondents, that is, defence counsel, prosecutors, police investigators and judges, were of the opinion that the current legal framework is not sufficient to support the use of open source evidence in legal proceedings in Kenya, especially in instances where the open source evidence has been posted anonymously. Similarly, as demonstrated by the systematic case study and feedback from the data collection process, significant importance has been placed on the requirement that the original author of open

---

shall be evidence of any matter stated in the certificate and for the purpose of this subsection it shall be sufficient for a matter to be stated to the best of the knowledge of the person stating it.

(5) For the purpose of this section, information is supplied to a computer if it is supplied thereto in any appropriate form and whether it is so supplied directly or (with or without human intervention) by means of appropriate equipment, whether in the course of activities carried on by any official, information is supplied with a view to its being stored or processed for the purpose of those activities, that information, if duly supplied to that computer, shall be taken to be supplied to it in the course of those activities.

7 [2018] eKLR. A similar position was held by the judges who were interviewed, with one stating expressly that they would not admit open source evidence without the certificate of authenticity.

source material should adduce the material in court in order to testify to its authenticity and consequent reliability. The proposed framework focuses on this aspect of the legal framework, the source requirement.

The Proposed Framework for the Assessment of the Admissibility of Open Source Evidence

Since section 106B of the Evidence Act categorises open source evidence as documentary evidence, the provisions of Part III of the Act, that is, section 64 to section 78, on documentary evidence, become operable in its entirety. Specifically, section 64 provides that "the content of documents may be proved either by primary or secondary evidence." This research proposes a conjunctive reading of this section together with section 78A(2) as a cure for the legal requirement for a source. The effect of such interpretation being that the absence of the original author of open source material should not be, in and of itself, a ground for its exclusion. As the Evidence Act clearly states that secondary evidence can equally be adduced in support. Section 68 of the Act provides for various exceptions to the general rule whereby secondary evidence can be adduced in *lieu* of primary evidence. Specifically, section 68(1)(a)(ii) states that:

> Secondary evidence may be given of the existence, condition or contents of a document in the following cases … when the original is shown or appears to be in the possession or power of … a person out of reach of, or not subject to, the process of the court.

Given that the conditions of anonymously posted open source evidence fall squarely within this provision, in that the original source is "out of reach of, or not subject to, the process of the court," it is this research's contention that the admissibility of open source evidence falls under the ambit of this section. And that there is no need for a new law to address the admissibility of open source evidence in legal proceedings in Kenya but rather adjudicators need to interpret Part III of the Evidence Act as proposed.

Further support for the proposal that this section should be interpreted in the suggested manner can be found in section 78A (3) (d) of the Evidence Act, which gives the adjudicator further leeway by providing that:

> In estimating the weight, if any, to be attached to electronic and digital evidence, under subsection (1), regard shall be had to … any other relevant factor.

And the "relevant factor" here is the fact that by the time this amendment was being introduced into the Evidence Act in 2014, there was no appreciation of the particularities of the impact of technology on evidentiary processes and specifically on open source evidence. Therefore, there could not have been a direct provision for it.

It is critical to note here that this interpretive approach has the support of one of the judges who was interviewed, whereby they acknowledged the fact that the law might not have foreseen certain technological evolutions, but there exists room for interpretation within it. The judge posited:

> Whatever short falls exist in the law, and even as we wait for amendments or as we push for law reform in certain areas, there are provisions of the Evidence Act that can serve as a guideline. These are the provisions that leave room for the discretion of the person interpreting that law.

Due to the fact that Kenya is a precedential legal system, such an interpretation by the higher courts would therefore become binding law.

Having stated the above, it is important to provide a justification for the reasoning behind the proposal for legal change through judicial interpretation of the existing law as opposed to an amendment of the law. This approach is based on the recognition that this area of the law is still developing rapidly and new standards are constantly being developed, especially as at the time of writing.[8] The need for elucidation of uncertain issues and adaptation to the ever-changing circumstances wrought by constant technological evolution will always be there. Furthermore, the progressive development of laws through judicial law-making is a well-entrenched and also a necessary part of legal tradition in Kenya.[9]

Therefore, the gradual clarification of rules pertaining to open source evidence through the channel of judicial interpretation on a case-by-case basis is the best way forward. This is because this research posits that any proposals that target law reform for this nascent type of evidence, at this stage in time, would be premature and could risk interfering with the predictability and consistency of this legislation. Risking the potential violation of the principle of

8 For instance, there is no binding international practice that regulates open source investigations which produce the open source information. The Berkeley Protocol is the closest instrument that holds such a status, but due to its non-binding nature and consequent lack of enforcement mechanisms, at best it can be considered a soft law. Another challenge connected to this is the fact that there appears to be a myriad of standards that are being presented to regulate this space; see for example the Report on Digitally Derived Evidence used in UN Human Rights Fact-Finding Missions: Approaches and Standards of Proof (also known as the Leiden Guidelines).

9 It should also be highlighted that this was a sentiment that was raised by one of the prosecutors who was interviewed during the data collection process. See also, generally, the court's overall sentiments and acknowledgement of this approach in the case of *Yüksel Yalçinkaya v Türkiye*, (Application no. 15669/20), Judgment, Grand Chamber, European Court of Human Rights.

legality, should there be a need for further amendments induced by further technological advancements.[10]

The second justification for this approach is the fact that courts have the benefit of interpreting laws in the context of the changes in society by virtue of the doctrine of judicial notice. This is a luxury that written laws do not have due to, among other things, the principle of legality and the rule of law requirements that laws should be predictable.[11] To that effect, section 60 of the Evidence Act provides for facts of which the court shall take judicial notice and section 1, sub-section (o) provides that:

> The courts shall take judicial notice of the following facts … all matters of general or local notoriety.

The fact of the impact of technological advancement on evidentiary standards and procedures is one of general notoriety and, as the systematic case study and survey have shown, it is also a fact of local notoriety. Based on this section, therefore, Kenyan courts are legally empowered to take judicial notice of technological advancements that impact evidentiary standards and procedures, such as open source evidence and its oddities specifically in relation to anonymously posted open source material.

This position also finds support from the litigants who were surveyed. While addressing the question as to what form a legal framework that specifically provides guidance on the admissibility of open source evidence would look like, one prosecutor observed that:

> Due to the fact that technology is constantly changing and legislation has no hope of keeping up with it, we need a fluid law. And the judiciary is best placed to provide such fluidity as through their decisions they are able to cater to every facet of open source evidence. This way we are able, as a jurisdiction, to have laws that are adaptable to the times and changing nature of the digital space as ours is a precedential legal system.

The last justification is the fact that there is room for training, sensitisation and overall capacity building for adjudicators on open source evidence.[12] Such an understanding of open source evidence by adjudicators would result in a proper appreciation of open source evidence within legal proceedings in

10 See OECD, "Predictability and Consistency of Legislation," 2023. Available: https://www.oecd.org/en.html, accessed 11 November 2023.

11 See generally, C Sampford, "The Rule of Law," in *Retrospectivity and the Rule of Law*, Oxford University Press (2012) Online Edn. Accessed 11 November 2023.

12 Through the Judicial Training Institute, for instance.

Kenya. Effectively harnessing its democratising power and thus enhancing accountability for human rights violations in Kenya through the courts.

This point provides a segue for a discussion of the framework that would guide the assessment of the admissibility of open source evidence once it reaches the courtroom.

Proposed Framework for Assessing Admissibility of Open Source Evidence in Kenya

Introduction

This section focuses on how the admissibility of open source evidence can be assessed in legal proceedings in Kenya. This section focuses on an authentication test.

Authentication

Before embarking on this research's proposed authentication test, it is important to first understand how Kenyan courts have approached this issue. Accordingly, the Kenyan court set out four steps to be considered in the authentication process of electronic and digital evidence in *Republic v Mark Lloyd Steveson*, the case *classicus* on authentication, as discussed in Chapter 4.[13] This authentication process, as provided by the court, includes the following steps:

I. First, the Court determines if the proposed evidence is relevant. Here, the Court simply determines the probative value of the proposed evidence: whether the proposed evidence has a tendency to make the existence of any fact that is of consequence to the determination of a fact in issue more or less probable than it would be without the evidence. If the proposed evidence passes the Relevancy Test, it proceeds to the second step.
II. Second, in the case of tangible exhibits (such as the two documents in the case in question), the Proponent for the evidence authenticates the proposed piece of evidence; that is, the Proponent must prove that the evidence is what the proponent claims it to be. The court only proceeds to the third step if the proposed evidence passes muster under the Authentication Test. It is important to explain here that the term "authentication," though the technically correct word which is widely used for this step, can be misleading. In fact, what is meant by "authentication" at this stage is merely that a proper foundation for admission of the document or exhibit has been laid. It does not, at all, mean that the exhibit must now be accepted and believed. The Trial Court, as the fact finder,

13 [2016] eKLR.

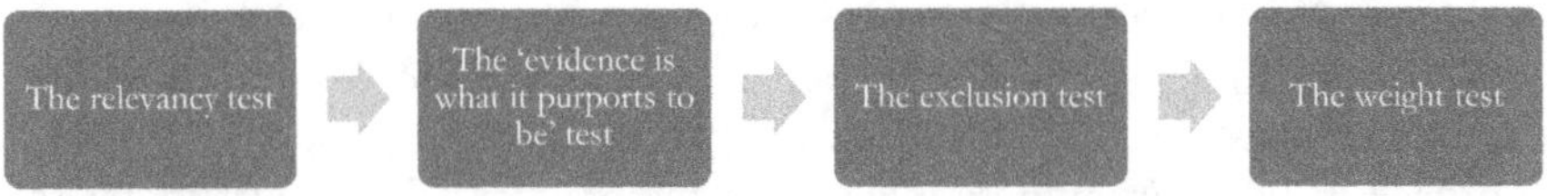

Figure 5.1 Framework for determination of authenticity of open source evidence

must ultimately weigh (in step 4 below) the admitted evidence in light of all the circumstances. The weighing can only happen after the foundation for the proposed evidence has been laid.

III. Third, the Court, at the urging of the parties or on its own motion, determines if there is any other rule of evidence that excludes the proposed evidence. Here the Court considers whether the evidence is excluded by the Constitution (for example, the right against self-incrimination discussed above, prohibition against hearsay evidence, or whether the proposed evidence would lead to unfair prejudice with its probative value substantially outweighed by the danger of unfair prejudice). If the proposed evidence survives this Exclusion Test, then the proposed evidence is admitted into evidence and the Court proceeds to the fourth step.

IV. Fourth, the Court considers the weight to be accorded to the admitted evidence. At this stage, the opponent may still bring to the Court's attention evidence opposing the authenticity of the evidence, thereby allowing the Court to give less weight to the evidence or no weight at all.[14]

The proposed authentication test for open source evidence builds on this authentication standard because of the fact that open source evidence is an aspect of electronic evidence and is therefore admissible under the current legislative framework as discussed in the first part of this chapter. It is of note that this authentication standard by the court in *Stevenson* closely reflects the three-pronged test set out by the ICC to assess admissibility of any evidence which includes an assessment of relevance, probative value and the absence of prejudicial effect.[15]

The proposed framework to guide the authentication of open source evidence in Kenya will accordingly comprise four hierarchical tests, that is, as shown in Figure 5.1, the relevancy test, the "evidence is what it purports to be" test, the exclusion test and the weight test.

The Relevancy Test

The relevancy test is the preliminary level of assessment of admissibility in which the court assesses the usefulness of the open source evidence to support

14 [2016] eKLR.

15 See, Rome Statute, Article 69(4) and Rule 63, the Rules of Procedure and Evidence.

the determination of the questions at issue in a dispute. The ICC defines relevance in the same way as *R v Stevenson* above, which definition this research adopts, as "existence of a fact at issue more or less probable."[16] The ICC's approach is, however, undesirable in that the practice of the court shows that the determination of the relevance of the evidence is left to the final determination stage. Such an approach would be undesirable for the Kenyan context as it would result in the placement of an onerous burden on the defence, or the prosecution for that matter, "to respond to all the submitted evidence regardless of its relevance or probative value.[17] An approach that would certainly have the effect of escalating equality of arms challenges by impacting access to justice thereby affecting the rights of the accused person."[18]

In England and Wales, the relevance of open source evidence is determined based on the presence of a demonstrable link between the material contained in the open source information and the subject matter of the case. This position was confirmed by the court in *Khan v R* where the court was ruling on the authenticity of screenshots which were held as being unreliable as there had been no demonstrable link between them and the accused person.[19]

While in the USA, by virtue of Rule 104(b) of the Federal Rules of Evidence, the first determination of any such assessment will have to be a test of its relevance resulting in this rule being referred to as the conditional relevance rule. In *Lorraine v Markel American Insurance Co* the court noted that relevance is one of the factors that need to be determined in order for digital evidence to be admissible.[20] The Canadian approach does not explicitly make a provision for relevance but, as seen in the analysis in the comparative chapter, it is a pertinent consideration for the admissibility of open source evidence.

The Kenyan position on relevance is reflected by the courts' holding in the *classicus* Stevenson case where the court emphasised the importance of this step by noting that just because section 78A of the Evidence Act provides for the admissibility of electronic evidence, "this section does not obviate the need for establishing the relevance of the proposed evidence."

Based on the foregoing, it is this research's proposal that the relevancy test, as set out in the *Stevenson* case, should be maintained as the standard for assessing the relevance of open source evidence in Kenya. The only addition to the *Stevenson* relevancy test, as proposed by this framework, is that such a determination should be conducted as and when the open source material comes to court, rather than being left for determination at the final stage. This

16 Articles 64(9)(a) and 69(4) of the Rome Statute, as read together with the REP, define relevance as denoting "existence of a fact at issue more or less probable."; Mehandru & Koenig (n 79 above).
17 Trevisan (n 340 above) p 8.
18 Trevisan (n 340 above) p 8.
19 [2015] EWCA Crim 1816.
20 241 F.R.D. 534 (D. Md. 2007).

is in order to avoid escalating equality of arms challenges by impacting access to justice and thereby affecting the rights of the accused person.

Once the assessment of the relevance of the open source evidence is complete and the material has been found to be relevant for the determination of the questions at issue in a dispute, the adjudicator should proceed to determine whether the said evidence is what it purports to be.

The "Evidence Is What It Purports to Be" Test

This next level of assessment relates to the proponent proving that the open source evidence is what the proponent claims it to be. In England and Wales, this step was discussed in the *R v Kay* case which dealt with the issue of Facebook messages that were edited.[21] Here the court noted *inter alia* that in order for this type of evidence to be admissible, it must be authentic and the authenticity was connoted to mean that the open source evidence is what it purports to be.[22] In order to prove this step, the English courts expect to see that there is continuity in the evidence, that is, the chain of custody. This can be proven in various ways such as through technical corroboration.[23] And through expert evidence, for instance in *Amjad v R* the court categorically stated, while considering open source material, that

> we were surprised the Crown made no effort to canvass expert evidence at least capable of establishing the provenance of some if not all open source material and perhaps of establishing authenticity and accuracy. Had it been able to lead any such the court might have been better served.[24]

An important aspect to be noted from the English approach to this step of the authentication process is the realisation that there cannot be a blanket test for authenticity in relation to the requirements of proving that open source evidence is what it purports to be. This is because of the diverse nature of open source evidence. This position was accurately summarised as "the tests of authenticity for digital data ... will vary, depending on the source and type of the data."[25] The process of establishing that open source evidence is "what it purports to be" in England and Wales courts has been summarised as:

21 [2017] EWCA Crim 2214, para. 20.
22 [2017] EWCA Crim 2214, para. 20.
23 See, 2009] EWHC 1435 (Comm) para. 60.
24 [2016] EWCA Crim 1618, para. 37.
25 Mason & Stanfield (n 120 above) p 193–194; see also *R v Mawji (Rizwan)* where the court refused the appellant's contention that "the provenance of the email could not be certain as it was relatively easy to produce a document that had nothing to do with the email address," and that for this reason, there should have been evidence that proved the audit trail. The court noted instead that the way through which this evidence was presented in court, through the

1. The data (both the content and associated metadata) relied upon in any legal proceedings can be shown to be an accurate representation of the prevailing and existing state of those data at the time relevant to the legal proceedings.
2. If the data have changed, for whatever reason, there is an accurate and reliable method of documenting the changes, including the reasons for any such changes from the moment they were identified (and possibly seized) as potential evidence in legal proceedings.
3. The continuity of the data can be demonstrated between the moment the data were obtained for legal purposes and their submission as an exhibit in legal proceedings.
4. Any techniques that were used to obtain, secure and process the data can be shown to have been appropriate for the purpose for which they were applied.
5. The technical and organisational evidence demonstrates that the integrity of the data is trustworthy, and can therefore be considered to be reliable and complete (insofar as the data can be complete), which in turn will depend on the circumstances surrounding the data at the time they were identified as being potentially relevant in legal proceedings.[26]

The Canadian position on this stage of the authentication process is contained under section 31.1 of the Canadian Evidence Act, which Canadian courts have interpreted as merely requiring the party seeking to adduce an electronic document into evidence to prove that the electronic document is what it purports to be.[27] Denoting the fact that the determination of the weight to be apportioned to an item is left to the judge at the end when balancing and

---

oral testimony of the victim, was sufficient to allow for its admission. In agreeing with this court's position, Mason and Stanfield observed that "the email did not have to be authenticated in the way suggested by the appellant because of the circumstances surrounding the events and the other evidence in the case." As the authenticity of a document in electronic format can be tested in other ways, for instance by analysing the metadata; *R v Skinner*, [2005] EWCA Crim 1439; and *Khan v R*, [2015] EWCA Crim 1816, para. 9.

26 Mason & Stanfield (n 120 above) p 247. This is the standard that has been included in the Draft Convention on Electronic Evidence – which has been said to be the first treaty dealing with the status of electronic evidence, covering civil and criminal proceedings; the investigation and examination of electronic evidence, and general provisions regarding the recognition and admissibility of electronic evidence from foreign jurisdictions and was published in 2016. An important clarification to make here is that even though the Draft Convention focuses on electronic evidence, the same standards can be transposed herein given that open source evidence falls under the electronic and digital evidence framework in Kenya. The second, yet very critical clarification is the fact that this Draft Convention has been drafted by Stephen Mason in consultation with various stakeholders such as the Institute of Advanced Legal Studies. It appears to be more of a proposal as opposed to an instrument that has been drafted under the aegis of a responsible international law making organ.

27 See, Saskatchewan Court of Appeal, 2017 SKCA 14, para. 18; *R. v Martin*, the Court of Appeal for Newfoundland and Labrador, [2021] NLCA 1 at para. 47.

weighing all the admitted evidence.[28] Therefore, the only consideration at this stage is the availability of some evidence that is logically probative of whether the electronic evidence is what it purports to be.[29] This test has been likened to the showing of a *prima facie* case for authenticity as opposed to full establishment of the same and follows a similar approach as Kenya, as envisioned by the court in the *Stevenson* case.

The challenge with the Canadian approach, however, is that this is a very low standard because it does not limit how or by what means it may be met, and neither does it impose a particular standard for threshold admissibility.[30] The benefit of the low standard is that it aligns the Canadian approach to the England and Wales approach in that there is no one blanket test on how to show that the open source evidence is what it purports to be. But on the other hand, the low standard does not guard against the complexities of open source evidence, particularly the potential abuse and manipulation that open source evidence is prone to.[31]

The American position can be summarised into two approaches, the Maryland and Texas approaches. The Maryland approach is considered to require a higher standard for the authentication of open source evidence, which strict approach is based on the likelihood of abuse and manipulation. The approach is summarised by the Maryland Court of Appeal as:

> "Authenticating electronically stored information presents a myriad of concerns because 'technology changes so rapidly, ... is "often new to many judges," and "requires greater scrutiny of "the foundational requirements"' than letters or other paper records, to bolster reliability."[32]

Therefore, the proponent of the open source evidence would have to prove a measure of the material's authenticity at this stage.

Conversely, the Texas approach only requires a sufficient showing of authenticity of the open source evidence to permit the trier of fact to find that it is authentic.[33] The consequence is that "authentic evidence is admitted, clearly inauthentic evidence is excluded, and everything in between is conditionally relevant and admitted for the jury to make the final determination as to authenticity."[34]

The Texas Approach also recognises the fact that there cannot be a blanket test for authenticity in relation to the requirements of proving that open source evidence is "what it purports to be." The Texas Criminal Appeal court

28 Gorman (n 175 above) p181.
29 Gorman (n 175 above) p181.
30 Gorman (n 175 above) p 181; see also, Silver (n 183 above) p 137.
31 See, *R v Aslami*, [2021] ONCA 249, para. 24, 29 and 30.
32 *Griffin v State*, 19 A.3d 415 (Md. App. 2011), para. 423.
33 135 Cal. Rptr. 3d 628 (Ct. App. 2011).
34 Grimm *et al.* (n 231 above) p 465.

observed that "as with the authentication of any kind of proffered evidence, the best or most appropriate method for authenticating electronic evidence will often depend upon the nature of the evidence and the circumstances of the particular case."[35] Which of course does not provide much guidance in terms of best practices that would support the development of a standardised framework for assessment.

It is important to reiterate here that these approaches are generally indicative of the practice in the states that follow the common law legal system and this can be testified to by the decisions from various appellate courts such as the California Court of Appeal, the Connecticut Appellate Court, the Arizona Court of Appeal, the Michigan Court of Appeal and of course the Maryland and Texas Appellate Courts.

However, both the Maryland and Texas approaches are not favourable in as far as standard setting for the Kenyan context is concerned. This is because the Maryland standard is too high and may have a deleterious effect on efforts that are aimed at streamlining the use of open source evidence within courts. This is because it would significantly increase the standard of proof that litigants would have to discharge. On the other hand, the Texas standard is too low and may not guard against the potential abuse and manipulation that open source evidence is prone to. A preferred approach would therefore be one that takes the middle ground between these two approaches.

At the ICC, there are various methods of determining that open source material is what it purports to be and therefore reliable. The first method is a process of proving that a digital file is genuine or not forged and that it has not been manipulated or altered.[36] The factors to consider under this process include: originality, integrity and date/location of recording.[37] The second method is "other *indicia*" which includes an assessment of factors such as bias of the source, public or private nature of the information, testimonial nature of the information, purpose for which the information was created, *inter alia*.[38]

Closely connected and equally necessary for the determination of the admissibility of open source evidence at the ICC is the concept of verification, a process of ensuring that a claim or assertion statement in some medium of communication is reliable and/or true.[39]

However, more recently, the ICC in the case of the *Prosecutor v Ali Muhammad Ali Abd-Al-Rahman ("Ali Kushayb")*, in the Situation in Darfur,

35 *Tienda v State*, 358 S.W.3d 633 (Tex. Crim. App. 2012), para. 639.

36 Dubberley *et al.* (n 317 above).

37 *The Prosecutor v Germain Katanga*, Situation in the Democratic Republic of the Congo, Trial Chamber II, Decision on the Prosecutor's Bar Table Motions, ICC-01/04-01/07-2635, 19 December 2010; See also, Mehandru & Koenig (n 79 above).

38 *The Prosecutor v Germain Katanga*, Situation in the Democratic Republic of the Congo, Trial Chamber II, Decision on the Prosecutor's Bar Table Motions, ICC-01/04-01/07-2635, 19 December 2010; See also, Mehandru & Koenig (n 79 above).

39 Dubberley *et al.* (n 317 above).

Sudan, held, with respect to its approach on the submission of evidence, the Court ruled that the Chamber "will ultimately assess the relevance, probative value and potential prejudice of the evidence (the 'standard evidentiary criteria') as part of the holistic assessment of all evidence submitted when deciding on the guilt or innocence of the accused, in its judgment pursuant to Article 74 of the Statute."[40] In making this determination, the Chamber noted that this is now an established practice of the Court.[41] This was in response to the document-specific objections that the Defence had raised while relying on the decisions in *Katanga and Ngudjolo*[42] and *Ruto and Sang*.[43]

The Court stated, in response to these cases that, "these cases are not applicable *vis-à-vis* the present ruling, on the basis that in these cases the Chambers adopted a different approach to the reception of materials into evidence, i.e., that of 'admission' rather than 'submission.'"[44] It seems that in instances where the Trial Chamber is following the "submission model," these factors will be taken into account at the deliberation stage, instead of at the judgement stage.[45] Regrettably, due to the flexible approach to evidence at the ICC, the standard is unpredictable and there is therefore not enough to be gleaned from this in so far as best practices are concerned.

Therefore, the proposed way for Kenyan courts to assess whether open source evidence is "what it purports to be" is enumerated in the box below. This approach is better than the ones enumerated above as it emulates only the

40 ICC-02/05-01/20, 27 February 2023, para. 25. It should be noted that in this decision, when it refers to open source information, it refers to journalistic accounts, NGO reports, *inter alia*.

41 The Chamber made reference to the following Court documents and decisions in support of the fact that it is an established practice: See Chambers Manual, Sixth Edition, 24 November 2022, para. 84 and confidential annex. See also, The Prosecutor v Dominic Ongwen, Trial Chamber IX, Decision on Prosecution's Request to Submit 1006 Items of Evidence, ICC-02/04-01/15-795, 28 March 2017; The Prosecutor v Al Hassan Ag Abdoul Aziz Ag Mohamed Ag Mahmoud, Trial Chamber X, Decision on the Prosecution's fourth, fifth and sixth requests for the admission of evidence from the bar table, ICC-01/12-01/18-2127, 23 February 2022; The Prosecutor v Alfred Yekatom and Patrice-Edouard Ngaïssona, Trial Chamber V, Decision on the First Prosecution Submission Request from the Bar Table, (Sexual and Gender Based Violence), ICC-01/14-01/18-1359, 12 April 2022.

42 The Prosecutor v Germain Katanga and Mathieu Ngudjolo Chui, Trial Chamber II, Decision on the Prosecutor's Bar Table Motions, ICC-01/04-01/07-2635, 17 December 2010, paras 12-13, 22-24, 27-35; The Prosecutor v Germain Katanga and Mathieu Ngudjolo Chui, Trial Chamber II, Decision on the Bar Table Motion of the Defence of Germain Katanga, ICC-01/04-01/07-3184, 21 October 2011, para. 17.

43 The Prosecutor v William Samoei Ruto and Joshua Arap Sang, Trial Chamber V(A), Decision on the Prosecution's Request for Admission of Documentary Evidence, ICC-01/09-01/11-1353, 10 June 2014, paras 44, 85-87.

44 Prosecutor v Ali Muhammad Ali Abd-Al-Rahman ('Ali Kushayb'), ICC-02/05-01/20, 27 February 2023, para. 26.

45 Prosecutor v Ali Muhammad Ali Abd-Al-Rahman ('Ali Kushayb'), ICC-02/05-01/20, 27 February 2023, para. 26. See also, McDermott *et al.* (n 366 above).

positive aspects from each case study and cures the negative aspects and thus provides an adequately balanced test.

Box 5.1 Framework for assessment of whether open source evidence is "what it purports to be"

I. In the first instance, the determination of whether the open source evidence is what it purports to be should be made at the point at which the evidence is adduced as opposed to being made during the final determination of the case.
II. The continuity of the open source evidence material can be demonstrated from the moment the material was obtained for legal purposes and its submission as an exhibit in legal proceedings.
III. There is an accurate and reliable method that documents the steps taken from the moment the open source material was identified/retrieved to the steps followed during the forensics analysis process – including any changes and the reasons for any such changes.
IV. Any techniques that were used to obtain, secure and process the open source material should be shown to have been appropriate for the purpose for which they were applied. Here, any software used should have licences and the analysts that are conducting the forensics analysis should also possess certification to engage in such analysis.
V. The presence of technical and independent corroboration to demonstrate that the integrity of the data is trustworthy, and can therefore be considered to be reliable and complete (insofar as the data can be complete). Here, expert evidence that shows the provenance of the open source material and establishes its authenticity and accuracy should be considered; witness accounts; and any "other indicia" which may include an assessment of factors such as bias of the source, public or private nature of the information, testimonial nature of the information, purpose for which the information was created.

The Exclusion Test

As enunciated by Ngugi J, this is the stage of the authentication process where the court determines whether there are any other rules of evidence that exclude the proposed evidence.[46] This determination includes a consid-

46 *Republic v Mark Lloyd Steveson* [2016] eKLR.

eration of whether the evidence is excluded: by the Constitution, for example, the admission of the evidence violates the right against self-incrimination, the right to privacy or an aspect of the right to fair trial; whether it violates the prohibition against hearsay evidence under the Evidence Act; or whether its probative value is substantially outweighed by the danger of unfair prejudice.

The predominantly addressed exclusion rule, and one which is a sub-theme of this research, is the prohibition against hearsay evidence and it is therefore discussed extensively. This is followed by a discussion of the relationship between open source evidence and fair trial considerations as this was one of the areas that the survey focused on. A standard cannot be provided for the remaining exclusionary grounds as these determinations can only be assessed on a case-by-case basis depending on the particular facts of a case and the evidence that has been adduced accordingly.

In England and Wales, open source evidence has been categorised as real evidence. The import of this categorisation is that open source evidence can be analysed directly as a primary source once it has been verified,[47] as opposed to it being treated as "any kind of statement made by a person".[48] It is therefore this categorisation that enables the admission of open source evidence, especially video evidence, if the "creator is not available to testify. This is because it would be hearsay if introduced as evidence of the truth of its contents."[49]

As demonstrated by the *Amjad v R* case, audio-visual open source evidence is not hearsay if it is not being relied upon for the truth of its content. The court, in ruling that there was no hearsay, stated that:

> Neither was the material on the internet relied on for truth, merely to show that it is similar to that which the Appellant possessed. Had the material on the internet been couched not in words but in images of individuals demonstrating exercises, the Crown would have advanced its case in the same way, relying on the striking similarity of the fitness poses *etc.* It would be odd to describe such images as hearsay. There is on these facts no hearsay and no anonymous hearsay issue.[50]

47 It is important to reiterate here the previous discussions that: open source evidence is a document under section 134 (1) of the Criminal Justice Act and although electronic evidence has very different characteristics to paper, "the rules of evidence that have developed with respect to the authentication of evidence, particularly documentary evidence, are still highly pertinent to electronic evidence."

48 In *McDonald v R*, [2011] EWCA Crim 2933 para 42, the court found that a printout from a mobile phone service provider, Vodafone, was real evidence as opposed to documentary hearsay. See also, *R v Spiby*, [1990] 91 Cr App R 186, the court accepted an automated computer process that monitored telephone calls and a printout of certain call details as real evidence because there was no human intervention in the production of the data and consequently held that it was not hearsay evidence. See also, Minogue *et al.* (n 109 above).

49 Minogue *et al.* (n 109 above).

50 [2016] EWCA Crim 1618, para. 32–33.

The converse is also true; open source evidence will be excluded as hearsay if there is no witness to testify to its contents on the grounds that there would be no way to test its reliability.[51] Even though Kenya categorises open source evidence as documentary evidence, thereby bringing it within the purview of secondary evidence, the position of the England and Wales court is interestingly similar to the Kenyan position. This was shown by the dataset; that is, a majority of the surveyed respondents, including the judges, were of the opinion that having a witness testify to the contents of open source material would be the best way to test its reliability.

The same holds true for text-based open source evidence as they fall under the categorisation of "statements" as under section 115 of the Criminal Justice Act 2003. They will not constitute hearsay if they are not relied on for the truth of the matter stated.[52] The contrary is also true; if these statements are submitted for the truth of the matter stated without a witness to authenticate the said material, it will constitute hearsay.[53] The Kenyan case, *Clement Kungu Waibara v Annie Wanjiku Kibeh & another*, holds a similar stance whereby the Court held, in relation to evidence that was derived from social media including Facebook and WhatsApp:

I do not think they amount to hearsay evidence if read in the sense in which they are offered: not to prove the veracity of the matters asserted in those statements but to prove that the Petitioner did actually become aware of the existence of the statements or the social media accounts.[54]

Gallavin and Mason highlighted the complexity of the hearsay rule, which increases where digital evidence is concerned, and it would be remiss not to mention it here. They posited that "while a communication written by a person and stored in a digital form is capable of being a statement for the purpose of the hearsay rule, 'statements' derived from software code are not. In the case of the latter, where raw data is entered into a programme and then processed by digital means, the resulting apparent statement may not qualify as a statement for the purpose of the hearsay rule."[55]

For this reason, they opine that:

> A distinction therefore needs to be drawn between the content of text messages and emails, the presentation of raw data (for example, the metadata in Gmail, Hotmail, graphs, charts, presentations etcetera), and the presentation of information derived as a consequence of action by software code (for example, conclusions resulting from predictive logic

51 Seng & Mason (n 160 above).
52 O'Floinn & Ormerod (n 114 above) p 9.
53 O'Floinn & Ormerod (n 114 above) p 9.
54 [2017] eKLR.
55 Gallavin & Mason (n 163 above) p 71.

> and the presentation of computer generated conclusions and advice drawn from data).[56]

To avoid such complexities, the UK Law Commission provided an alternative position that:

> It is unnecessary to complicate our hearsay rule by extending it to statements made by machines on the basis of human input. On the other hand we do not think it would be safe to assume that everyone will share this view. We must anticipate the argument that, if such statements are inadmissible at present, that is because they are hearsay; that, under our recommendations, they would no longer be hearsay, because our formulation of the rule would apply only to representations made by people; and that they would therefore cease to be inadmissible.[57]

The Canadian position can be summarised by the Supreme Court of Canada's holding in *R v Khelawon*,[58] where the Court held that in cases where hearsay evidence does not fall under a traditional exception, it may still be admitted if *indicia* of necessity and reliability are established.[59] The converse was also held as being true, that is, "in rare cases, hearsay evidence which falls under a traditional exception may be excluded on the ground that it lacks necessity and reliability in the specific circumstances of the case."[60] Therefore, simply put, the Canadian position as far as hearsay is concerned is that even if the open source evidence does not fall under a traditional exception, it may still be admitted if *indicia* of necessity and reliability are established.

The American position is quite interesting in that hearsay rules and exceptions are applied to open source evidence in the same way that they are applied to other evidence, and this conclusion was supported by the fact that the judge in *R v Oyerinde* applied the test as it would be applied to any other out-of-court statement and determined that Facebook messages sent by the defendant were not hearsay.[61]

Before the ICC, hearsay is admissible but it is apportioned lesser weight.[62] In *Prosecutor v Al Hassan*, the question relating to hearsay was whether due to the "non-attribution of the source of the information," anonymous hearsay concerns were triggered.[63] The Prosecutor relied on the *Bemba et al.* case

56 Gallavin & Mason (n 163 above) p 71.
57 Law Commission (n 165 above) paras. 7.48–7.49.
58 2006 SCC 57, [2006] 2 S.C.R. 787.
59 2006 SCC 57, [2006] 2 S.C.R. 787.
60 *R. v Simpson*, 2007 ONCA 793, [2007] O.J. No. 4510.
61 Gilliland (n 274 above).
62 Freeman (n 75 above).
63 *Prosecutor v Al Hassan*, Trial Chamber X, Prosecution's Second Request for the Admission of Documentary Evidence from the Bar Table, ICC-01/12-01/18-1412, 13 April 2021, para. 19.

and the Appeals Chamber decision in *Ngudjolo* to defend this evidence and opined that "the fact that evidence is hearsay does not necessarily deprive it of probative value, and that the weight or probative value afforded to it will depend upon 'the infinitely variable circumstances which surround hearsay evidence.'"[64] The Defence's argument against this evidence was tied to the issue of anonymous hearsay, that is, the prejudice occasioned by the open source evidence eclipsed its probative value:

> it is nonetheless necessary to exercise "caution when items are submitted without any corresponding witness to comment on them." The prejudice caused through the inability to examine the source of information is particularly aggravated in the current instance as first, several items could and should have been submitted through a witness, and second, the majority of the tendered documents deny any assessment of the source/s of information. Without any means to verify even whether the hearsay is, for example, first-hand, third-hand, rumour circling in the civilian or military populations, a comment spreading on social media, or a government-promoted narrative fed to international agencies[.][65]

It is important to highlight here that this Defence argument reflects the sentiments of the Kenyan defence counsel who were surveyed. In that, the said defence counsel's main concern with the adducing of open source evidence without the source of information is the fact that it denies the defence an opportunity to verify the veracity of this material through cross-examination. One defence counsel noted, for instance:

> Article 50(2)(k) of the Constitution provides for the right to challenge the evidence in a criminal proceeding by way of cross-examination. In the absence of the maker of the evidence, the accused person cannot exercise this right.

However, the ICC did not determine the admissibility of the open source evidence and similarly rule on the objections raised by the Defence in that matter. The Trial Chamber instead recognised the admission of this evidence without ruling on relevance and/or admissibility of the open source evidence

64 *Prosecutor v Al Hassan*, Trial Chamber X, Prosecution's Second Request for the Admission of Documentary Evidence from the Bar Table, ICC-01/12-01/18-1412, 13 April 2021, para. 19.

65 *Prosecutor v Al Hassan*, Trial Chamber X, Defence Response to Prosecution's Second Request for the Admission of Documentary Evidence from the Bar Table, ICC-01/12-01/18-1446, 26 April 2021, para. 9.

and deferring this determination to "the part of the holistic assessment of all evidence submitted" in the final judgment.[66]

The Chamber's approach was criticised as presenting an extremely problematic precedent given the nature of open source evidence in which more often than not the source of information cannot be identified.[67] This is an important observation, and one with which this research agrees, in that the Chamber's approach falls below international standards on open source verification. The standards require that open source investigators verify open source information using different techniques such as those listed in the discussion of the Berkeley Protocol.[68]

Therefore, by leaving this determination to the final judgment, the Defence is tasked with "an onerous burden to respond to all the submitted evidence regardless of its relevance or probative value escalating equality of arms challenges and affecting the rights of the accused person as a whole."[69] Such a position will ultimately raise questions relating to the concept of access to justice and whether the use of open source evidence, by virtue of an approach such as the ICC's, would impede such access. Furthermore, due to the flexible approach to evidence at the ICC, the assessment and reliance on hearsay evidence is unpredictable. There is therefore not enough to be gleaned from this in so far as best practices are concerned.

The Kenyan position can be summarised by the decision of the court in *Francis Wambugu Mureithi v Owino Paul Ongili Babu & 2 others* where the court held that video evidence from a social media platform was inadmissible on the basis that there was a failure of the source of the videos to testify, rendering the same as hearsay.[70] The court stated that it was persuaded by the decision of Ochieng, J. in the case of *Ndwiga Steve Mbogo v I.E.B.C & 2 others Election Petition no. 7 of 2017* and held *inter alia* that "the person who produced the original record would be the most appropriate person to produce the record in evidence."[71] This categorisation of anonymous open source evidence, that has not been adduced through a witness, as hearsay is one that finds support from the litigants who were surveyed. Some of the defence counsel were of the opinion that they would have objected to the production of the video evidence in the hypothetical case as such videos do not meet the

66 *Prosecutor v Al Hassan*, Trial Chamber X, Decision on Prosecution application submitting 63 open source exhibits into evidence, ICC-01/12-01/18-1514, 15 June 2021, para. 4.

67 Trevisan (n 340 above).

68 Trevisan (n 340 above). These include, for example, geolocation, chronolocation, source analysis, and triangulating documentary, physical, and testimonial evidence.

69 Trevisan (n 340 above).

70 [2018] eKLR.

71 *Abdullahi v Independent Electoral & Boundaries Commission & 3 others* (Election Petition E006 of 2022) [2022] KEHC 15079 (KLR) (2 November 2022) (Ruling).

required legal threshold for admission in evidence and offend the rules against admission of hearsay evidence.[72]

The proposed way through which Kenyan courts should therefore assess whether open source evidence is excluded based on the prohibition against the hearsay rule is listed in the box below. This approach is better than the ones enumerated above as it emulates only the positive aspects from each case study and cures the negative aspects and thus provides an adequately balanced test.

Box 5.2 Framework for assessing whether open source evidence is excluded by the hearsay rule

I. In the first instance, even if the open source evidence does not fall under a traditional exception, its admissibility should be determined by a consideration of whether other *indicia* (which includes an assessment of factors such as "bias of the source, public or private nature of the information, testimonial nature of the information, purpose for which the information was created," *inter alia*) of necessity and reliability are established. This proposal is influenced by the Canadian approach where Justice Paciocco's assertion provides a succinct argument for this position: "computer generated information consisting of data created by a computer system is not hearsay even when offered to prove the facts it asserts. Admissibility depends on its reliability which can be established by expert evidence, or in appropriate cases, by taking judicial notice. Electronic documents containing statements of fact may still be admitted without the need for the hearsay exception to be triggered if, by their nature, they lead to relevant circumstantial inferences."

II. The second proposal is, in evaluating hearsay and open source evidence in Kenya, there should be a distinction between a communication written by a person and stored in a digital form and statements made by machines on the basis of human input. This can be done by employing the suggestion by Gallavin and Mason who propose that a distinction needs to be drawn between the content of text messages and emails, the presentation of raw data (for example, the metadata in Gmail, Hotmail, graphs, charts, presentations etcetera), and the presentation of information derived as a consequence of action by software code (for example, conclusions resulting from predictive logic and the presentation of computer-generated conclusions and advice drawn from data). Once this distinction is made, the assessment of whether open source evidence is hearsay would then be: a

72 One judge was also of the opinion that in some instances, they would categorise the open source evidence as secondary evidence.

communication written by a person and stored in a digital form is capable of being a statement for the purpose of the hearsay rule – which should be assessed based on the first proposal above; 'statements' derived from software code are not hearsay, that is, where raw data is entered into a program and then processed by digital means, the result should not qualify as a statement for the purpose of the hearsay rule.

As far as the assessment of the impact of open source evidence on the right to fair trial goes, the Kenyan approach is the only example that will be analysed and from whence the framework will be derived. This is because it is the only case study where this theme was revealed by the analysed data.

A majority of the defence counsel who were surveyed were of the opinion that the admission of open source evidence would interfere with the right to fair trial as guaranteed under Article 50(2) of the Constitution of Kenya.[73] The reasoning was mainly focused on the fact that the defence would be denied an opportunity to challenge the originator of the videos through cross-examination.[74] Interestingly, as noted in the foregoing discussion, the Defence's first point of objection to the admission of open source evidence in the *Prosecutor v Al Hassan* case before the ICC, though not argued on the basis of fair trial grounds, is similar to that of this majority. This objection at the ICC was directed at the fact that the open source evidence was not admitted through a witness, thereby denying the Defence a chance to proceed with an in-court testimony to verify the reliability and authenticity of the adduced items, disadvantaging the rights of the accused. This discloses the fact that there appears to be a uniform position, in as far as defence counsels are concerned, on the need for a witness to adduce open source evidence in court. Therefore, any proposed framework needs to be vigilant of this potential challenge to such evidence and ensure that there is a foolproof way of verifying the authenticity and reliability of open source material even without the source of the information being in court. This verification can be determined by following the steps that have been provided for in this framework.

On the other hand, the prosecutors were of the opinion that by virtue of their duty to present their case in a way that does not prejudice the accused person, various measures need to be taken to ensure that the right to fair trial is not violated by reliance on open source evidence. These measures include: disclosure of all evidence that the prosecution seeks to rely on to the defence,

73 A majority ratio of 17 out of 20 of the defence counsel.

74 A smaller number of the defence counsel, 3 out of 20, were of the contrary opinion, that is, that this evidence does not violate any fair trial considerations provided the existence of proper safeguards.

ensuring that the open source evidence is authenticated and ensuring that there exists independent corroboration before open source information is relied on as the basis and/or in support of a criminal charge. Another important measure that was stated as being critical to ensuring that fair trial rights are respected is the exclusion of improperly obtained evidence especially if irregular investigative measures were used. Such exclusion was reported as being in line with the ODPP's obligation under Article 157(11) of the Constitution of Kenya to ensure that all the rules of evidence are observed and a duty on prosecutors to prevent abuse of the process.

The judges, while commenting on the right to fair trial and its connection to the principle of inequality of arms, were of the opinion that at the end of the day, the Kenyan legal system is adversarial in nature. For these reasons, they would be guided by two principles, that is, any doubt the court has will be resolved in favour of the accused person and the *maxim* that he who alleges must prove. Such that, even if it is a human rights violations case, the burden required to discharge the evidentiary standard is on the party who is alleging a violation.

Based on the foregoing, in determining whether the right to fair trial has been violated due to the reliance on open source evidence, a Kenyan court should consider, whether at the urging of the parties or on its own motion, the following non-exhaustive issues as a guide:

Box 5.3 Framework for assessing whether the right to fair trial has been violated

I. That the open source evidence has undergone proper verification.
II. That there exists other independent corroboration, be it expert testimony, witness account, *inter alia*.
III. That any disclosure requirements have been fulfilled by the party seeking to rely on the said open source evidence.
IV. That the opposing party has been accorded sufficient opportunity to challenge the said open source evidence.

The Weight Test

This is the final stage at which point the court considers the weight to be accorded to the admitted open source evidence.

In Canada, the determination of the weight to be apportioned to an item is left to the judge at the end when balancing and weighing all the admitted evidence. In the *R v Aslami* case, the court provided a caution to guide an adjudicator when assessing the weight of an open source evidence and provides insight into some of the issues that the court could take into consideration when determining such issues. The court opined:

> Be very careful in how they deal with electronic evidence of this type. There are entirely too many ways for an individual, who is of a mind to do so, to make electronic evidence appear to be something other than what it is. Trial judges need to be rigorous in their evaluation of such evidence, when it is presented, both in terms of its reliability and its probative value … Put simply, it is too easy to use various pieces of software to create, or manipulate, messages such that they can appear to be from someone when, in fact, they emanate from an entirely different person. Similarly, the timing of the messages can be altered to suit a particular purpose.[75]

The determination of the weight of the open source evidence at the final stage is also the approach taken by the ICC and this was noted in *Prosecutor v Jean-Pierre Bemba Gombo* where the majority noted that:

> the Chamber will evaluate, in accordance with Rule 63(2) of the Rules, the probative value and appropriate weight to be given to the evidence as a whole, at the end of the case when making its final judgement. The Chamber would then make the appropriate determinations on whether the probative value of the evidence is out-weighed by its prejudicial effect.[76]

In making this determination, the main question before a court is whether the said open source evidence is reliable. The assessment of reliability before the ICC can be encapsulated into two approaches: the first method is by authentication, which entails proving that a digital file is genuine or not forged and that it has not been manipulated or altered.[77] The factors to consider under authentication include: originality, integrity and date/location of recording.[78] The second method is "other *indicia*" which includes assessing factors such as bias of the source, public or private nature of the information, testimonial nature of the information, purpose for which the information was created, *inter alia*.[79] Closely connected and equally necessary for the determination of the admissibility of open source evidence is the concept of verification.[80]

75 [2021] ONCA 249, para. 30.

76 Trial Chamber III, Decision on the admission into evidence of materials contained in the prosecution's list of evidence, ICC-01/05-01/08, 3 May 2011, p 9.

77 Dubberley *et al.* (n 317 above).

78 Mehandru & Koenig (n 79 above).

79 Mehandru & Koenig (n 79 above).

80 Dubberley *et al.* (n 317 above).

To surmise the position of the ICC on assessment of the weight to be apportioned to open source evidence, the court in *Prosecutor v Jean-Pierre Bemba Gombo* noted that this is done by assessing the:

> provenance, source or author, as well as their role in the relevant events, the chain of custody from the time of the item's creation until its submission to the Chamber, and any other relevant information.[81]

In Kenya, the determination of the weight to be apportioned to electronic evidence is governed by section 78A (3) of the Evidence Act, which provides that:

> In estimating the weight, if any, to be attached to electronic and digital evidence, under subsection (1), regard shall be had to –

(a) the reliability of the manner in which the electronic and digital evidence was generated, stored or communicated;
(b) the reliability of the manner in which the integrity of the electronic and digital evidence was maintained;
(c) the manner in which the originator of the electronic and digital evidence was identified; and,
(d) any other relevant factor.

In consonance with the above, one of the judges, speaking in reference to the hypothetical case, emphasised the importance of the following things that would enable them to assess the weight to apportion to open source evidence: authentication of the material and specifically having the person who recorded the material adducing it in court, the existence of expert evidence to confirm the technical integrity of the open source evidence and other independent corroboration. The judge noted:

> This is even more important for video and photo evidence, which I believe is the form that most open source evidence will take. And of course, only after receiving and assessing that evidence post cross-examination, will I be able to determine the weight to be apportioned to the said evidence. For the chain of custody issues, the Evidence Act section 78A is very clear about the certificate – without it I will absolutely not admit this kind of evidence.

Therefore, in as far as a framework goes, for the determination of the weight to be apportioned to open source evidence in Kenya, the provisions of section 78A

81 Freeman (n 75 above).

(3) of the Evidence Act are sufficiently all-rounded and adequately reflect the approaches from the case study jurisdictions. For this reason, it is proposed that the provisions of section 78A (3) of the Evidence Act are maintained as the standard for the assessment of the weight test. Only a slight addition, that is, an explicit requirement that a certificate of authenticity should accompany any such evidence should be included.

Furthermore, section 106B of the Evidence Act which sets out the admissibility standard for electronic evidence, needs to be amended to accommodate the nature of open source evidence. This is because this section, as set out *verbatim* in the foregoing sections, currently predominantly focuses on the "computer" that produces the output. In the first instance, due to the nature of anonymous open source evidence, the 'computer' that produced that output is more often than not available to the investigators. Therefore, attaching the admissibility of open source evidence to a computer would be in variance with reality. Connectedly, the standards set out by section 106B do not, therefore, clarify what an admissibility standard should be, given the extensively discussed peculiar nature of open source evidence.

Therefore, being the operative law that provides for the admissibility of electronic evidence in Kenya, section 106B of the Evidence Act should be amended to include provisions that reflect the presence of electronic evidence that does not conform to the traditional conceptualisation of electronic evidence. That is, as frequently pointed out throughout this research, as far as open source evidence is concerned, the device from whence this material originated is often not available to be subjected to any verification process. Secondly, and perhaps more importantly, the existence of this device is not the only marker of the material's authenticity. Therefore, an admissibility standard that prioritises the device/computer as the basis of such an assessment is not sufficient to enable the open source evidence.

It is therefore proposed that there be an amendment to section 106B of the Evidence Act; this would ideally be subsection 6, as in Box 5.4.

Box 5.4 Proposed amendment to section 106B of the Evidence Act

Section 106B (6): Notwithstanding the conditions mentioned in subsection (2), (3) and (4), in any proceedings where it is desired to give evidence that has been sourced from open sources, in determining the admissibility of such open source evidence, the court should assess the appropriate weight to be apportioned to such material. For the purpose of this subsection, the assessment of the weight to be apportioned to the open source evidence will be guided by a hierarchical test that assesses: the relevancy test, the "evidence is what it purports to be" test and the exclusion test. The conditions set out in subsections (2), (3) and (4) may be taken into consideration when making such an assessment.

Investigation of Open Source Evidence in Kenya

As highlighted continually in this research, the Berkeley Protocol is an internationally accepted document that provides guidance on how open source investigations should be conducted to ensure that the deriving open source evidence is credible and reliable, thereby enhancing its acceptability within legal proceedings. Despite the fact that the Protocol is not a legally binding instrument, being a product of the OHCHR, and as canvassed in the chapter on the comparative study, it has arguably acquired the status of soft law. Therefore, it is proposed that Kenyan investigators should use this Protocol as an important source of guidance on best practices.

It is important to note that the Chief Inspector also concurred with this proposal whereby he noted that:

> We require guidelines on how to conduct open source investigations and we can borrow from the Berkeley Protocol as it will assist our law enforcement officers to adopt the best practices in terms of investigations and prosecution of cases by use of open sources.

However, in order to ensure that effective open source investigations are conducted, the conclusions of this research under the theoretical framework that underpins it have to be considered. That is, a need to ensure that before international standards are applied at the municipal level, a consideration of the prevailing circumstances of a specific municipal jurisdiction must be taken. Accordingly, the following proposals are made to enhance the effectiveness and acceptability of the said Berkeley Protocol in guiding open source investigations in Kenya. These proposals are derived from the data arising from the survey and from the best practices that were gleaned from the comparative analysis of the leading common law jurisdictions.

This framework focuses on challenges that surround the open source investigation process in Kenya as raised by the respondents from the Department of Criminal Investigations. These are: the issue of the capacity of investigators and analysts to adequately conduct these investigations, the potential of the use of open source evidence to exacerbate inequality of arms issues, and ensuring the safeguarding of the right to fair trial.

On the issue of the capacity of investigators and analysts to adequately conduct open source investigations, it is proposed that the concept of reasonable lines of inquiry from England and Wales be implemented in Kenya. As discussed in the comparative chapter, it is a concept that has the effect of protecting actors from being overwhelmed by the vastness of open source information by ensuring that any such inquiry is reasonable. The reasonableness is assessed based on whether there is something beyond a purely speculative search.[82]

82 Crown Prosecution Service (n 280 above).

This therefore requires that before an open source investigation is conducted the involved parties should be able to: set out what they expect to find by conducting such an investigation; determine what is reasonable in the circumstances and how best to seek that information/material; take a proportionate approach to the investigation – here proportionality means ensuring that all related fair trial rights as contained in the Constitution of Kenya are upheld.

The second issue relates to ensuring that open source investigations in Kenya do not result in exacerbating inequality of arms concerns between the state apparatus and the defence and/or parties claiming violation of their human rights and ensuring the safeguarding of the right to fair trials. This risk can be mitigated under the umbrella of section 106B(4) of the Evidence Act certificate. That is, adjudicators should interpret this section as requiring investigators to provide information, in that certificate, that shows the requirements in Box 5.5:

Box 5.5 Open source investigation certificate of authentication

I. How the open source information was downloaded. Here the investigators and/or analysts should provide details of the software that was used.
II. What has been searched for and any limitations on the results of the download such as whether or not it can be guaranteed that all deleted messages were retrieved.
III. If there was a manual download of open source material resulting from a manual examination of a device, the investigator and/or analyst must also provide a statement exhibiting any information found, such as any screenshots taken during the examination.

In conclusion, therefore, the following principles, which reflect the provisions of the Berkeley Protocol and are heavily influenced by the Association of Chief Police Officers (ACPO) Good Practice Guide for Digital Evidence, should be the foundation of open source investigations in Kenya, as they reflect the prevailing international best practices on open source investigations, see Box 5.6:

Box 5.6 Foundational principles to guide open source investigations

I. Principle 1: No action taken by investigators/analysts should change open source information which may subsequently be relied upon in court.

II. Principle 2: In circumstances where an investigator/analyst finds it necessary to access original data, for instance by contacting a social media platform administrator, they must be competent to do so and be able to give evidence explaining the relevance and the implications of their actions.
III. Principle 3: An audit trail or other record of all processes applied to the open source evidence should be created and preserved and included in the certificate discussed above. Further, an independent third party should be able to examine those processes and achieve the same result.
IV. Principle 4: The person in charge of the investigation has overall responsibility for ensuring that the law and these principles are adhered to.

Conclusion

There exist foundational laws and practices within the Kenyan legal system that provide for the admissibility and the assessment of the weight to be apportioned to open source evidence as guided generally by sections 78A and 106B of the Evidence Act. However, the reliance on these legal provisions as the framework to support the admissibility of open source evidence in Kenya is wrought with challenges which, if left unchecked, will have a deleterious effect on the use of open source evidence in legal proceedings in Kenya. This will have the effect of hampering the efforts of harnessing its democratising power to ensure accountability for the violation of human rights.

This chapter has therefore provided a framework that addresses the various phases of concern starting with a proposal relating to the legal requirements for the determination of the admissibility of open source evidence in legal proceedings in Kenya, followed by a proposed framework for assessing the admissibility of open source evidence in Kenya and concluded with a proposal on how open source investigations should be conducted in Kenya. The premise of this proposal being underpinned by this research's theoretical framework, which supports a context-based application of international standards, the comparative studies and the data from the field research and interviews.

Bibliography

Books

Mason, S (ed) *Electronic evidence* (LexisNexis Butterworths 2012).

Minogue, D, Siobhán, A, Andrews-Briscoe, C & McDermott, Y, 'Putting principles into practice: Reflections on a mock admissibility hearing on open source evidence' in *International criminal law before domestic courts* (Vienna MANZ Verlag 2023). help_outline

Sampford, C, 'Retrospectivity and the rule of law,' Oxford University Press (2012)

Book Chapters

Dubberley, S, Koenig, A & Murray, D 'Introduction: The emergence of digital witnesses' in S. Dubberley, A Koening & D Murray (Eds) *Digital witness: Using open source information for human rights investigation, documentation, and accountability* (Oxford University Press 2020).

Freeman, L 'Prosecuting atrocity crimes with open source evidence: Lessons from the International Criminal Court' in Dubberley, S, Koeing, A & Murray, D (eds) *Digital witness: Using open source information for human rights investigation, documentation and accountability* (Oxford University Press, 2019).

Gallavin, C & Mason, S 'Hearsay' in Mason, S & Seng, D (eds) *Electronic evidence* (Institute of Advanced Legal Studies 2017).

Seng, D & Mason, S 'Hearsay' in Seng, D & Mason, S (eds) in *Electronic evidence and electronic signatures* (Institute of Advanced Legal Studies, University of London 2021).

Journal Articles

Gilliland, J 'The admissibility of social media evidence' (2013) 39 *Litigation* 20.

Gorman, WK 'The admissibility of social media evidence in Canada: Part 2: The Canada Evidence Act' (2021) 57 *Court Review: Journal of the American Judges Association.*

Grimm, PW, Bergstrom, YL & O'Toole-Loureiro, MM 'Authentication of social media evidence' (2013) 36 *American Journal of Trial Advocacy* 433.

Mehandru, N & Koenig, A 'ICTS, social media, & the future of human rights' (2019) 17 *Duke Law & Technology Review* 129.

O'Floinn, M & Ormerod, D 'Social networking material as criminal evidence' (2012) 7(7) *Criminal Law Review* 486.

International Instruments

OECD, 'Predictability and consistency of legislation,' 2023. Available: https://parportal.sigmaweb.org/areas/2/indicators/17/#:~:text=The%20consistency%20of%20laws%20is,of%20interpretatio n%20of%20business%20regulations, accessed 11 November 2023.

Rome Statute of the International Criminal Court, adopted on 17 July 1998, entered into force on 1 July 2002.

National Legislation, Policies and Bills

Kenya Information and Communication (Amendment) Bill, 2022.

Internet Sources

Crown Prosecution Service 'Social media and other electronic communications' 19 December 2022 https://www.cps.gov.uk/legal-guidance/social-media-and-other-electronic-communications.

Goldstraw-White, J 'Legal and policy framework for digital forensics: A resource for practitioners. A policy and practice briefing from the digital forensics and social media project funded by the Dawes Trust' September 2022 https://perpetuityresearch.com/wp-content/uploads/2022/09/Final-LegalProceduraland-Guidance.pdf.

Law Commission, 'Evidence in criminal proceedings: Hearsay and related topics' https://cloudplatforme218f50a4812967ba1215eaecede923f.s3.amazonaws.com/uploads/sites/30/2015/03/lc245_Legislating_the_Criminal_Code_Evidence_in_Criminal_Proceedings.pdf.

Trevisan, S 'Open-source evidence at a crossroad: the (pending) case against Mr Hassan at the International Criminal Court and the fundamental right to fair trial,' *Giurisprudenza Penale Web*, 27 January 2022 https://www.giurisprudenzapenale.com/2022/01/27/open-source-evidence-at-acrossroad-the-pendingcase-against-mr-hassan-at-the-international-criminal-court-and-thefundamental-right-to-fair-trial/.

Table of Cases

International Criminal Court

The Prosecutor v Al Hassan Ag Abdoul Aziz Ag Mohamed Ag Mahmoud, Trial Chamber X, ICC-01/12- 01/18-T-027-Red-ENG 21 September 2020.

The Prosecutor v Ali Muhammad Ali Abd-Al-Rahman ("Ali Kushayb") Trial Chamber I, ICC-02/05- 01/20 27 February 2023.

The Prosecutor v Germain Katanga, Trial Chamber II, ICC-01/04-01/07-2635 19 December 2010.

The Prosecutor v Jean-Pierre Bemba Gombo, Aime Kilolo Musamba, Jean-Jacques Mangenda Kabongo, Fidele Babala Wandu & AridoNarcisse , Trial Chamber VII, ICC-01/05-01/13-1498-Conf 30 November 2015.

National Case Law

United Kingdom

Amjad v Regina (2016) EWCA Crim 1618.
Khan v R (2015) EWCA Crim 1816.
McDonald v R, (2011) EWCA Crim 2933.
R v Kay (2017) EWCA Crim 2214.
R v Skinner (2005) EWCA Crim Crim 1439, (2006) Crim. L.R. 56.

United States of America

Griffin v State, 419 Md. 343, 19 A.3d 415 (2011)
Lorraine v Markel American Ins. Co. 241 F.R.D. 534 D. Md. (2007)
The People v Albert Jerome Beckley JR, 110 Cal. Rptr. 3d 362 Ct. App. (2010)
Tienda v State, 358 S.W.3d 633 Tex. Crim. App. (2012)

Canada

R v Aslami (2021) ONCA 249.
R v Hirsch, Saskatchewan Court of Appeal, 2017 SKCA 14.
R v Khelawon (2006) SCC 57.
R v Martin, the Court of Appeal for Newfoundland and Labrador, [2021] NLCA.
R. v Simpson (2007) ONCA 793, (2007) O.J. No. 4510.

Kenya

Abdullahi v Independent Electoral & Boundaries Commission & 3 others (Election Petition E006 of 2022) [2022] KEHC 15079 (KLR) (2 November 2022) (Ruling).
Francis Wambugu Mureithi v Owino Paul Ongili Babu & 2 others [2018] eKLR.
Idris Abdi Abdullahi v Ahmed Bashane & 2 others, [2018] eKLR.
Republic v Mark Lloyd Steveson, [2016] eKLR.

6 Conclusion and Recommendations

Conclusion

In light of the realisation that news often spreads faster on social media than through conventional media, and the unprecedented autonomy that comes with self-publishing, it has been observed that citizens are increasingly uploading vast amounts of digital imagery and videos to social media platforms to spread awareness of atrocities and human rights violations. As discussed in Chapter 1, McDermott *et al.* have acknowledged this potential of open source evidence to democratise the collection of evidence.[1] In that, it "allows access to a much broader range of sources and voices than would normally be consulted through traditional methods of information gathering."[2] Further, it has the ability to provide immediate access to evidence and thereby preserve evidence that might otherwise be lost or destroyed by the time investigators get involved.[3]

The importance of this information as evidence in legal proceedings has been underscored throughout this research. For instance, the International Criminal Court issued its first arrest warrant based entirely on evidence collected from social media against Mahmoud Mustafa Busayf Al-Werfalli on 15 August 2017. Similarly, some national jurisdictions such as the 28 member states of the European Union and Norway have been shown to use online open source information in trial proceedings. Furthermore, there is evidence of this usage within common law jurisdictions as evidenced by the discussions in Chapter 2 and in UN processes as evidenced by Chapter 3. Clearly, there is existing evidence to denote the fact that open source evidence could easily be harnessed to enhance accountability for human rights violations. And this was the premise that this research operated on within the context of Kenya, that is, that open source evidence can be harnessed to enhance accountability for human rights violations in Kenya.

1 McDermott *et al.* (n 366 above).
2 McDermott *et al.* (n 366 above).
3 Hamilton (n 37 above).

DOI: 10.4324/9781003770343-6

In spite of its apparent ubiquitous role in legal proceedings even within domestic jurisdictions, comparatively little has been written about the use of open source evidence within domestic common law jurisdictions. There is however an extensive presence of literature on how this type of evidence can be used in international legal proceedings and investigations. Accordingly, the dilemma as to how to design a process that will allow for these transformative impacts of open source evidence while at the same time answering the various procedural and technical questions that are attendant to such a process within a domestic common law jurisdiction still remains.

It is based on the foregoing that this research sought to contribute to the existing body of literature on open source evidence by filling those gaps. This research has contributed to the body of literature by providing a framework through which open source evidence can be used in legal proceedings in Kenya to enhance accountability for human rights violations. This research further asserts that even though this framework specifically focuses on Kenya, it can certainly be adapted for use in other domestic common law jurisdictions.

Summary of Key Findings

This research set out to determine how open source evidence, which has been demonstrated as having the potential to radically transform the way investigations are conducted, and how information is collected and analysed, can be harnessed to enhance accountability for human rights violations in Kenya. In order to do this, various questions were raised in the research. The overarching research question was: How can open source evidence be harnessed to enhance accountability for human rights violations in Kenya? To adequately answer this question, further questions had to be posed. In aligning with the TWAIL framework on the fact that international standards affect domestic processes, it was first critical to ascertain the prevailing standards at the international level.[4] Thus, the first two research questions sought to assess: "what guidance is available on the use of open source evidence in legal processes from other national jurisdictions?" and "what guidance is available from international case law and the practice of UN human rights investigations to date?"

The next set of questions was context specific; this too is in line with the TWAIL framework's clarion call, as discussed extensively in Chapter 1, that the only way to ensure that standard setting is devoid of traditional hegemonic tendencies characteristic of international law is to make certain that the idiosyncrasies of a particular domestic jurisdiction are taken into consideration. The third question therefore sought to assess whether Kenya's legal framework is suitable in relation to open source evidence. Once the *status quo* was ascertained by answering that question, the final question posed was, 'how

4 International is construed to mean the practices of other domestic jurisdictions and of international bodies.

should open source evidence be litigated and judicially evaluated in Kenyan courts?' These research questions then formed the chapter titles.

Accordingly, Chapter 2 sought to determine the available guidance on the use of open source evidence from the jurisprudence in other countries. This was done by conducting a comparative analysis of the national jurisprudence from leading common law jurisdictions, that is, England and Wales, Canada and the United States of America. The analysis sought to determine how questions of admissibility and authentication of open source evidence have been dealt with in these jurisdictions in order to glean best practices that would potentially influence the proposed framework from Kenya. The comparative analysis demonstrated that various domestic jurisdictions have interacted extensively with open source evidence in their legal processes and this was denoted by the presence of considerable judicial evaluation of questions that relate to the admissibility of open source evidence. It was similarly established that in these jurisdictions, the predominant themes in the judicial evaluation related to the authentication of open source evidence, questions regarding its form and categorisation, and discussions on exclusionary rules such as the rule against hearsay.

As to the specific findings of Chapter 2, the first finding from the comparative analysis was the substantiation of the fact that open source evidence has been admitted as evidence in courts in various domestic legal processes across the world. For instance, in some European countries such as Sweden, Germany, Finland and the Netherlands, evidence derived from digital open sources has been used to prosecute domesticated international crimes under the concept of universal jurisdiction. The best practices that can be gleaned from these jurisdictions are therefore limited. This notwithstanding, their inclusion in this analysis was still relevant as they serve as an exemplification of the acceptance of this type of evidence in national judicial processes. The use of user-generated video evidence to bring historical crimes to a domestic court in the Democratic Republic of Congo by eyeWitness, TRIAL and WITNESS in which two commanders of the Democratic Forces for the Liberation of Rwanda were found guilty of crimes against humanity and their victims were awarded reparation was also an apt example of its presence within the African region.[5]

The second finding from this chapter related to the comparative analysis of the practice of the leading common law jurisdictions such as England and Wales, Canada and the USA. This analysis revealed the presence of extensive interaction with open source evidence in their legal processes denoted by the

5 Ndayambaje Gilbert and Nizehimana Evariste, Tribunal Militaire de Garnison Bukavu (Bukavu Military Tribunal), RP No. 1215/2017, RMP No. 6043/YM/017, 2018; AS Macumu, "Bringing Historical Crimes to Domestic Court in the Democratic Republic of Congo," eyeWitness. Available: https://www.eyewitness.global/Bringing-historical-crimes-to-a-domestic-court-in-the-DRC, accessed 11 November 2023. It is important to highlight here that.

presence of considerable judicial evaluation of the admissibility and reliability of open source evidence. However, there were marked differences in the approaches taken by each jurisdiction in assessing the admissibility of open source evidence. In England and Wales, the assessment of whether the material is what it purports to be is based on "whatever way the court may approve." This denotes a lack of a common standard in the assessment of the admissibility of open source evidence in legal proceedings in England and Wales. Open source investigations were also discussed in the context of England and Wales. The research established the existence of an extensive legislative and regulative framework that governs these investigations. The concept of reasonable lines of enquiry was also highlighted as being essential to managing the voluminous nature of open source information.

In Canada, the authenticity threshold is "evidence capable of supporting a finding that the electronic evidence sought to be admitted is what it purports to be." This denotes the fact that the determination of the weight to be apportioned to an open source item is left to the judge for determination at the end, when balancing and weighing all the admitted evidence. For that reason, the only consideration at the admission stage is some evidence that is logically probative of whether the electronic document is what it purports to be.[6] The Canadian test has therefore been likened to the showing of a *prima facie* case for authenticity as opposed to full establishment of the same.[7] The threshold has consequently invited criticism as being low based on the fact that it does not limit how or by what means it may be met, and neither does it impose a particular standard for threshold admissibility.[8]

In the United States of America, there are two approaches to this assessment, the Maryland Approach which is generally considered as requiring a higher standard for the authentication of open source evidence, and the Texas Approach which is generally considered as requiring a lower standard. The Texas Approach requires the adducing party to simply adduce some evidence that the open source item is what it purports to be. Questions as to proof or accuracy of the open source item are only considered under the determination of the weight of the item and not as a determination of its admissibility. On the other hand, the Maryland Approach places a higher burden on the party that seeks to adduce the open source evidence. The adducing party is required to prove that the open source evidence has an *indicia* of authenticity in order for the evidence to be admissible. It was also underscored that these approaches are generally indicative of the practice in the states that follow the common law legal system and accordingly the cases that were analysed came from various appellate courts such as the California Court of Appeal, the Connecticut

6 Gorman (n 175 above) p 181.
7 *R v JV*, 2015 ONCJ 837, para. 10.
8 Gorman (n 175 above) p 181. See also, Silver (n 183 above).

Appellate Court, the Arizona Court of Appeal, the Michigan Court of Appeal and of course the Maryland and Texas Appellate Courts.

The analysis from the comparative study in Chapter 2 therefore showed a lack of standardised approach in the assessment of the admissibility of open source evidence. Furthermore, each approach revealed several issues that consequently became stumbling blocks to their complete inclusion in the proposed framework, as discussed.

Chapter 3 examined international case law and the practice of UN human rights investigations to answer the research question, "what guidance is available on the use of open source evidence in legal processes from international practice?" This was done by looking at the legal framework and relevant decisions of international criminal courts and tribunals. OHCHR official guidance was also analysed. This included the analysis of the Commissions of Inquiry and Fact-Finding Missions on International Human Rights and Humanitarian Law: Guidance and Practice and the Berkeley Protocol on Digital Open Source Investigations (Berkeley Protocol). Reports of UN-mandated human rights investigations such as the Independent International Commission of Inquiry on the Syrian Arab Republic, the Independent International Fact-Finding Mission on Myanmar (FFM), *inter alia,* were also reviewed. The overall aim of Chapter 4 was therefore to draw parallels between the discussed examples and to distill lessons that can inform the proposed framework for the use of open source evidence in Kenya.

This chapter established that there is a steady development of international practice from various legal, policy and investigative processes that can be studied comparatively in order to distill best practices. At the international and regional level, the ICC emerged as the leading source of judicial best practice. This is due to its substantial interaction with open source evidence in both the OTP investigations and judicial evaluation. However, it is of note that the Court is yet to pronounce itself conclusively and directly on open source evidence. This is because, thus far, no case that seeks to probe these issues has progressed to the hearing and judgment stages.

As far as open source investigations/evidence collection are concerned, the Berkeley Protocol emerged as the internationally accepted source of best practice. This is owing to the fact that it is a practical guide on the effective use of digital open source and information in investigating violations of, among other things, human rights law. In addition, it was noted that the OTP's methodology seems to follow that which has been enunciated in the Berkeley Protocol and primarily focuses on relevance, reliability, credibility and completeness of the open source item.

Non-judicial investigative bodies mandated by UN organs have been shown to also use open source information and evidence in their investigations. Examples of these bodies include: the Independent International Fact-Finding Mission on Myanmar, the Independent International Commission of Inquiry on the protests in the Occupied Palestinian Territory, Commissions of Inquiry into the Syrian Arab Republic, Libya, Sri Lanka, Yemen, Burundi and South Sudan. This has consequently fed into various judicial processes such as the investigation in Myanmar which resulted in a case before the ICJ. Conversely, this evidence has been used by these investigative bodies to make legal findings. For instance, the Commission of Inquiry in the Occupied Palestinian Territory has used open source evidence to substantiate the violation of international human rights by the IFS. Regrettably, these reports have not provided any substantive disclosure of the steps that were taken by the investigative bodies to authenticate the open source material.

The OHCHR has also recognised the emergence and significance of this type of evidence, noting its importance in providing an insight into modern conflicts. To wit, open source evidence has been included in the OHCHR's "Commissions of Inquiry and Fact-Finding Missions on International Human Rights and Humanitarian Law: Guidance and Practice" document.

Beyond the best practice that can be gleaned from these discussions, this chapter also established the existence of support for one of this research's contentions. That open source evidence is a type of evidence that the Kenyan legal system will have to contend with imminently, necessitating a framework for its use in legal practice.

Chapter 4 addressed the question that sought to assess whether Kenya's legal framework is suitable in relation to open source evidence. Accordingly, a survey that was based on a hypothetical case was conducted, targeting defence counsel, prosecutors, police investigators and judges. A systematic case study was also conducted to assess how open source evidence has been used in legal proceedings. The analysis of the data demonstrated that litigants and judicial actors in Kenya possess a good grasp of the concept of open source evidence. The data also revealed that the same standards apply when adducing 'normal' digital evidence and open source evidence in Kenya. This means that the admissibility of open source evidence is currently governed by sections 78A and 106B of the Evidence Act.

It was, however, evident that a reliance on this legal framework to assess the admissibility of open source evidence, especially the anonymously posted open source evidence, is not sufficient. This is because, in such situations, if that evidence is not corroborated, the court may not admit it due to a lack of sufficient probative value. Therefore, the weight to be attached to open source evidence would be dependent on the fulfilling of the threshold set out in section 78A as read together with section 106B.

The data showed that in order for open source evidence to be admissible and reliable, it has to be authenticated. Further, the need to have the original author of the open source material to adduce it in court was emphasised. The existence of expert evidence and other independent corroboration to confirm the credibility of open source evidence was also deemed crucial. The important considerations in as far as authentication is concerned, therefore, are to ensure the integrity of the open source material, the underlying chain of custody and providing an opportunity for the open source evidence to be tested through cross-examination.

As far as the majority of the respondents were concerned, the current legal framework in Kenya is not sufficient to support the use of evidence that has been gathered from social media, within circumstances such as in the hypothetical case. Relatedly, the Kenya Information and Communication (Amendment) Bill, 2022 is under discussion to form a regulatory regime for social media in Kenya. To wit, the predominant opinion is that it has the potential to ultimately impact the use of evidence derived from social media in Kenya as it seeks to regulate social media. Therefore, there is a need for a legal framework that provides guidance on the admissibility of open source evidence, provides clarity on how this evidence can be authenticated, and how the probative value of this type of evidence can be assessed.

Chapter 5 addressed the final research question which sought to determine how open source evidence should be litigated and judicially evaluated in Kenyan courts. The assessment established that section 78A of the Evidence Act provides a legal foundation for the admissibility of open source evidence in Kenya. On the other hand, section 106B of the Evidence Act provides for the assessment of the weight to be apportioned to open source evidence. However, this legal framework is wrought with challenges that largely relate to the fact that these sections were conceptualised to cater for traditional digital and electronic evidence. The reliance on the current legal framework, despite the challenges, would have a deleterious effect on the use of open source evidence in legal proceedings in Kenya.

In order to provide a solution that addresses these challenges, a tripartite framework that is based on the overarching themes of this research was proposed. This was based on the conclusion that maintaining the *status quo* would result in a situation where valuable evidence from open sources is not considered because it is either “overlooked, under-analysed, or not analysed at all” due to the lack of an adequate admissibility framework, thus impeding the benefits that can be harnessed from this type of evidence.[9] Furthermore, the framework was cognisant of the fact that, within the Kenyan context and based on the findings of Chapter 4, an overhaul of the entire evidentiary framework was not necessary in order to make it more suitable for the use of open source evidence.

Accordingly, the first part of the framework proposes a legal framework that would enable the use of open source evidence in legal proceedings, even in instances where this material is posted anonymously. The second part of the framework focuses on an authentication test. The test incorporates steps that can be followed to systematically adduce open source evidence and to

9 JW Hak, “Non-textual Evidence in International Criminal Prosecutions: Discovering the Best Practices for Audiovisual Materials in a Digital Age,” unpublished PhD thesis, Leiden University, 2023, p 243.

determine its admissibility. These proposals were mainly hinged towards an adjudicator's interpretation of the existing legal provisions based on a set of tests as seen in Chapter 5. The third and final part of the framework focused on open source investigations in Kenya and proposed a framework that reflects both the prevailing international best practices and particularities of the investigatory landscape in Kenya. A framework that targets the investigatory part was provided based on the accepted fact that investigatory practices will ultimately impact the admissibility of open source evidence.

It is important to highlight here that the proposed framework differs from the approaches taken by the international court and the practice of the other national jurisdictions due to various reasons. Firstly, and as elaborated extensively throughout this research, due to the theoretical framework that underpins it, it is important that any proposed framework that seeks to influence the Kenyan legal system takes into consideration the idiosyncrasies of this system. Thus, an analysis of the Kenyan legal space revealed that the best way to ensure its suitability for the use of open source evidence was through judge-led amendments as opposed to overhauling the evidentiary laws. This is because there already exists a sufficient foundation and all that is needed is an interpretation of these provisions to enable the integration of open source evidence.

The other reason that informed the difference in approach is the fact that there are obviously clear distinctions between the nature of proceedings at the ICC and national proceedings in Kenya. That is, the ICC favours the civil legal system due to its flexible approach to evidentiary processes in that "the compromise was to eschew generally the technical formalities of the common law system of admissibility of evidence in favour of the flexibility of the civil law system."[10] This limitation necessitated a cautious application of its approach on the evaluation of open source evidence in the consequent development of the proposed framework for Kenya. Furthermore, due to its nature as an international court, the admissibility standard is generally low compared to a common law country like Kenya and the judges have significant discretion with respect to evidentiary matters.[11]

The reason for a departure in approach with the national comparators derives from the fact that most of the comparable national examples that were analysed related significantly to a particular type of open source evidence, that is, communications involving either the accused or the victim, whereas this research focuses on instances where open source information is imputed with evidentiary value in the absence of a witness. This variance therefore limited the extent of transferability of the approaches.

10 *Prosecutor v Jean-Pierre Bemba Gombo*, Trial Chamber III, "Decision on the Admission into Evidence of Materials Contained in the Prosecution's List of Evidence," ICC-01/05-01/08, 19 November 2010, p 17.

11 Rule 63(2) of the Rules and Article 69(4) of the Rome Statute; Khan *et al.* (n 306 above).

Despite efforts to ensure that the analysis of the topic is thorough, there are some limitations to this research which arose as a direct consequence of the methodology that was employed, as was highlighted in the introduction. The data collection was constrained in four respects: the first constraint related to the sampling in that some targeted respondents were not able to take part in the study due to time constraints. The second limitation related to the fact that only a small number of respondents took part in the study; hence, the findings are anecdotal. The third limitation derives from the fact that the research used purposive sampling, and there thus exists a selection bias towards respondents who are known to have a measure of understanding of digital evidence generally. The final limitation relates to the systematic case study that was conducted in Kenya. This is because there were scant reported cases that directly probed this research's objective and fit within its parameters, as all cases at the lower court level are unreported. However, despite these limitations, the data was still able to disclose sufficient findings to enable an adequate assessment of whether the Kenyan legal system is suitable for the use of open source evidence, as seen in the foregoing discussions.

Lastly, it is important to also acknowledge that a discussion of the admissibility of open source evidence within a domestic legal system, especially a common law one, is extensive and quite multifaceted. Accordingly, in as far as implications for future research are concerned, there exists room for future research which can target a broader section of legal practitioners, for instance by surveying the entire Law Society of Kenya. Closely related to this, future research can benefit from a comparative design between legal practitioners who have a good grasp of digital evidence versus those who do not to explore similarities and differences between these groups to determine whether the proposed framework needs to be varied further to accommodate both groups. Furthermore, future research could also include an assessment of whether all open source evidence in Kenya should be submitted within the regime of digital and electronic evidence, as has been proposed by this research. Or whether the definition of open source evidence can be expanded, beyond the definition that is used in this research, to consequently assess whether there is a need for developing a separate framework for audio-visual open source evidence within the Kenyan context.

Recommendations

In order to provide achievable policy strategies and targets with a view to ensuring that the proposed framework can be used to influence practice vis-à-vis the use of open source evidence in Kenya, the following recommendations can be explored to promote the realisation of this goal.

The first recommendation is directed to the Government of Kenya. As noted earlier, states bear the primary responsibility under international law to protect their populations from human rights violations. It is based on this obligation that the development of legislation and their consequent implementation derives. Accordingly, this research recommends that there should be law reform that targets the Evidence Act. Specifically, section 106B of this Act should be amended, as per the proposed framework in Chapter 5. As such an amendment will bring the Act to par with technological advancements by creating room for an interpretation that takes into consideration the impact of these advancements on digital and electronic evidence.

It is crucial to highlight that these amendments can be made through other legislations and that they do not require the Evidence Act itself to go through the law review process. That is, in light of the fact that the KICA (Amendment) Bill 2022 is currently undergoing deliberations that are targeted at amending it, advantage can be taken of this process and it can be an avenue through which the proposed amendment to section 106B can be made. This is keeping in mind that the Evidence Act has been previously amended in this manner. For instance, the inclusion of section 78A to the Evidence Act was done through the Security Laws (Amendment) Act, 2014.

The second recommendation similarly relates to the legal framework and is directed to the Judiciary of Kenya, as an arm of the Government. This recommendation urges judicial officers to interpret the Evidence Act based on the framework proposed in Chapter 5 above. That is, judicial officers should interpret the Evidence Act as already containing provisions that support the assessment of admissibility of open source evidence in legal proceedings in Kenya, as discussed throughout this research. Such a supportive interpretation by judicial officers will ensure that the use of open source evidence is ensconced in legal proceedings in Kenya.

The justification for employing the proposed framework is that it provides a standardised approach to the determination of the admissibility of open source evidence in Kenya, thus preventing a fragmented approach. In that, the framework reflects prevailing best practices drawn from the comparative case study, data from the field which includes a survey of members of the Law Society of Kenya, respondents from the Office of the Director of Public Prosecutions, investigators from the Department of Criminal Investigations, and judges.

The third recommendation calls upon judicial officers to be vigilant against the misuse of open source evidence whenever it is adduced as evidence in legal proceedings. Indeed, the court cannot move *suo moto*. However, the Constitution of Kenya of 2010 has a very clear emphasis on the requirement that the aims of justice should outweigh procedural considerations, as illustrated in the foregoing discussions. Accordingly, they should be able to employ this vigilance in that adducing doctored or manipulated open source evidence is an offence under Chapter 11 of the Penal Code of Kenya. Section 108 of the Penal Code provides that "any person, who in any judicial proceeding, or for the purpose of instituting any judicial proceeding, knowingly gives false testimony touching on any matter which is material to any question then pending in that proceeding or intended to be raised in that proceeding, is guilty of ... perjury." Further, sub-section (2) states that "any person who aids, abets, counsels, procures or suborns another person to commit perjury is guilty of the misdemeanour termed subornation of perjury." The offence of perjury attracts a punishment of seven years' imprisonment under section 110 of the Penal Code.

It is important to also clarify that there is a basic requirement of a criminal offence in Kenya that "a person cannot be convicted unless some element of mental culpability is proved with respect to each material element of the offence," that is, the *mens rea* element of an offence must be proved.[12] Therefore, in instances where the intent of the "manipulator" and/or "misattributor" of the open source evidence was not to influence a judicial proceeding, then such lack of intent would be an important factor in the determination of their criminal culpability. Nonetheless, it is hypothesised that the deterrent effect caused by the risk of a seven-year imprisonment term can be instrumental in ensuring that open source evidence is not misused in legal proceedings in Kenya.

The fourth recommendation targets the regulatory mechanisms that regulate actors within the judicial sector. For advocates, that is, prosecutors and defence counsel, they are regulated by a Bar Association known as the Law Society of Kenya. While the regulatory framework for investigators is under the auspices of the Department of Criminal Investigations, it is recommended that a duty of care is imposed on all judicial actors, as an aspect of existing obligations of the professional code of conduct, to ensure that only authentic open source evidence is adduced in legal proceedings.[13] So that any complicity in the use of manipulated open source evidence will be considered a violation of the existing professional code of conduct, inviting the relevant consequences for such a breach.

In order to support the observance of this duty of care, it is recommended that guidelines should be provided to regulate the use of open source evidence in legal proceedings. For the Judiciary, it is recommended that the guidelines are created by the office of the Chief Justice under the framework of Practice Directions. This is because such Directions will have a far-reaching impact as all court users, including defence counsel, prosecutors and police investigators, would be subject to them. Similar guidelines should also be created for investigators to provide guidance on open source investigations. These can be modelled after the Association of Chief Police Officers (ACPO) Good Practice Guide for Digital Evidence that guides the police in England and Wales, as discussed in Chapter 2.

12 See for instance the case of *RC v R* [2005] 2 KLR on the mental element requirement of intention. See also generally, William Musyoka, *Criminal Law*, Law Africa (2013).

13 This proposal of a duty of care has been canvassed extensively by B van der Sloot, Y Wagensveld & B Koops, "Deepfakes: The Legal Challenges of a Synthetic Society," Tilburg Institute for Law and Technology, November 2021.

The final recommendation targets a broader group that is classified in this research as stakeholders. This recommendation focuses on the need for capacity building and awareness-raising initiatives across the justice sector. Stakeholders from civil society organisations such as Amnesty International, policymakers and academia can convene engagements with judicial officers, legal practitioners and other court users for the purposes of capacity building and raising awareness. These initiatives can be in the form of training that targets all these different actors. Accordingly, judges can be trained and engaged with through the Judicial Training Institute. Defence counsels and prosecutors can be trained and engaged with through the Continuous Professional Development system, under the auspices of the Law Society of Kenya. While the investigators can be trained under the aegis of the Department of Criminal Investigations.

The justification for such initiatives is that they provide a good platform through which stakeholders can engage with judicial actors, legal practitioners and other court users to create awareness and enhance their knowledge on the use of open source evidence in legal proceedings. These forums are also an ideal opportunity to tackle contemporary issues that impact open source evidence such as the rise of artificial intelligence. Lastly, these initiatives provide fertile ground for dialogue between the stakeholders and actors within the Kenyan legal space that may result in the development of context-specific best practices. This will have the effect of enriching knowledge on the use of open source evidence thus enhancing its acceptability and use in legal proceedings in Kenya.

Bibliography

Books

McDermott, Y Proving international crimes (Oxford University Press 2023)

William Musyoka, CriminalLaw, Law Africa (2013)

Journal Articles

Gorman, WK 'The admissibility of social media evidence in Canada: Part 2: The Canada Evidence Act' (2021) 57 *Court Review: Journal of the American Judges Association.*

Hamilton, RJ 'User-generated evidence' (2018) 57(1) *Columbia Journal of Transnational Law* 1–61.

van derSloot, B, Wagensveld, Y & Koops, B 'Deepfakes: The legal challenges of a synthetic society,' Tilburg Institute for Law and Technology, November 2021.

International Instruments

Rome Statute of the International Criminal Court, adopted on 17 July 1998, entered into force on 1 July 2002.

Table of Cases

International Criminal Court

The Prosecutor v Jean-Pierre Bemba Gombo, Aimé Kilolo Musamba, Jean-Jacques Mangenda Kabongo, Fidèle Babala Wandu and Narcisse Arido, Trial Chamber VII, ICC-01/05-01/13-1524, 14 December 2015.

International Tribunals

Ndayambaje & Evariste, RP No. 1215/2017, RMP No. 6043/YM/017, Military Tribunal Bukavu 21 September 2018.

National Case Law

Kenya

RC v R [2005] 2 KLR

Canada

R v JV (2015) ONCJ 837.

Other Sources

JW, Hak, 'Non-textual evidence in international criminal prosecutions: Discovering the best practices for audiovisual materials in a digital age', unpublished PhD thesis, Leiden University, 2023.

Appendices

Appendix 1: Questionnaire – Defence Counsel

Reasearch Project:

An Assessment of How Open Source Evidence Is Being Litigated and Judicially Evaluated in Kenya

By Claire Adionyi

Questionnaire – Defence Counsel

- This questionnaire will be uploaded onto an online form, google forms and the link will be shared with the research participants *via* email.
- Before commencing to fill out the questionnaire, the respondent will be required to read and sign the Informed Consent Form.
- The Questionnaire will take approximately one hour to answer.

Themes

- Current uptake and use of social media evidence in litigation and judicial evaluation of human rights cases in Kenya.
- How is this evidence categorised?
- How has it been used, if at all?
- Is there a legal framework in place that would support the use of evidence that has been gathered from social media?
- Assessment of the necessary conditions for the uptake of social media evidence

Aims

- Assess how evidence derived from social media platforms is categorised in Kenya

- Assess the extent to which evidence derived from social media platforms has been used by defence counsel in Kenya.
- Assess the challenges that defence counsel may face in an attempt to adduce evidence that has been derived from social media platforms.
- Assess whether there is a legal framework in place that would support the use of evidence that has been gathered from social media.

Preliminary

1) Are you a litigating advocate?
    - Yes
    - No
2) If yes, how long have you been a litigating advocate?
    - Less than 3 years
    - 3 to 5 years
    - 5 to 10 years
    - More than 10 years
3) Have you appeared before the Criminal and the Constitutional & Human Rights Division?
    - Yes
    - No
4) Have you ever adduced digital evidence? Responses:
    - Yes
    - No
5) Have you ever used evidence that has been obtained from social media? Responses:
    - Yes
    - No

    If yes, please explain what type of evidence you used: ________________
    ____

    If yes, please explain how you used this evidence: ________________
    ____

6) Do you think there is a difference between "digital evidence" and "social media evidence" as

categories?

Yes? If yes, please explain why you think so:
____

No? _____ If not, please explain why you think so:
I don't know

Hypothetical Case

The ODPP seeks to submit six videos that have been downloaded from YouTube as corroborative evidence to some other piece of evidence in a human rights violations case before the Constitutional & Human Rights Court. As the Prosecution does not have direct access to YouTube's servers or data, it relied on videos that had been downloaded from a user's account on YouTube. The Prosecution did not provide metadata, such as time stamps or IP addresses of the uploaders, to assist in the authentication of the videos. Consequently, there was no way to either determine the identity of the person who posted them or the veracity of the content of the videos.

The facts of the case was that the said six videos had been posted anonymously on YouTube and were downloaded by an investigator from the Criminal Investigations Department (CID) thereby constituting their "ordinary activities." There was therefore no information as to who took the videos, when they were taken, where they were taken and who posted them. Furthermore, no information was provided on how the Prosecution (through the CID) had gone about extracting the videos from YouTube and consequently verifying them.

The ODPP has called one witness, the CID Investigator (PW1) to persuade the court that the videos were admissible in evidence, pursuant to the provisions of the Evidence Act. The petitioner also provided the court with links to the said videos.

NOTE: The following questions are to give the researcher an insight into the thinking behind your preparation for this case: arguments, pre-empting the questions that the ODPP and the court would ask and the responses given. The overall goal being to establish how you would deal with issues of: authentication, relevance, probative value and prejudicial effect on trial fairness when dealing with social media evidence.

7) How would you categorise this evidence?

____

____

8) The Prosecution has failed to provide any explanation or justification as to why this material is not being tendered through the original author of the material. How would you as a defence counsel address this issue?

Please explain: ____________________________________

I do not know: ____________________________________

9) Would you argue against the admissibility of these videos as evidence?

If yes, how would you structure your argument keeping in mind the provisions of the Evidence Act under section 78A and 106B?

10) What further information would you have expected to accompany the videos that had been downloaded by the CID investigator? (In addition to the video file, what other data would you expect to have been adduced in court?)

Please explain ______________________________

None______________________________

11) Would you still require the ODPP to call the investigator to testify in relation to the methodology and results of their investigation?

If yes, why? ______________________________

Ifno,why?______________________________

12) Would you have been able to interpret any other data relating to how the videos were acquired, should it have been provided by the CID investigator?

If the answer is Yes, please explain how you would have interpreted this data.

____

If the answer is No, to whom would you turn for assistance in interpreting such data? Please explain.

____

13) In your opinion, does the admission of this evidence interfere with your client's right to a fair trial?

If the answer is Yes, which particular component of the right to a fair trial?

____

Please also explain how you would approach the argument for the rectification of this violation and/or request for a counterbalance.

____

If the answer is No, please explain why you think so.

____

____

14) In the event that the six videos supported your client's case, how would you have addressed the issue of credibility of sources and reliability of the content?

Please explain:

____

I don't know

____

____

15) Do you think the current legal framework is sufficient to support the use of evidence that has been gathered from social media within circumstances such as in the hypothetical case?

Yes? ________ If yes, please explain why you think so:

____

If yes, in your opinion, are there any inconsistencies between the said legal framework and this type of evidence?

____

If No, please explain why you think so:

16) In your opinion, do you think the Kenya Information and Communication (Amendment) Bill, 2019 will impact the use of evidence derived from social media in Kenya?

Yes? Please explain why you think so:

____

____

If No, please explain why you think so:

____

____

I don't know

____

____

17) In your opinion, what are the challenges that practitioners would face in an attempt to adduce evidence that has been derived from social media platforms in Kenya?

____

____

Additional Information

Do you have any additional comments you would like to provide with respect to the use of evidence that has been derived from social media platforms?

In case we need further clarification on your responses, are you okay if we reach out to you for further discussions?

If yes, kindly share your email address and contact number.

Appendix 2: Key Informant Interview Guide – Prosecutors

Research Project:

An Assessment of How Open Source Evidence Is Being Litigated and Judicially Evaluated in Kenya

By Claire Adionyi

Key Informant Interview Guide – Prosecutors

- The questions below are meant to guide the key informant interview with prosecutors.
- Before commencing the interview, the Principal Investigator will begin by introducing the project and addressing the Informed Consent issues. The interview will commence once the Informant has read and signed the Informed Consent Form.
- The interview will take approximately 1 hour.

Themes

- Current uptake and use of social media evidence in litigation and judicial evaluation of human rights cases in Kenya.
- How is this evidence categorised?
- How has it been used, if at all?
- Is there a legal framework in place that would support the use of evidence that has been gathered from social media?
- Assessment of the necessary conditions for the uptake of social media evidence

Aims

- Assess how evidence derived from social media platforms is categorised in Kenya
- Assess the extent to which evidence derived from social media platforms has been used by defence counsel in Kenya.
- Assess the challenges that defence counsel may face in an attempt to adduce evidence that has been derived from social media platforms.
- Assess whether there is a legal framework in place that would support the use of evidence that has been gathered from social media.

Part A – Preliminary Questions

1. How long have you been a prosecutor?

2. Have you ever appeared before the Criminal and the Constitutional & Human Rights Division?
3. Have you worked on cases from the Independent Policing Oversight Authority (IPOA)?
4. Have you ever adduced digital evidence?
5. Have you ever used evidence that has been obtained from social media?
6. If the answer to 5 is yes, what type of evidence?
7. What are the main differences, if any, between "digital evidence" and "social media evidence" as

categories?

8. Have you ever heard of the term open source evidence?

    - What do you understand the term to mean?

Part B – Hypothetical Case

The ODPP seeks to submit six videos that have been downloaded from YouTube as corroborative evidence to some other piece of evidence in a human rights violations case before the Constitutional & Human Rights Court. As the Prosecution does not have direct access to YouTube's servers or data, it relied on videos that had been downloaded from a user's account on YouTube. The Prosecution did not provide metadata, such as time stamps or IP addresses of the uploaders, to assist in the authentication of the videos. Consequently, there was no way to either determine the identity of the person who posted them or the veracity of the content of the videos.

The facts of the case was that the said six videos had been posted anonymously on YouTube and were downloaded by an investigator from the Criminal Investigations Department (CID) thereby constituting their "ordinary activities." There was therefore no information as to who took the videos, when they were taken, where they were taken and who posted them. Furthermore, no information was provided on how the Prosecution (through the CID) had gone about extracting the videos from YouTube and consequently verifying them.

The ODPP has called one witness, the CID Investigator (PW1) to persuade the court that the videos were admissible in evidence, pursuant to the provisions of the Evidence Act. The petitioner also provided the court with links to the said videos.

NOTE: The following questions are to give the researcher an insight into the thinking behind your preparation for this case: arguments, preempting the questions that the respondent and the court would ask and the responses given. The overall goal being to establish how you would deal with issues of: authentication, relevance, probative value and prejudicial effect on trial fairness when dealing with social media evidence.

9. As the prosecutor seeking to tender this as evidence, how would you address admissibility and the issue of the probative value of these videos, keeping in mind the provisions of the Evidence Act under section 78A and 106B?
10. An inferential step will almost always be required to connect the dots and to link the perpetrator to the atrocity on the ground – how would you achieve this?
11. The Prosecution has also failed to provide any explanation or justification as to why this material is not being tendered through the original author – how would you, as a prosecutor, respond to this question?
12. How do you maintain the right to a fair trial?

    - Especially the human rights principle of equality of arms, the related right to examine witnesses and challenge evidence, and the right to be tried without undue delay – How would you address this with respect to open source evidence?
    - How do you counterbalance?
13. It will be essential for the fairness of proceedings for the Prosecution to involve the defence earlier in the process and analysis of raw data as required by rules on discovery and/or pretrial conferences.

    - What challenges do you perceive will arise from such a requirement?
    - How will you address these challenges?
14. How would you deal with the issue of exclusion of improperly obtained evidence, especially if irregular investigative measures have been used?
15. How would you ensure the balancing of the right to privacy in the investigative process?
16. How would you respond to a challenge by the respondent with respect to the credibility of sources in light of the anonymity of the source and questions on the reliability of content?
17. How would you preserve this evidence?
18. Do you think the current legal framework is sufficient to support the use of evidence that has been gathered from social media within circumstances such as in the hypothetical case?
19. Do you think the Kenya Information and Communication (Amendment) Bill, 2019 will impact the use of evidence derived from social media in Kenya?
20. What are the challenges that practitioners would face in an attempt to adduce evidence that has been derived from social media platforms?

Appendix 3: Key Informant Interview Guide – Investigators

Research Project:

An Assessment of How Open Source Evidence Is Being Litigated and Judicially Evaluated in Kenya

By Claire Adionyi

Key Informant Interview Guide – Investigators

- The questions below are meant to guide the key informant interview with investigators.
- Before commencing the interview, the Principal Investigator will begin by introducing the project and addressing the Informed Consent issues. The interview will commence once the Informant has read and signed the Informed Consent Form.
- The interview will take approximately one hour.

Themes

- Current uptake and use of social media evidence in the investigation of human rights cases in Kenya.
- How is this evidence categorised?
- How has it been used, if at all?
- Is there a legal framework in place that would support such investigations?
- Assessment of the necessary conditions for the uptake of social media evidence

Aims

- Assess how evidence derived from social media platforms is categorised in Kenya
- Assess the extent to which evidence derived from social media platforms has been used in the investigation of human rights cases in Kenya.
- Assess whether there is a legal framework in place that would support such investigations.
- Assess the challenges that investigators face in these investigations.

Part A – Preliminary Questions

1. How long have you worked as an investigator? With the DCI?
2. Do you use evidence derived from social media platforms in your day-to-day investigations? Please speak to that process?

- What does the process entail?
- Do you require authority to conduct such a search beforehand?
- Or does such a search fit into your overall authority to conduct investigations?

3. At what stage of an investigation do you resort to these platforms? What is the sequence of an investigation that involves deriving evidence from a social media platform?
   - Does it come at the beginning, the end, or does it depend on the specific investigator?
   - How important is it in investigatory processes?
4. Are there any evidentiary rules and standards that you are required to observe in that process?
5. How would you deal with the authentication, provenance and chain of custody issues?
   - Through external indicators, such as?
6. How do you preserve this evidence that has been derived from social media platforms?
7. The amount of available data continues to grow exponentially with increased connectivity and integration of portable electronics. This will overload investigative resources and create an unmanageable digital evidence backlog – how do you intend to deal with that?
8. Since the creation of social media accounts such as a Facebook account does not require any valid identity information, it is impossible to forensically ascertain, even on a *prima facie* basis, that a Facebook account under a certain name is attributable to a person of the same name.
   - How will you evaluate credibility of sources and reliability of this content?
9. How do you balance the legal rights that are affected in such a process, such as the right to privacy?
10. Have you ever presented this evidence to a prosecutor as part of the police file?
    - Were there any challenges that you faced in trying to include that evidence in the Police File?
    - How did you mitigate these challenges in future investigations?
11. Have you ever appeared in court as a witness to speak to the step-by-step process that you undertook in deriving evidence from social media platforms?
    - What questions were posed by the defence counsel with respect to the investigatory steps?
    - In your opinion based on practice, are these the same standards that apply when trying to adduce "normal" digital evidence?
12. Have you received training/specialised training in investigating social media platforms for information to be used as evidence in court?
13. Would such a training be desirable?

14. How do you deal with the psychosocial impact of constantly being exposed to such graphic material?
15. Is there a need to adapt your policies and practices to address novel legal issues involving digital evidence?
16. Have you ever heard of the term open source investigations?
    - What do you understand the term to mean?
      -Have you used it in the course of your investigations?
17. Have you ever heard of the Berkeley Protocol on Digital Open Source Investigations?
    - Do you use it to guide your open source investigations?
    - Are you willing to take part in a training on this Protocol?

Part B – Hypothetical Case

The ODPP seeks to submit six videos that have been downloaded from YouTube as corroborative evidence to some other piece of evidence in a human rights violations case before the Constitutional & Human Rights Court. As the Prosecution does not have direct access to YouTube's servers or data, it relied on videos that had been downloaded from a user's account on YouTube. The facts of the case was that the said six videos, which had been circulating on various social media platforms, had initially been posted anonymously on YouTube and were downloaded by an investigator from the Criminal Investigations Department (DCI) thereby constituting their "ordinary activities."

The ODPP has called one witness, the DCI Investigator (PW1) to persuade the court that the videos were admissible in evidence, pursuant to the provisions of the Evidence Act. The petitioner also provided the court with links to the said videos. You are the DCI Investigator.

18. How would you categorise this evidence?
19. As PW1, based on your practical experience as an investigator, how would you persuade the court on the issue of authentication given the fact that the video was posted anonymously? (Here, the researcher will guide the respondent towards a discussion of issues relating to metadata, such as time stamps or IP addresses of the uploaders).
    - How would you respond to the defence counsel's question on the fact that the defendant's right to confront their accuser has been violated in light of the fact that the videos were posted anonymously?
20. As PW1, based on your practical experience as an investigator, how would you persuade the court on the issue of reliability? (Here, the researcher will steer the respondent towards a discussion of how they had gone about extracting the videos from YouTube and consequently verifying them.

21. Are you aware of any legal framework that is in place in support of the use of open source evidence within circumstances such as in the hypothetical case?
    - If yes, please give examples
    - If yes, in your opinion, is this legal framework effective?
    - If yes, in your opinion, are there any inconsistencies between the said legal framework and this type of evidence?
    - If no, what legal framework do you usually rely on to support your investigations that relate to deriving evidence from social media platforms?
22. In your opinion, what are the challenges that investigators face in conducting investigations that entail deriving evidence from social media platforms?
    - How do you mitigate these challenges?

Appendix 4: Key Informant Interview Guide – Judge

Research Project:

An Assessment of How Open Source Evidence Is Being Litigated and Judicially Evaluated in Kenya

By Claire Adionyi

Key Informant Interview Guide – Judge

- The questions below are meant to guide the key informant interview with judges.
- Before commencing the interview, the Principal Investigator will begin by introducing the project and addressing the Informed Consent issues. The interview will commence once the Informant has read and signed the Informed Consent Form.
- The interview will take approximately 1 hour and 30 minutes.

Themes

- Current uptake and use of social media evidence in litigation and judicial evaluation of human rights cases in Kenya.
- How is this evidence categorised?
- How has it been used, if at all?
- Is there a legal framework in place that would support the use of evidence that has been gathered from social media?
- Assessment of the necessary conditions for the uptake of social media evidence

Aims

- Assess how evidence derived from social media platforms is categorised in Kenya
- Assess the extent to which evidence derived from social media platforms has been used by litigants in Kenya.
- Assess the challenges that the court may face in dealing with evidence that has been derived from social media platforms.
- Assess whether there is a legal framework in place that would support the use of evidence that has been gathered from social media.

Part A – Preliminary Questions

1. What are the main differences, if any, between "digital evidence" and "social media evidence" as categories?

2. Based on your experience in adjudication of disputes, are you comfortable with litigants adducing evidence that has been obtained from social media before you?
3. What do you understand the term open source evidence to mean?

Part B – Hypothetical Case

You were the presiding Judge in the case of **Ndwiga Steve Mbogo v Independent Electoral and Boundaries Commission & 2 others.**

Where, the petitioner sought to submit six videos that had been downloaded from YouTube and Facebook as evidence in support of his election petition. The petitioner called two witnesses, plaintiff witness 7 (PW7) and plaintiff witness 8 (PW8) to persuade the court that the videos were admissible in evidence, pursuant to the provisions of the Evidence Act. The petitioner also provided the court with links to the said videos. The facts of the case relevant to this study were: PW7, who is a law student, signed a certificate on 5th September 2017, indicating that the videos in question were downloaded by her. Having downloaded the videos, PW7 had made available to the court, both the hard-disc and the transcript. PW 7 also provided the particulars of the laptop which she used to download the videos. During cross-examination, PW7 informed the court: that she had downloaded the videos from YouTube and Facebook; that the videos had not been recorded by her, nor was she present when the videos were being recorded; that she did not know when the videos were recorded; that she would be unable to confirm whether or not the contents of the videos had been stage-managed; that she was unaware of the identity of the persons who had shot the videos; and, that she had no way of confirming whether or not the events captured actually occurred.

PW8 identified himself as an ICT expert who had completed a degree course on computer science and was yet to graduate. PW 8 said he obtained the videos from PW7 and also indicated that PW7 neither disclosed to him the identity of the person who shot the videos nor the identity of the person who had posted the videos on YouTube and Facebook. PW8 told the court that it was possible to identify the person who had posted the videos on YouTube and Facebook, however in this case he did not identify the person who had uploaded the videos. According to PW8, he could not tell either the time when, nor the location where the videos were taken. PW8 however informed the court that he had ability to verify whether or not the contents of the video were an act or a play stating that there is software which could enable him to determine the authenticity of the videos concluding that the said videos had not been edited. PW8 did not identify the equipment which had been used to shoot the videos.

The court ruled that video evidence from social media was inadmissible due to the fact that, among other things, downloading social media videos did not constitute part of the responsible person's 'ordinary activities' as required by Section 106 B (2) of the Evidence Act. The implication being that, for a litigant to adduce evidence obtained from social media, they would have to procure the services of an individual whose ordinary activities entails downloading media from these platforms. The Court did not interact with the technical questions surrounding the use of social media evidence due largely to procedural considerations.

How would you have ruled in this case, keeping in mind issues of authentication, reliability and the weight of the evidence, had the facts been as follows?

"the said six videos had been posted anonymously on Facebook and YouTube; the videos were downloaded by an investigator thereby constituting their 'ordinary activities'; they were adduced in court by a prosecutor or a human rights actor as corroborative evidence to some other piece of evidence in a human rights violations case. As the prosecution/human rights actor does not have direct access to YouTube and Facebook's servers or data, it relied on screenshots, which meant that the prosecution could not provide metadata, such as time stamps or IP addresses of the uploaders, to assist in the authentication of the photos. Consequently, there was no way to determine the identity of the person who posted them."

The next questions seek to assess how you would go about ruling on the authentication and reliability of this evidence.

4. How would you deal with the authentication, weight of evidence, and chain of custody issues
   - – Through external indicators, such as?
5. How will you evaluate credibility of sources (when the source is anonymous) and the reliability of content?
   - Would you require the investigator to testify as to the methodologies used during the online open- source investigation, when, where and how the video was found and how its contents were verified?
   - Why?
6. What type of corroborative evidence would you require for you to consider open source evidence to be authentic and reliable?
   - What if the OSE was posted anonymously?
   - No legislative framework that directly touches on OSE, so how would you bridge the gap?
7. In your opinion, does the admission of this evidence interfere with the right to a fair trial?
   - If the answer is Yes, which particular component of the right to a fair trial?
   - Please explain how you would approach the determination of the rectification of this violation and/or request for a counterbalance – equality of arms

8. Is the legislative framework in Kenya sufficient to support the use of such evidence in Kenya?
    - Or is there a need to adapt our policies and practices to address novel legal issues involving digital evidence?
9. What are the challenges that the Court would face in analysing evidence that has been derived from social media platforms?
10. Has the Judiciary received specialised training on dealing with evidence derived from social media platforms?
    - If not, would such training be desirable?

Appendix 5: Hypothetical Cases

Hypothetical Case for the Defence Counsels

The ODPP seeks to submit six videos that have been downloaded from YouTube as corroborative evidence to some other piece of evidence in a human rights violations case before the Constitutional & Human Rights Court. As the Prosecution does not have direct access to YouTube's servers or data, it relied on videos that had been downloaded from a user's account on YouTube. The Prosecution did not provide metadata, such as time stamps or IP addresses of the uploaders, to assist in the authentication of the videos. Consequently, there was no way to either determine the identity of the person who posted them or the veracity of the content of the videos.

The facts of the case were that the said six videos had been posted anonymously on YouTube and were downloaded by an investigator from the Department of Criminal Investigations (DCI) thereby constituting their "ordinary activities." There was therefore no information as to who took the videos, when they were taken, where they were taken and who posted them. Furthermore, no information was provided on how the Prosecution (through the DCI) had gone about extracting the videos from YouTube and consequently verifying them. The ODPP has called one witness, the DCI Investigator (PW1) to persuade the court that the videos were admissible in evidence, pursuant to the provisions of the Evidence Act. The petitioner also provided the court with links to the said videos.

Hypothetical Case for the Prosecutors

The ODPP seeks to submit six videos that have been downloaded from YouTube as corroborative evidence to some other piece of evidence in a human rights violations case before the Constitutional & Human Rights Court. As the Prosecution does not have direct access to YouTube's servers or data, it relied on videos that had been downloaded from a user's account on YouTube. The Prosecution did not provide metadata, such as time stamps or IP addresses of the uploaders, to assist in the authentication of the videos. Consequently, there was no way to either determine the identity of the person who posted them or the veracity of the content of the videos.The ODPP seeks to submit six videos that have been downloaded from YouTube as corroborative evidence to some other piece of evidence in a human rights violations case before the Constitutional & Human Rights Court. As the Prosecution does not have direct access to YouTube's servers or data, it relied on videos that had been downloaded from a user's account on YouTube. The Prosecution did not provide metadata, such as time stamps or IP addresses of the uploaders, to assist in the authentication of the videos. Consequently, there was no way to either determine the identity of the person who posted them or the veracity of the content of the videos.

The ODPP seeks to submit six videos that have been downloaded from YouTube as corroborative evidence to some other piece of evidence in a human rights violations case before the Constitutional & Human Rights Court. As the Prosecution does not have direct access to YouTube's servers or data, it relied on videos that had been downloaded from a user's account on YouTube. The Prosecution did not provide metadata, such as time stamps or IP addresses of the uploaders, to assist in the authentication of the videos. Consequently, there was no way to either determine the identity of the person who posted them or the veracity of the content of the videos.

The ODPP seeks to submit six videos that have been downloaded from YouTube as corroborative evidence to some other piece of evidence in a human rights violations case before the Constitutional & Human Rights Court. As the Prosecution does not have direct access to YouTube's servers or data, it relied on videos that had been downloaded from a user's account on YouTube. The Prosecution did not provide metadata, such as time stamps or IP addresses of the uploaders, to assist in the authentication of the videos. Consequently, there was no way to either determine the identity of the person who posted them or the veracity of the content of the videos.

The facts of the case were that the said six videos had been posted anonymously on YouTube and weredownloaded by an investigator from the DCI thereby constituting their "ordinary activities." There was therefore no information as to who took the videos, when they were taken, where they were taken and who posted them. Furthermore, no information was provided on how the Prosecution (through the DCI) had gone about extracting the videos from YouTube and consequently verifying them. The ODPP has called one witness, the DCI Investigator (PW1) to persuade the court that the videos were admissible in evidence, pursuant to the provisions of the Evidence Act. The petitioner also provided the court with links to the said videos.The facts of the case were that the said six videos had been posted anonymously on YouTube and weredownloaded by an investigator from the DCI thereby constituting their "ordinary activities." There was therefore no information as to who took the videos, when they were taken, where they were taken and who posted them. Furthermore, no information was provided on how the Prosecution (through the DCI) had gone about extracting the videos from YouTube and consequently verifying them. The ODPP has called one witness, the DCI Investigator (PW1) to persuade the court that the videos were admissible in evidence, pursuant to the provisions of the Evidence Act. The petitioner also provided the court with links to the said videos.

The facts of the case were that the said six videos had been posted anonymously on YouTube and were

downloaded by an investigator from the DCI thereby constituting their "ordinary activities." There was therefore no information as to who took the videos, when they were taken, where they were taken and who posted them. Furthermore, no information was provided on how the Prosecution (through the DCI) had gone about extracting the videos from YouTube and consequently verifying them. The ODPP has called one witness, the DCI Investigator (PW1) to persuade the court that the videos were admissible in evidence, pursuant to the provisions of the Evidence Act. The petitioner also provided the court with links to the said videos.

The facts of the case were that the said six videos had been posted anonymously on YouTube and were

downloaded by an investigator from the DCI thereby constituting their "ordinary activities." There was therefore no information as to who took the videos, when they were taken, where they were taken and who posted them. Furthermore, no information was provided on how the Prosecution (through the DCI) had gone about extracting the videos from YouTube and consequently verifying them. The ODPP has called one witness, the DCI Investigator (PW1) to persuade the court that the videos were admissible in evidence, pursuant to the provisions of the Evidence Act. The petitioner also provided the court with links to the said videos.

Hypothetical Case for the DCI Investigator

The ODPP seeks to submit six videos that have been downloaded from YouTube as corroborative evidence to some other piece of evidence in a human rights violations case before the Constitutional & Human Rights Court. As the Prosecution does not have direct access to YouTube's servers or data, it relied on videos that had been downloaded from a user's account on YouTube. The facts of the case was that the said six videos, which had been circulating on various social media platforms, had initially been posted anonymously on YouTube and were downloaded by an investigator from the Department of Criminal Investigations (DCI) thereby constituting their "ordinary activities." The ODPP has called one witness, the DCI Investigator (PW1) to persuade the court that the videos were admissible in evidence, pursuant to the provisions of the Evidence Act. The petitioner also provided the court with links to the said videos. You are the DCI Investigator.The ODPP seeks to submit six videos that have been downloaded from YouTube as corroborative evidence to some other piece of evidence in a human rights violations case before the Constitutional & Human Rights Court. As the Prosecution does not have direct access to YouTube's servers or data, it relied on videos that had been downloaded from a user's account on YouTube. The facts of the case was that the said six videos, which had been circulating on various social media platforms, had initially been posted anonymously on YouTube and were downloaded by an investigator from the Department of Criminal Investigations (DCI) thereby constituting their "ordinary activities." The ODPP has called one witness, the DCI Investigator (PW1) to persuade the court that the videos were admissible in evidence, pursuant to the provisions of the Evidence Act. The petitioner also provided the court with links to the said videos. You are the DCI Investigator.

The ODPP seeks to submit six videos that have been downloaded from YouTube as corroborative evidence to some other piece of evidence in a human rights violations case before the Constitutional & Human Rights Court. As the Prosecution does not have direct access to YouTube's servers or data, it relied on videos that had been downloaded from a user's account on YouTube. The facts of the case was that the said six videos, which had been circulating on various social media platforms, had initially been posted anonymously on YouTube and were downloaded by an investigator from the Department of Criminal Investigations (DCI) thereby constituting their "ordinary activities." The ODPP has called one witness, the DCI Investigator (PW1) to persuade the court that the videos were admissible in evidence, pursuant to the provisions of the Evidence Act. The petitioner also provided the court with links to the said videos. You are the DCI Investigator.

The ODPP seeks to submit six videos that have been downloaded from YouTube as corroborative evidence to some other piece of evidence in a human rights violations case before the Constitutional & Human Rights Court. As the Prosecution does not have direct access to YouTube's servers or data, it relied on videos that had been downloaded from a user's account on YouTube. The facts of the case was that the said six videos, which had been circulating on various social media platforms, had initially been posted anonymously on YouTube and were downloaded by an investigator from the Department of Criminal Investigations (DCI) thereby constituting their "ordinary activities." The ODPP has called one witness, the DCI Investigator (PW1) to persuade the court that the videos were admissible in evidence, pursuant to the provisions of the Evidence Act. The petitioner also provided the court with links to the said videos. You are the DCI Investigator.

Hypothetical Case for Judges

You were the presiding Judge in the case of Ndwiga Steve Mbogo v Independent Electoral and Boundaries Commission & 2 others. Where, the petitioner sought to submit six videos that had been downloaded from YouTube and Facebook as evidence in support of his election petition. The petitioner called two witnesses, plaintiff witness 7 (PW7) and plaintiff witness 8 (PW8) to persuade the court that the videos were admissible in evidence, pursuant to the provisions of the Evidence Act. The petitioner also provided the court with links to the said videos.The facts of the case relevant to this study were: PW7, who is a law student, signed a certificate on 5th September 2017, indicating that the videos in question were downloaded by her. Having downloaded the videos, PW7 had made available to the court, both the hard-disc and the transcript. PW 7 also providedYou were the presiding Judge in the case of Ndwiga Steve Mbogo v Independent Electoral and Boundaries Commission & 2 others. Where, the petitioner sought to submit six videos that had been downloaded from YouTube and Facebook as evidence in support of his election petition. The petitioner called two witnesses, plaintiff witness 7 (PW7) and plaintiff witness 8 (PW8) to persuade the court that the videos were admissible in evidence, pursuant to the provisions of the Evidence Act. The petitioner also provided the court with links to the said videos.The facts of the case relevant to this study were: PW7, who is a law student, signed a certificate on 5th September 2017, indicating that the videos in question were downloaded by her. Having downloaded the videos, PW7 had made available to the court, both the hard-disc and the transcript. PW 7 also provided

You were the presiding Judge in the case of Ndwiga Steve Mbogo v Independent Electoral and Boundaries Commission & 2 others. Where, the petitioner sought to submit six videos that had been downloaded from YouTube and Facebook as evidence in support of his election petition. The petitioner called two witnesses, plaintiff witness 7 (PW7) and plaintiff witness 8 (PW8) to persuade the court that the videos were admissible in evidence, pursuant to the provisions of the Evidence Act. The petitioner also provided the court with links to the said videos.

The facts of the case relevant to this study were: PW7, who is a law student, signed a certificate on 5th September 2017, indicating that the videos in question were downloaded by her. Having downloaded the videos, PW7 had made available to the court, both the hard-disc and the transcript. PW 7 also provided

You were the presiding Judge in the case of *Ndwiga Steve Mbogo v Independent Electoral and Boundaries Commission & 2 others*. Where, the petitioner sought to submit six videos that had been downloaded from YouTube and Facebook as evidence in support of his election petition. The petitioner called two witnesses, plaintiff witness 7 (PW7) and plaintiff witness 8 (PW8) to persuade the court that the videos were admissible in evidence, pursuant to the provisions of the Evidence Act. The petitioner also provided the court with links to the said videos.

The facts of the case relevant to this study were: PW7, who is a law student, signed a certificate on 5th September 2017, indicating that the videos in question were downloaded by her. Having downloaded the videos, PW7 had made available to the court, both the hard-disc and the transcript. PW 7 also provided

the particulars of the laptop which she used to download the videos. During cross-examination, PW7 informed the court: that she had downloaded the videos from YouTube and Facebook; that the videos had not been recorded by her, nor was she present when the videos were being recorded; that she did not know when the videos were recorded; that she would be unable to confirm whether or not the contents of the videos had been stage-managed; that she was unaware of the identity of the persons who had shot the videos; and, that she had no way of confirming whether or not the events captured actually occurred.

PW8 identified himself as an ICT expert who had completed a degree course on computer science and was yet to graduate. PW 8 said he obtained the videos from PW7 and also indicated that PW7 neither disclosed to him the identity of the person who shot the videos nor the identity of the person who had posted the videos on YouTube and Facebook. PW8 told the court that it was possible to identify the person who had posted the videos on YouTube and Facebook, however in this case he did not identify the person who had uploaded the videos. According to PW8, he could not tell either the time when, nor the location where the videos were taken. PW8 however informed the court that he had ability to verify whether or not the contents of the video were an act or a play stating that there is software which could enable him to determine the authenticity of the videos concluding that the said videos had not been edited. PW8 did not identify the equipment which had been used to shoot the videos. The court ruled that video evidence from social media was inadmissible due to the fact that, among other things, downloading social media videos did not constitute part of the responsible person's "ordinary activities" as required by Section 106 B (2) of the Evidence Act. The implication being that, for a litigant to adduce evidence obtained from social media, they would have to procure the services of an individual whose ordinary activities entails downloading media from these platforms. The Court did not interact with the technical questions surrounding the use of social media evidence due largely to procedural considerations.

How would you have ruled in this case, keeping in mind issues of authentication, reliability and the weight of the evidence, had the facts been as follows:

> the said six videos had been posted anonymously on Facebook and YouTube; the videos were downloaded by an investigator thereby constituting their "ordinary activities;" they were adduced in court by a prosecutor or a human rights actor as corroborative evidence to some other piece of evidence in a human rights violations case. As the prosecution/human rights actor does not have direct access to YouTube and Facebook's servers or data, it relied on screenshots, which meant that the Prosecution could not provide metadata, such as time stamps or IP addresses of the uploaders, to assist in the authentication of the photos. Consequently, there was no way to determine the identity of the person who posted them.

Index

Note: Page numbers in *italics* indicate figures. Page numbers in **bold** indicate table.

www.ingramcontent.com/pod-product-compliance
Lightning Source LLC
LaVergne TN
LVHW010549300926
849162LV00002B/273

* 9 7 8 1 0 4 1 2 9 6 0 3 4 *